The
Family Book
About
Sexuality

Other books by the authors

By Mary S. Calderone, M.D.

Sexuality and Human Values *(editor)*
Manual of Family Planning and Contraceptive Practice *(editor)*
Release from Sexual Tensions
Abortion in the United States *(editor)*
Talking with Your Child About Sex *(with James W. Ramey)*

By Eric W. Johnson

How to Live Through Junior High School
Love and Sex in Plain Language
Love and Sex and Growing Up
Sex: Telling It Straight
People, Love, Sex, and Families: Answers to Questions That Preteens Ask
Guide to the Subject of Sex—For Teachers
How to Relate to Sex Education Programs: A Guide for Parents
How to Achieve Competence in English
You Are the Editor
Teaching School: Points Picked Up
How to Live with Parents and Teachers
Raising Children to Achieve
Older and Wiser
Guilt, Guffaws, and Guinea Pigs: Humorous Stories about the Human
    Condition

The
Family Book
About
Sexuality

Revised Edition

Mary S. Calderone, M.D., and Eric W. Johnson

Drawings by Vivien Cohen

1817

HARPER & ROW, PUBLISHERS, New York
Cambridge, Philadelphia, San Francisco, London
Mexico City, São Paulo, Singapore, Sydney

Grateful acknowledgment is made for permission to reprint:

Table on page 91 from *Contraceptive Technology, 1988–1989,* 14th revised edition, by Robert A. Hatcher, M.D., et al.; published by Irvington Publishers, 740 Broadway, New York, NY 10003.

Library of Congress Cataloging-in-Publication Data

Calderone, Mary Steichen.
    The family book about sexuality / Mary S. Calderone and Eric W. Johnson ;
drawings by Vivien Cohen. — Rev. ed.
        p.   cm.
    Bibliography: p.
    Includes index.
    ISBN 0–06–016068–3 : $
    1. Sex—Handbooks, manuals, etc.   I. Johnson, Eric W.   II. Title.
HQ21.C24   1989
306.7—dc19   88–45889
                                                                      CIP

89 90 91 92 93 CC/HC 10 9 8 7 6 5 4 3 2 1

Contents

About This Book

This book is about the nature and development of human sexuality. It tells everything that most members of any family will want to know about sex.

The main part of the book, Chapters 1–12, is written so that it can be read straight through. But people often want to find out about a specific matter quickly. That is what the Concise A–to–Z Encyclopedia (beginning on page 215) is for. In this Encyclopedia you can immediately find just about any item concerning sex and sexuality that you might have a question about. From there you may be referred to other items in the Encyclopedia. Thus the book attempts to give you the best of both worlds: the world of making sense, and the world of quickly found facts.

The General Index at the back of the book will help you to locate discussions of any subject, whether in the main chapters or in the Encyclopedia.

Preface

As we write this preface, a tragedy is building in the United States: because of AIDS, many Americans are beginning to think of human sexuality primarily as danger or disaster, instead of as a profoundly human endowment essential to all of us and normally active at all age levels. While our society seems to be implying that sex kills, the media din into our ears, "*Be* sexy: *have* sex!"

As one result the Surgeon General of the United States is being quoted with narrow-minded literalness as urging schools to rush into sex education in the primary grades. To most this can only mean anti-disease, or protection-from-sure-disaster, education. The news we have for you in this book is that human sexuality is not a disease, but is quite literally a God-given human endowment, full of wonder for its potential for what is good and normal in all human lives. Yes, AIDS *is* a deadly and alarming result of human ignorance, and *yes,* we applaud Surgeon General C. Everett Koop for expressing the truth well: "Information is the best protection." Now we need to specify that information on sexuality as given in schools must be based on truths: it must be balanced information that is accurate, sound, nonthreatening, and not disease-oriented.

In this book, we view AIDS as a previously unknown disease of previously unknown nature that can directly or indirectly threaten unaware people in long- or short-term relationships, or even in no intimate relationship (see Chapter 10). Some of these people may lead lives of relatively little discipline, but many others may be involved entirely innocently. For the sake of succeeding generations we cannot afford to permit our society to be blind to its own great need for education in the *truths* about *healthy* human sexuality.

Why did we write this book? So that more and more people might begin to understand the vital truths about the sexual part of their lives, the roles that sex plays in all lives, the many new facts being learned from research about sex, sexuality, and human behavior. We also wanted to explain and put into perspective some of the more informed attitudes that scientific and religious leaders are developing about human sexuality. These can help make sex less something to be afraid of or ashamed of, and more understandable—and therefore easier to manage responsibly. Despite AIDS, we need to make the sexual parts of all lives as wonderful and rewarding as they have ever been, or even more so.

This book is for anyone of any age who can read and is genuinely interested in sexuality. People from around ten right on through old age will find in it valid and helpful information from reliable scientific sources. Even young children rightfully have many wondering questions about sex. If they know that their family has a book from which even grownups can learn, and if they are helped to feel free to leaf through it whenever they wish, they too will find parts that are helpful and useful to them. This can make them comfortable in taking part in family discussions about sexual questions. What they don't yet need to understand will slip right past them, yet the experience will verify for them the importance of sharing family knowledge and honesty about all aspects of life.

We, the two authors, are old friends. We are also Friends, that is, members of the Religious Society of Friends, known as Quakers. Quakers believe that all human beings have a right to all the information that can help them arrive at rational and responsible decisions about the conduct of their lives. Quakers also have concerns about the rights of others, and so our concern as authors is to share with other families what we have come to know about sex. We try to describe rather than advocate, to explain all sides of a subject on which serious professionals in the field might disagree, to not take any specific position on an issue other than to indicate, when possible, where most workers, researchers, therapists, and religious counselors in the field of human sexuality do tend to agree.

Sexuality is part of life from the beginning to the end of our days. We know that two aspects of sex, pleasure and procreation, have often been used without any sense of responsibility for their consequences—present and future—for the individuals involved, for others not directly involved, and for society. Any irresponsible use of sex is likely to damage individuals and society; therefore such lack of responsibility is, in the broadest and deepest sense, immoral.

Because of the work in which both of us have been involved over the past thirty years, we share the conviction of countless others that sexuality is one of three great human endowments, comparable to the mind and the body in importance, and partaking of both. Pleasure and joy from the use of these great faculties are enhanced by sound knowledge about their many aspects, including strong convictions about the infinite worth of each and every person.

The family is surely the best setting for learning how one's sexuality develops. But we recognize that many parents need help in educating their children about the normal aspects of sexuality, because their own mothers and fathers had not known how to carry this out as a family task. We also believe that schools have important roles to play in supplementing what the family teaches. So we devote most of Chapter 11 to how schools and families can work together or, where more appropriate, separately. We have kept in mind, too, that teachers need a book about sexuality to use for reference, in which they can comfortably look up what *they* feel they need to know and comprehend.

We believe that values relate to all of life, and that sex and sexuality are intrinsic to human life. We believe that sexuality has no morality peculiar to itself, but that morality or immorality will always lie in the way each of us uses our gifts of life, including sexuality, in our life's relationships. We also believe that our society as a society must never lose sight of the primary goal of educating all of its members for *healthy* and *responsible* sexuality.

For all these reasons we originally wrote, and have now revised, this book for you and for your family to share together.

Mary S. Calderone, M.D.
Eric W. Johnson
1988

1
Understanding Ourselves as Sexual People

What factors today influence how people develop and live their lives as sexual persons? Ever since Dr. Alfred Kinsey first published his research findings on men (1948) and on women (1953), we have become ever more aware of the factors that can influence the long process of creating a sexually well-balanced man or woman out of a tiny newborn. The facts in this chapter can help us understand ourselves as sexual persons, and think through what we may have taken for granted about the role of sex in human lives.

The assumptions on which this book is based are these: Each of us is sexual, all of our lives, and at any given moment each in our own unique way; there are as many different ways of being sexual persons as there are people in the world; and for each one of us individually, there are as many different ways of being a sexual person as there are days in our lives! Our sexuality may prove to be the second most important thing about us; having been born with the body and mind of a human being is the first. It is clear that humans are made sexual for the purpose of reproduction. It is equally clear that if we humans did not enjoy our sexuality there would be notably less reproduction. Do we enjoy it? Too much? Not enough? These and other questions will be touched on as we go along.

To avoid misunderstandings, it will help to keep clearly in mind how we use the words *sex, sexuality,* and *sexual.*

Sex: today this noun is most often used in two ways: (1) to label gender, that is, whether a person belongs to the male or the female gender or *sex:* and (2) to refer to the physical part of a relationship that differentiates that relationship from others. People use the word in the second way when they say, "I had sex last night," meaning a physical, erotic, or genital experience. But there are many more subtle meanings: a high school senior thanking a lecturer at school remarked with sincerity and warmth, "You've taught me that there's more to sex than just doing it." The lecturer was pleased that for that young man at least, the evening may have marked the beginning of a whole new way of thinking about and dealing with the sexual part of his life.

The word *sexuality* is used in a broader sense, meaning the whole person, including his or her sexual thoughts, experiences, learnings, ideas, values, and imaginings, as these have to do with being male or female.

The descriptive term *sexual* is used in the same broad sense as its noun, sexuality: your sexual self is your entire self as girl or boy or man or woman; your sexual feelings may be those having to do not only with the physical, but also with your own present or future male or female role in life. Your sexual feelings may also involve the relationships you may be having with people of the opposite sex, your own sex, or with yourself, at whatever age. Very often these experiences totally occupy your thoughts yet have nothing at all to do with physical activity, existing only in your mind as remembering or planning or wishing or daydreaming.

Sexual relationships do not always involve sex in the physical sense, but bear strongly on the sense of dealing with another equal as human to human: child to child, adolescent to adolescent, parent to parent. Parents and children, friend and friend, man and woman, man and man, woman and woman, employer and employee, student and student, student and teacher, colleague and colleague—all are daily experiencing at least one "sexual" relationship in the sense that they are, in part, sharing something with each other as the male or the female each of them has developed into, at any given moment. While genital sexual activity is an important part of some of our human relationships, (and can indeed become obsessive in some people for all of their adult lives), it takes up a quite small portion of waking time in a relatively small proportion of all the people we deal with from day to day.

The Process of Sexualization

As children develop, some of the most important things they learn have to do with their sense of self. Children are always learning, by observation, by being taught, or by experiencing or sensing, what their society considers desirable for a male or a female to be or to do. We can label this aspect of growth and development as a male or as a female the process of sexualization. It is integral to becoming a fully developed sexual person. This process, like other life processes, such as acquiring knowledge or developing the mind or the spirit, begins at birth and goes on throughout life. It is a dynamic process, one that is never still, never finished, never lastingly balanced, and that certainly plays a vital part in the process of "getting to know *me.*"

Throughout history, most societies have had fixed patterns by which they molded the natures and relationships of their boys and girls; in these societies, every child was taught to do or learn certain things at a given stage in his or her life, and thus grew up knowing exactly what was expected of him as male or of her as female at each stage. Today some Western societies maintain the sexual patterns of centuries, but ours no longer appears to standardize and fix sex patterns. And so the process of sexualization in one child often turns out to be quite unlike that experienced by another, even a brother or sister, except perhaps in the case of identical twins or triplets.

It is essential to distinguish the process of sexualization from the development of reproductivity, the capacity to reproduce (see Chapter 3). The term "reproductivity" simply means that a female has matured physically and is now capable of becoming pregnant, and that a male has matured physically and is now capable of making a female pregnant—and that both have reached puberty. But puberty does not mean that either of them is physically or intellectually or sexually mature, in the full sense of the word *sexual,* or that she is now fully a woman and he fully a man. And it must be pointed out that girls actually can—and not infrequently have—become pregnant even before menstruation, and without having fully developed sexually. The same is not true of a boy, for unless he can ejaculate he cannot impregnate, and he cannot ejaculate without experiencing powerful sexual feelings.

The step-by-step process by which sexuality is developed takes a number of years, from even before birth through puberty, and indeed a long time after. There are many components of this maturation process, most dependent on the kind and quality of a family's interrelationships. Negotiating this long process intelligently and safely requires much participation by the parent(s) in the form of reading, discussions of the reading, and family discussions of parent(s) with each other and all the children. Around the family dinner table, at quiet times during vacations and on trips, this type of discussion, coming from the family,

is by far the most important sex education that a child can have between six months of age and the sixteenth birthday, and can be the most
productive of all time/energy investments a family can make.

PRENATAL SEXUAL DEVELOPMENT

The moment of conception marks the very beginning of the sexual
development of each and every human being. In Chapter 3 you'll read
how a single sperm from the father fertilizes an ovum (egg) from the
mother. When the two meet and fuse, at the very moment of fertilization, the gender of the future baby is determined by which of the two
sex chromosomes is carried by that single successful sperm. Sperms are
of two kinds: (1) those carrying an X (female-producing) chromosome;
and (2) those carrying a Y (male-producing) chromosome. The egg's sex
chromosome is *always* X, so when the sperm fertilizing it also carries
an X chromosome, the baby-to-be will be like its mother, XX and female; if the fertilizing sperm has a Y sex chromosome, then the baby-to-
be will be like its father, XY and male. At the instant of penetration by
the sperm cell, the way into the ovum is barred for all other sperm, and
division of the cells of the new human being now proceeds with extraordinary rapidity to create all its organs and parts.

It should thus be understood that the sperm and the ovum each
contribute a specific packet of a specific number of chromosomes, producing pairs of chromosomes that, together, dictate color of hair and
eyes, body size and many other complex factors. The sex chromosomes'
main function, however, is to pass on the genetic signal, XX *or* XY, to
all the cells already multiplying with astonishing rapidity—especially to
a special group of cells that, with the sex chromosome in command, are
now coded to develop into testicles (XY) or ovaries (XX). And, to ensure
that the sex organs of the baby match its gender, the group of cells with
the task of producing a girl or a boy begin their life work by manufactur-
ing the corresponding female (XX) or male (XY) hormone. It is this
self-manufactured hormone in the tiny embryo that ensures that the
special organs characterizing male or female will develop correctly: the
cells that make up the digestive organs need not and will not be involved in this critical business of the genetic code, while the male or
female sex organs that together govern the sexual functions of the two
sexes, are from the start controlled by one of the two codes. The female
hormone estrogen is produced to ensure the birth of a girl baby complete with female sex organs. In addition, the making of a girl baby is

backed up by the mother's own blood, which carries estrogen from *her* ovaries. The total production of estrogen assures development of the complex of female organs—uterus, fallopian tubes, ovaries, vagina, clitoris, and labia (see the drawings on pages 39 and 41). These will remain small and undeveloped until puberty, when the flood of estrogen will assure normal development for the girl turning into a woman, culminating in menstruation every 28–30 days.

On the other hand, when the sperm carries a Y, an XY message instructs a group of cells to become testicles. These begin to secrete the male hormone testosterone and thus to bring about development of the male genital organs—penis, scrotum, testicles, prostate, seminal vesicles, etc. (see the drawing on page 34). These remain small and almost dormant until puberty, when their maturation assures development from boy to man. Just as first menstruation in the girl will signal the power to conceive, first ejaculation in the boy will announce his power to impregnate.

The above relates specifically to the formation of anatomy that is male or female. One of the anatomy's two functions, reproduction, has been thoroughly researched and commands specialties in medical practice: gynecology and obstetrics in the female, urology in the male. A new finding has provided a solid basis for understanding how and when another function of the same anatomical organs develops in the human being, but with a different time frame and purpose. In the early 1980s, scientists using relatively new techniques combining ultrasound and amniocentesis noted periodic erection of the penis in the male fetus, and in addition determined that the erections occurred regularly every ninety minutes. No one quite knew how to interpret this phenomenon, until reminded that sleep laboratories had found that normally healthy adult sleeping males also had erections about every 90 minutes.

We call human beings' ability to respond sexually *the human sexual response systems*. In the face of societal changes that have released many children and young people from adult control, we need to develop more understanding of these human sexual response systems. To continue denial of normal sexual awareness or activity until puberty is clear error: in females sexuality is lifelong, though reproductivity has a specifically limited span. In males sexuality is likewise lifelong, but reproductivity is not as sharply limited as in the female.

To punish or shame a child for his or her own normal body function, or to deny the existence and recognition of this newly identified body system, is neither supportive of the child's natural processes nor of his or her personal development, and is all too reminiscent of the antiquated and destructive use of corporal punishment during toilet training. We must emphasize that parents and professionals should learn to recognize and respect a baby's sexuality, feelings, and functions.

ACQUIRING GENDER IDENTITY

At birth, the first announcement "It's a boy" or "It's a girl" is rapidly followed by an announcement of its physiological status: "healthy". It is important that both be accurate: if a baby is identified as of the gender other than its own, psychological problems can later arise that might be difficult or impossible to correct. Wrong gender identification can occur on rare occasions when the genitals of a baby are not clearly identifiable as belonging specifically to one or the other of the two sexes.

During a child's first two years, parents and others frequently provide many cues as to the baby's gender. American mothers dress their girl babies in pink and their boy babies in blue—in France, just the opposite. Almost all mothers talk even to a tiny baby—"What a fine big boy!" or "Mommy's lovely little girl!" Studies show that parents tend to handle a girl baby or toddler quite differently from the way they handle a boy of the same age. Both parents may give the baby toys or play games with it that identify it as male or female. They make definite statements that tell the toddler to which sex it belongs: "When you go to the toilet we put the seat back and you stand up just like Daddy," or, "Girls don't stand up to the toilet like Daddy but sit down like Mommy." There are constant cues to identify girls with females, boys with males. Thus, by age two or three boys and girls should be correctly sure of their own gender identity, aware that "I'm a boy" or "I'm a girl."

LEARNING GENDER ROLE BEHAVIOR

What do girls and women do—or *not* do?

What do boys and men do—or *not* do?

Through childhood and well into adolescence, children become more and more aware of differences in behavior that most adults consider appropriate for a boy or a girl. Formerly, a boy would scorn learning to cook, announcing loudly, "That's for *girls!*" Then, about thirty years ago, the backyard barbecue took hold as fun and status symbol, and daddies began liking to barbecue, for friends as well as for family. Little boys grew up with this, so it is not surprising that as this

barrier went down so did others. Boys could experiment with varieties of cooking, even in the kitchen, without feeling that they would become professional chefs or sissies as a result. Men began to find home cooking fun too, often leaving cleaning up to the women! Today men are routinely cooking for wives, children, and friends, perhaps some meals during the week, perhaps alternating with a wife who also works outside the home; sometimes even making all the meals. This is a good example of how gender role behavior can adapt to changing times. Another example is in Scotland, where knitting is enjoyed by men. Also, men increasingly share in the care of babies and young children.

It is important to keep in mind that possession of male or female chromosomes and organs is not what determines how people feel about their masculinity or femininity. Rather, it is how they are brought up to feel about themselves, their lives, and the opinions and attitudes of people around them, that carries the most weight. So broad social patterns change gradually over time.

REACHING PUBERTY

Puberty, the months-long process of reproductive maturation, though no mystery, does mark a unique milestone in every life: *You* do not reach puberty, puberty reaches *you* and all other human beings, male and female.

At a certain period, usually in the early teens, a sudden spurt of body development indicates that the sex glands (ovaries or testicles) are increasing their output of sex hormoness enough to begin the transformation of boy into man or girl into woman. These hormones determine both reproductive maturation and the bodily changes characteristic to being an adult female or adult male. Dr. John Money, long-time head of the Gender Identity Center at Johns Hopkins University, has said that puberty "is also the moment when the revelation of the identity and orientation that were already programmed occurs." The adolescent suddenly realizes "I'm getting to be a *man!*" or "I am becoming a *woman!*" And as Money astutely noted, for a small minority of people, puberty can be when a boy or a girl may first discover that falling in love seems to happen only with someone of his or her own gender—the first intimation of homosexuality.

For unprepared girls or boys, the first menstruation or "wet dream" may cause a mixture of fear and shame at the resulting soiling of underclothes or sheets. This indicates lack of intimacy and trust on

both sides, in marked contrast to families in which signs of maturation are discussed with pride and satisfaction.

But, unfortunately, too many adults continue to be fearful of openness about sexuality with their children and fearful of sexual pleasure itself, and continue to believe that simple rules and prohibitions are necessary and will be effective. However, they may only shut down whatever communication has been previously built between parents and child. There is no safe substitute for accurate sexual knowledge. Trust and a flow of truth between parents and children should be the rule. Facing the fact that sex can lead to the creation of a new life can be done in a family setting, where orderly, reasonable, ethical patterns for living can be discussed and then supported by the whole family.

Other Factors in Sexualization

As children grow, they are in contact with others who affect their development—brothers and sisters, relatives, friends, teachers and professionals, even strangers. Anyone who comes in contact with children or young people provides a role model of a certain kind of man or a certain kind of woman for them to weigh, accept, or reject. Children or young people, often without realizing it, absorb too much from today's movies, magazines, and TV, and may react unconsciously with "I would *like* to be like that person" or "I would *not* want to be that kind of person." Our entire society, especially as revealed in the media, plays a heavy role in the process of sexualization. Right now many of the role models presented to us are those we would hope and pray our children would choose *not* to follow.

Parents' groups, therefore, might begin considering what they might do toward providing better, more realistic role models. What is it, what does it mean, what does it take, to be a man, to be a woman? What kinds of men and women does our society need today in order to survive, to get better? Spirited family discussions can center on such questions. They are important questions for everyone to think about, to talk about together, at the dinner table, in the evening after homework, on weekends, or on long trips. One way children and parents can move closer to each other is to learn how to talk trustingly and freely with one another about the many kinds of feelings that need to be aired in dealing with sex-related problems in today's society.

Our adolescents can be helped to become aware that society has changed since they were born. One important reason for this is that women are evolving rapidly from their imposed role as inferiors of men to a new role as partners. Women today are freer to do or become what they wish. Some choose to stay at home and bring up their children, others choose to combine mothering and homemaking with job or career, still others delay childbearing until their thirties or perhaps forgo it entirely. This increasing freedom for women also offers men more freedom—to choose to be homemakers, for instance, so they can write during school hours. It will be some decades before the effects of these new attitudes on all family members can be fully evaluated.

To summarize: by the time children of today enter kindergarten, they probably have already experienced the most long-lasting sex education they can ever have, but its quality and results cannot be judged until several decades hence. Did the child have enough, not enough, prejudiced, incorrect, or prematurely offered information? For good or for ill, the parents have been *the* primary sex educators, not only in terms of information offered or not offered, but even more in terms of their attitudes about themselves as male or female, about their child as girl or boy, about each other as workers outside the home, and about sex itself, whether as an erotic experience or as an integral part of a relationship.

Fortunately, ongoing research is helping to fill gaps by developing new concepts and knowledge about expanded sex roles and relationships for men and women required by society's changes. Many of today's young parents have moved away from their own parents' concepts of sexuality. They do not want the sexual ignorance, discomforts, anxieties, distastes, fears, and shame that they may have experienced to continue to be passed on from generation to generation. They want to help their children move forward, not backward, in sexual knowledge and attitudes—to become healthier and happier sexually.

2
The Human Sexual Response Systems

How They Develop and How They Work

Every human being is born with the capacity to experience sexual pleasure and responsiveness, and in the last decades research has greatly increased our understanding of *the sexual response system.* But we still need to understand it better as a previously unidentified organ system that is distinct from the reproductive system, with its own unique ways of functioning. Whereas almost all body systems function the same in males and females, reproduction and sexual response are the two that function differently, not only from each other but from all other systems. Learning about and allowing for such differences can go a long way toward creating and supporting a harmonious relationship between two people in a relationship, and will be especially helpful in guiding them when they are bringing up a child.

The major difference between the workings of the reproductive and sexual response systems in the male and the female is this: After puberty, reproductive and sexual functioning are one and the same in the male, but not in the female. In the male, reproductive functioning is attained automatically with the achievement of ejaculation at puberty, and by the age of eighteen, practically 100 percent of males have experienced erection and ejaculation, without which the male could not play his part in reproduction. In the female it is different. Though she too reaches reproductive maturity at puberty, it is entirely possible, and sometimes happens, that she can become pregnant without experiencing sexual pleasure then or perhaps ever. This difference between the two sexes is basic, and important to understand. The process of reproduction in the female is automatic, for the brain areas controlling it do not operate consciously. But the brain areas affecting her sexual response system operate at both the conscious and unconscious levels, and things can happen in childhood that may interfere with her sexual response functioning in adult life.

Compare the drawing on page 39, showing the female reproductive system, with the drawing on page 41, the exterior organs of the female sexual response system. In reproductive functioning, the organs principally involved are the ovaries, the fallopian tubes, and the uterus, with the vagina involved passively at the very beginning of the reproductive process, when it is the passageway by which the sperm move toward the egg, and again at the very end, nine months after fertilization, when it is the passageway through which the baby enters the world.

In the diagram of the female sexual response system, notice that the organs principally involved in sexual response are the clitoris, as the main source of pleasure and the labia, or internal and external lips of the vulva. The muscular tissues that surround the vagina within the pelvis, at both its outer and deeper areas, also play a role in sexual response. It is these muscles, becoming engorged with blood and fluid during arousal in preparation for intercourse, that provide the pleasurably rhythmic contractions of orgasm as the culmination of intercourse. The further contribution of the vagina in sexual pleasure is not entirely passive, and is important: as soon as sexual stimulation begins, the small blood vessels in the muscular walls of the vagina become engorged with blood, causing a flow of clear slippery fluid to seep into the vagina in a kind of sweating mechanism. That fluid acts not only as an efficient lubricant but also as a beneficial environment for the sperm released at the culminating orgasm.

Also, for years women have claimed that the vagina is an organ for stimulation and sensations of pleasure. Recent research has identified a small area in the front wall of the vagina, the G-spot, named for its original observer, Ernst Gräfenberg (see the A–to–Z Encyclopedia). The mouth, the lips, the breasts, the anus, and the entire skin surface all act together as secondary sex organs to provide sensations of pleasure that can facilitate penetration, heighten pleasure, and culminate in orgasm.

Different women may give the primary and secondary sex organs different weights of importance for sexual pleasure, not only according to their individual experiences and preferences, but also at different moments in their lives. Most women also give different weights to different sources of stimulation. It is well known that whereas most men find intercourse the most desirable form of stimulation, many women do not, but find more pleasure and a higher degree of stimulation arising out of mouth or finger contact. The researchers William H. Masters and Virginia E. Johnson found consistently that women appeared to be more highly aroused in sexual self-pleasuring than in sexual intercourse, and many found it easier to experience orgasm following masturbation than during intercourse. But most of the women studied enjoyed and desired most the orgasm resulting from sexual intercourse, even though orgasm following masturbation might be more intense.

The capacity of females for orgasm differs from individual to individual more than it does in males. Some women never experience orgasm in their lives; some experience it as babies, even before conscious memory, and continue to experience it throughout their lives; some never experience more than one orgasm for each sexual episode; some experience single orgasms for some time before they discover that they have a capacity for multiple orgasms; and some experience multiple orgasms throughout their lives. The range is great. Many of the differences depend on circumstances; others are independent of circumstances. Many explanations have been offered as to why at least one third of all women have difficulty in experiencing orgasm during intercourse, but without shedding much light on the problem. One explanation offered is that during the most common position in intercourse (man on top), the penis is not in position to stimulate the clitoris directly, and clitoral stimulation is often necessary for a woman to have an orgasm.

The Sexual Response Cycle

Basically, what is called the sexual response cycle works about the same way for those men and women who experience arousal. Whether in self-pleasuring or in pleasuring each other, whether heterosexually or homosexually, there are four stages, each one leading to the next.

1. *The excitement stage.* In the excitement stage the body begins to respond to sexual stimulation, as from thoughts, imaginings, dreams, sights, sounds, body odors, body touch, and memories. It begins with erection in the male and with lubrication of the vagina, which results from engorgement of the vaginal blood vessels, in the female. Various movements or caresses provide stimulation and, if these are continued, excitement increases and the plateau stage is reached.

2. *The plateau stage.* Depending upon the intensity of reaction and the desire of the people involved, the plateau stage can be quite short or very prolonged. It is called "plateau" because it can be continued for variable lengths of time, until the sense of tension and pleasure increases to that moment when orgasm is felt by one partner or both as inevitable. During the plateau stage the blood trapped in the sex organs of both males and females causes pleasurable swelling, ultimately leading to the orgasmic stage.

3. *The orgasmic stage.* Once a certain pitch of tension has been reached in the plateau stage, orgasm is triggered. In both male and female it consists of a series of muscular contractions in or about the sex organs. According to the research of Masters and Johnson, the contractions number from perhaps six to fifteen—each lasting a little less than one second. In the male, the focus of orgasm is concentrated in the mind, which perceives it as taking place in the penis, the prostate gland, and the seminal vesicles. In the female the focus of orgasm is also concentrated in the mind, which perceives it as taking place in the muscles and tissues around and deep in the vagina. In both male and female, the whole body is often involved in muscle tension resulting in spasmodic contractions of limbs, fingers, toes, or face, especially in the female. Those women who are multi-orgasmic may experience several orgasms before satisfaction.

4. *The resolution stage.* For males, immediately after orgasm comes the resolution stage, during which tensions relax and pulse, breathing, and blood pressure return to their usual rates. Then there follows a refractory period, during which the man cannot respond as quickly to new stimulation. In young men this period is brief—minutes or hours. In others, especially in older men, it can last several hours or days, depending on age, vigor, and interest. In women, the resolution stage is immediate and shorter, but lengthens with age.

The Early Development of Sexuality

Examination of the wide range of differences in the sexual responses of women, compared to the narrower range of differences in the responses of men, has led to a search for explanations. The variations have been shown to result from early childhood experiences when natural erotic tensions were expressed, and responded to by rigid or fearful adults. Natural eroticism begins to be expressed in very early infancy. The widely differing ways in which adults react to such expression in their children may well have effects on the responsiveness of these children once they are grown. To understand the sexuality of women and of men, it is helpful to understand the evolution of sexuality in children.

THE SEXUALITY OF INFANCY

Most people don't wish to think of babies and young children as sexual, so if they observe some behavior that might be interpreted as such, they resist it as frightening or bad and try to stop it. Yet it is now increasingly understood that sexuality develops in the normal child more or less in the following sequence:

Newborn babies begin life with breathing, and their first cry is eagerly listened for as an indication that the breathing or respiratory system is functioning properly. Signs of functioning of other systems of the body are also watched for: the first bowel movement shows that the intestinal tract is working; the first feedings, not vomited, prove the same about the digestive system; the heart is listened to; tests for reflexes (like tapping the knee or the heel with a rubber hammer or seeing how the pupils of the eye react to light) show that brain and nervous system are working normally; and so forth.

At birth, two signs may serve as indicators that the sexual response system is working normally: a boy baby has one of what will be a lifelong series of erections and often is born with penis erect. Occasionally a girl baby may every few hours show a vaginal discharge heavy enough to crust over the vaginal opening. This is the infantile equivalent to the lubricating fluid that will eventually be produced whenever she is sexually aroused. That normal babies are sexual creatures is a surprise to many people, but it is a fact. Babies have been observed very early in infancy to become tense, rigid, and flushed: this sequence of responses peaks in quivering and rapid breathing, with sudden relaxation into instantaneous sleep.

It is just as automatic for the sexual response system to function at this time in the baby's life as it will later be automatic for the reproductive system to function in early puberty. You would think, then, that the sexual response system would continue working smoothly throughout life as a natural, normal thing, and that we would not see so many people who experience difficulties in one way or another with their own or their children's sexual-erotic functioning. Unfortunately, however, things happen on the way to adult life that can in the end interfere with the normal success of sexual response functioning.

A comparison can be made with the digestive system, at the lower end of which, for instance, trouble can begin with the parents' too-rigid approach to and early insistence on bowel training. This can lead to poor attitudes in young children about going to the toilet or even to constipation or other disturbances in later life. In the same way, mothers or fathers who insist on feeding children a certain amount of food in a certain way often end up with a child whose natural appetite has been distorted and who has problems with eating. We have had to learn how to avoid these problems by teaching parents to let their young children eat what they choose of the right foods, keeping wrong foods from them, and not feeding them again until the next meal—but never forcing them to eat.

In the same way, parents with the best intentions in the world have tended to interfere with the natural evolution of their children's sexuality. For one thing, not enough American babies receive the close body contact with their parents, particularly their mothers, that they need. It is good to see more and more young mothers today breastfeeding their babies and carrying them around close to their bodies with a carrying sling. It is good to know, too, that an increasing number of young parents enjoy holding their babies against their bare skin and gently stroking or massaging the baby's body.

Meeting the other needs of the baby is also important. When the baby cries, he or she is simply telling you of his or her needs or wants, which include need for regular body, voice, and eye contact. The job of a parent is to learn to interpret what the baby's needs might be at that moment. By having their needs and wants met, babies very early learn to trust the world around them, and become more and more able to bear frustration and meet the world confidently rather than in fear, loneliness, uncertainty, or anger.

The first contact of mother and baby is very important. The first hour or two, even the first few minutes, are those in which it is easiest and most rewarding for both to form their first bond. The baby should be given to the mother at once, before it is clothed or even bathed, so that with her own fingers she can touch it all over to make sure it is all right—and to give it its first sensation of direct relation to another person.

New mothers have been observed to touch the feet and hands first, then the body, and then the baby's face, after which their hands return to the body, to smooth and massage it. Meanwhile, the mother is looking intently at the baby, looking straight into his or her face, and, wonderfully, almost every normal baby is usually gazing straight back into her eyes, even though the baby's vision is not acute. These two human

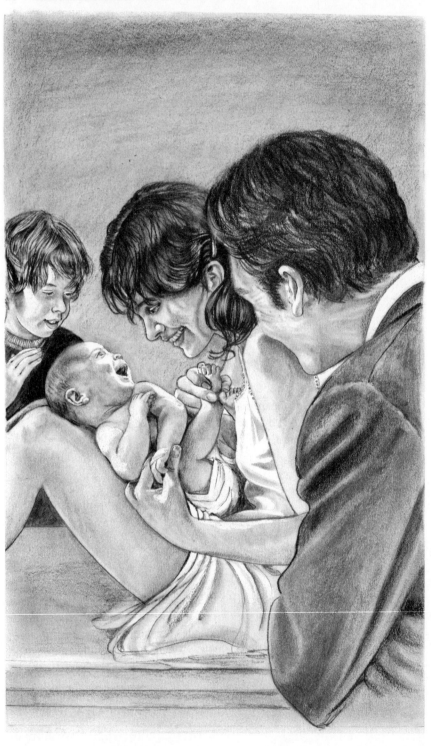

beings so important to each other are wordlessly saying many things that lay the foundation for a strong relationship together. As long as the baby is breathing well, all this should happen even before eyedrops, weighing, or examination by the doctor.

Studies show that those babies whose mothers had been helped to have this experience with their brand-new infants thrived and gained weight better, and that the mothers were more likely to be successful at nursing them, as compared with other mothers and babies who had not been given this opportunity to bond.

As soon after the baby's birth as possible, the father should have the same experience, as it is very important for him and for the baby, and for exactly the same reasons. Thereafter, both mother and father will find it always more rewarding to continue this strong, close-touching relationship with their baby, and the baby will thrive on it.

Just as important later are the attitudes of the parents about the baby's own good bodily feelings. The baby's fingers will eventually explore its body, discover the various fascinating things such as its nose, its ears, its hair, its belly button, its toes. Parents express delight over these discoveries, but when it comes to discoveries in the area between belly button and knees—that is too often a different story.

When the baby boy's fingers find his penis while the mother is bathing or diapering him, she usually begins her interference right then, afraid her child may break the taboo on the pleasure of sex "too early." She is thinking of sex in the adult sense, of course, but only because no one has helped her understand that childhood sexual feelings are quite different from those of an adult and that they occur naturally as part of the pleasure of touch. The reactions of mothers may vary. One might simply remove the baby's hand from his genital area; another might cover the baby quickly with the diaper; another might slap the baby's hand and speak angrily to him.

If the baby is a girl, the mother's panic may be even greater and her reaction stronger. If the father is standing by, the mother may be terribly embarrassed and upset; she might be even more upset if one of the baby's grandmothers is also watching. She wants to prevent any activity that they could interpret as "abnormal."

Rarely does anyone ever reassure the mother that not only is it normal for a baby to find pleasure in his or her own body, but it is also an essential part of the baby's growth and development that should not be interfered with. Rather, the mother may hear neighbors tell tales of the supposed harms and evils of masturbation. She has no way of knowing that these are myths and untruths handed down from the dark ages.

Neither does she know that masturbation for release of tension and to experience pleasure occurs throughout the lives of most people, with only positive effects—unless they are made to feel anxious or guilty about it. Parents do not have to teach their children to masturbate, but they should teach privacy in its practice.

When a baby discovers his or her genital organs, he or she is actually initiating the active functioning of the sexual response system which, years later, will be physiologically ready enough to permit normal sexual functioning accompanied by a sense of competence, fulfillment, ownership, and pleasure. Each system of the body—the heart and blood vessels, the respiratory, the digestive, the nervous system, and so forth—has inbuilt its specific purpose in life, its specific way of functioning. The sexual response system is no exception. But unlike the other body systems, the functioning of this system is not a life-or-death matter. Many people live satisfying and creative lives even if they choose to ignore or repress their sexual functioning. The possibility of such repressions, however, should not be forced upon children. The choice need be considered only by mature adults who have all the facts in their possession and who elect not to exercise their erotic powers.

SEX ROLES AND THE SEXUALITY OF CHILDHOOD

The young child will also be learning what her or his nongenital sex role should be in life. Here again the principal teachers are the parents, who by their words or their attitudes hammer in answers to these questions: What should little girls do or not do? What should little boys do or not do? What may both girls and boys, women and men, do or not do? Each parent, each family unit, and each society usually has quite specific convictions about the "correct" answers to these important social questions; there will be marked differences in these answers in various parts of the world or even in parts of the same country. The convictions based on the answers will be conveyed to the child both directly and indirectly day after day by the parents, and they will affect the child's eventual patterns of sexual beliefs and behavior. In the United States, these beliefs are not uniform and they are changing. Men and women and boys and girls can today do and be many more of the same things in everyday life than they were permitted even a decade or two ago.

Some people worry about what, since the late 1960s, is sometimes called "unisex." They worry that children will grow up confused about their gender roles. Children might get confused about changing gender roles today if the adults around them get confused. But if the child grows up knowing that the primary difference between males and females has to do with their reproductive function—men produce sperm, and women produce eggs that can be fertilized by the sperm and carried until birth—and if children can be taught to name and take pride in their own special organs that will perform those functions, then the wage-earning occupations of men and women become of less importance in distinguishing between them: mothers can be bus drivers and fathers can be cooks and still be looked upon as mothers and fathers, real women and real men.

If parents are aware that their child has been born with the same natural capacities for erotic feelings that every other child has, they will find it easier to learn the attitudes of calm and noninterfering yet socializing acceptance of this part of life. This, in turn, will assure the child that his or her body does indeed belong to him or her and to no one else. Naturally, parents' efforts must be exercised in relation to what is acceptable social behavior. For example, the child must understand early that today most people believe one's sex life should be private. Children will believe this until they watch soap operas and late-night films. There is no need for furtiveness, but there is a need to respect the feelings of others.

THE LESSONS OF NUDITY

One question that comes up in almost every family concerns nudity: Should parents and children see each others' bodies in the nude? If so, when and where? And how?

Unless the idea of nudity is entirely comfortable for parents, if they are going to try it at all they should do so gradually over time, not suddenly. Older children cannot easily learn to take nudity for granted if it has not been a part of family routine during their early years. But with very young children accustomed from the beginning to nudity in themselves and their parents, a great deal is taken for granted, and it doesn't seem to be much of an issue to them. What nudity does is make it easy for children to become absolutely certain about just how men and women are made. This knowledge is of great importance in assuring the child of his or her own correct gender. The differences in body states and sizes—and in body organs—can then be taken for granted and will provide an accurate image of how they themselves, or the

opposite sex, will look when grown up. Children whose parents feel at ease in such natural events as stepping out of the shower, toweling, and walking back to their room to dress are fortunate.

As children get older, they may copy their age-mates and express comfort if nudity is *not* practiced, even though they grew up with it. They will demonstrate this by choosing to be clothed or covered where before they were happy to prance around with nothing on. This becomes almost inevitable with the coming of adolescence. Parents can read these signs and be sensitive to them without necessarily changing their own preferred patterns. Privacy must always be respected, by grownups and children alike.

INCREASED INTEREST IN SEX

Extreme curiosity or repeated questions about sex should be carefully analyzed: Why is the child so curious? Why is she or he not satisfied with simple answers? What basic needs for information or reassurance do the questions indicate? Studies have shown that most parents tend to be convinced their children are less capable (by about two years) of absorbing knowledge about sexual matters than they are about other things, but this is not so.

It may be helpful for parents to know that many of the anxieties young children have that result in their heightened interest in the area of sex or greater activity in masturbation may not be related to sex at all but may spring from quite different causes: a recent severe illness or a death in the family, loss of a job or heavy pressures on the job of one or both parents, the arrival of a new brother or sister, heavy academic demands at school, a bullying child on the block, recent hospitalization, and so on. Such anxieties can cause a sense of being overwhelmed, with the child coming to feel as if the illness or death or loss of job was really in some way his or her responsibility. Such pressures can add greatly to the other factors that may already be pressing on the child, even though he or she may be too young to talk about it. The child may turn to the familiar self-touching that is pleasurable, to relieve these anxieties, and find comfort.

Sometimes parents get upset when they think their children show too much interest in sex when they play. Children do a lot of what scientists have come to call "rehearsal play": "I'll be the mommy and you be the daddy. I'll cook and you read the paper." They go through the motions of identification with the grown-up world, which enjoys and encourages this. Early grade school rooms have housekeeping areas where rehearsal play can be carried out by both boys and girls.

But suppose the children's rehearsal play is about heterosexual activities, and they pretend to go through those motions? "I'll be the daddy and put the seed in you." "And I'll be the mommy and push the baby out of my belly button." To many parents that's not cute; it's disgusting or frightening. For the children, however, such play does not have the sexual meanings it does for the parents. Actually, the parents should be helped to see this kind of play as accomplishing two things: First, it helps children to grow up solidly sure of how their sex roles are differentiated from one another's, primarily by the eventual reproductive functions of their sex organs: the man's penis to release sperm, and the woman's vagina to act as a passageway for the sperm to reach the egg to fertilize it. A baby thus created will be carried in the woman's body until it is born. Second, it provides opportunities for parents to check on the soundness and realism of their child's information. Thus, the situation described above would give a parent a chance to overhear and to say, "Daddy doesn't put a seed in, seeds are for plants. Daddies have sperm that join with the mother's egg to start a baby growing. And when a baby is born, it is never through the belly button. Instead, the mother pushes it right out through her vagina." Such sure knowledge, and their satisfaction in having received it directly from their parents, is part of the development of the sense of security that children need about their present sexual and future reproductive roles in life.

Sex rehearsal play takes place because of the need of young children to confirm any kind of important knowledge, not once but many times in many ways. Harm occurs when there are outcries or punishment by adults. Gentle but firm supervision and calm handling will make it easier to meet with positive and creative attitudes the many other sexual situations that will be inevitable with children growing up, particularly in today's open and sex-saturated society. In general, the balance between "What will the neighbors say?" and the evolution of one's own sexually healthy child must be tipped in favor of the child, not the other way around.

When confronted by sexual situations like sex rehearsal play in their young children, parents can say such things as: "Bodies are made to feel good in many different ways. Cool water on your skin, good smells, lovely tastes—all these experiences of your body are good. But touching is special—so special you must learn to feel that having your body touched should come only from yourself. Special places in your body that feel good when they are touched are your sexual places, and that should be a private thing, just for you alone, for now."

MASTURBATION

The development of understanding the sexual response system needs to continue smoothly throughout infancy, childhood, and adolescence. One of its most important functions is its role in developing a strong sense of the self. An increasing number of sexologists and sex therapists now agree that masturbation has a specific role to play in the sexual evolution and total life cycle of the human being. They recognize also that great numbers of adults, well into old age, utilize self-stimulation as a form of release and pleasure, sometimes in painful situations such as illness of the partner, or separation by long periods of travel, death, or divorce, but usually as part of ordinary life.

Masturbation can also be looked upon as rehearsal for mature sex. Just as adolescents are constantly trying all sorts of new ways to test their bodies—in sports, in activities like driving a car, in going without food or sleep—so too they need to find out how their bodies perform sexually. Masturbation is a safe way to do this, because it does not involve another person. In a sense, too, the young person learns how to relate to himself or herself sexually, and this helps prepare for eventually relating to another person. Getting to know yourself intimately is good rehearsal for getting to know another person intimately.

While professional people and researchers do not consider masturbation to be a problem itself, society makes it one when it looks upon it as somehow harmful, mentally unhealthy, sinful, or, at best, immature behavior that mature people should outgrow.

According to the most careful studies we have, in the United States and Canada well over 95 percent of males and 75 percent of females do masturbate at one or more periods in their lives, and the amount of masturbation and the ages at which people masturbate are unrelated to religious affiliation or frequency of church attendance. Also, we know of no studies showing that masturbation causes or is evidence of disorder. However, the fact that many people who do masturbate are also aware of strong statements against it, especially by religious groups, can cause them needless suffering, guilt, and worry. We can say today that one of the main sources of failure to achieve sexual satisfaction in adult life is interference by parents early in life with the child's discovery of his or her own body as a source of pleasure.

PARENTS AS ROLE MODELS

Children who have loving parents—parents who are loving with each other and with their children—will find it easy to accept the good examples set by their parents. They follow bad examples too. Fathers and mothers are usually not aware of how closely and constantly their children watch them and copy them. In this way, children learn how men and women deal with each other—honestly, trustingly and kindly, or sharply and hurtfully, playing games against each other.

Parents are bringing up not just their child but a probable future husband or wife of some other person, who also will bring to the marriage the effects of the role-modeling of his or her parents. How will the two sets of parents be reflected, years later, in the lives of the family that will include their future grandchildren?

The relationship of a mother and a father, and how they themselves feel about each other and about erotic sex, is inevitably an important influence on every child. One of the difficulties that children face today in growing up is the wide variety of attitudes parents have about sex and how their children should learn and feel about it:

• Some parents have fine sex lives but don't want to talk to or teach their children about sex.

• Some parents believe that sex is a bad thing, to be repressed or enjoyed seldom, even in marriage.

• Some parents would like to have better, warmer sex lives, but their own upbringing has made letting go with enjoyment almost impossible for them.

• Some parents look upon sex as a piece of cake—to be had and enjoyed with almost anyone.

• Some parents regard sex primarily as a joking matter.

• Some parents experience practically no sex feelings and don't understand what all the fuss is about.

• Some parents limit sex with so many rules and restrictions and ceremonies that it is never a spontaneous and free experience for them.

• Some parents have been taught by life experiences to link sex with violence and anger.

• Some parents have found it impossible to enjoy sex except under unusual circumstances, and so they seek out these circumstances constantly.

• And many parents, of course, have joyous, rewarding sexual lives and are living examples of love and consideration for their children.

Some parents who read this may feel that something very important is missing from their lives, deeply concerned that they do not fall into the last group. These couples, if they wish, can seek help from accredited marriage or sex counselors. They can obtain the names and addresses of qualified counselors in their area by contacting AASECT—the American Association of Sex Educators, Counselors and Therapists—in their own community or by writing to AASECT at 11 Dupont Circle N.W., Suite 220, Washington, DC 20036 (phone 1-202-462-1171) for referral to a member in their area.

Learning Sexual Techniques

There really are no recipes for concocting a perfect sexual relationship. Two unique individuals get together and develop a relationship which they may eventually decide will involve sexual intercourse. From then on they are probably largely on their own as they find out what pleases, satisfies, and fulfills them as individuals and as a couple.

There certainly are books that can help, particularly those which describe or illustrate various positions and techniques. Provided the couple is flexible about trying things, these can help them to develop the kind of spontaneous and free experimentation that remains, for many, the best way for discovering the most satisfying ways of sexual pleasuring. Furthermore, just as one does not try to take a course in calculus before one has learned simple arithmetic, so there is a natural progression from the earlier and simpler elements of sexual loving to the more sophisticated, and this enjoyable progression can continue for many years.

What is most important is not time but how both people feel about themselves and about each other, what the motives are in their exploration, and how well they are able to talk together by words and body language about their emotions and bodily feelings. Obviously, if one partner finds certain sexual activities pleasurable and acceptable but the other does not, then the one should not force these on the other. However, the one who is moving more slowly into sexual experience can try to be open to learning new ways of expressing physical pleasure, so that in the end a harmonious balance can be achieved between the desires and sexual capacities of the two.

In the Victorian era it was not considered proper for married people even to talk about their sexual preferences and habits. In the 1920s there was more openness, but at the same time books began to be published that indicated there were only certain ways to experience sexual relationships if one wanted to get the most satisfaction out of them. People believed these ideas and began to measure themselves against what the books said. This had very poor results, because competitiveness in sexual matters never helps enjoyment or performance but, rather, impedes both. In this period there was always the difficulty, too, that a Victorian-minded man could marry a woman with freer and more spontaneous approaches to sexual life, or the other way around: such differences in attitude often resulted in great difficulties in adjustment between them.

Gradually, in the past few years, a more open and simpler attitude has been adopted by an increasing number of people: do what you enjoy, don't force yourself for the other person, let your imagination be your guide, but communicate, so that each can know what the other is feeling. Above all, don't strive grimly and compulsively for orgasm every time. Grimness, compulsiveness, speed, and competitiveness are death blows to sexual enjoyment. Spontaneousness, warmth, freedom, communication, time, laughter, and trust—these are its life breath. Sexologists recommend that enjoyment be enhanced by mutual pleasuring, with no exclusive concern as to whether or not an orgasm occurs. Given this kind of approach, orgasms do happen and many relational difficulties resolve themselves. All the above applies equally to heterosexual and homosexual relationships.

Special Needs in Sexual Response

We referred earlier to the fact that childhood events can affect sexual response later in the adult. For example, some adults cannot achieve sexual satisfaction except under very special sets of circumstances and could benefit from sex therapy. A sexual dysfunction is a part of the sexual process that doesn't work right. Some sexual dysfunctions in the male are inability to achieve ejaculation or erection (called impotence), and ejaculation too soon, usually almost before intercourse has really begun (called premature ejaculation). Some sexual dysfunctions in the female are inability to experience orgasm (often called frigidity), uncontrollable tightening of the muscles around the entrance of the vagina, preventing the penis from entering (vaginismus), and painful intercourse (dyspareunia). Masters and Johnson identified these dysfunctions clearly and indicated successful ways of treating them. Since publication of their work, much research has been done by other sex therapists, and modifications of the Masters and Johnson methods as well as new methods have been developed for the treatment of the dysfunctions that can have such painfully adverse effects on the sexual part of an otherwise happy relationship.

Other kinds of sexual dysfunction have also been identified by therapists. One, studied particularly by Dr. Helen Kaplan, is lack of sexual desire. This can occur in both men and women as a condition that begins during adolescence and continues, or that develops in the course of a relationship. Such a lack of sexual desire is not specifically related to impotence or frigidity. After a thorough examination to make sure that there is no physical reason for it, its roots should be searched for in the possibility that something happened in the childhood or adolescence of a person that, unconsciously, operates to "turn off" that person's capacity to be sexually "turned on."

The sexuality of aging also has come in for a good bit of research. Older men and older women have for a long time been expected to lose their interest in sex, and very often they have obliged by carrying out what seemed to be expected of them. When this is *not* the case, aging individuals often undergo hardship either by denying and trying to stifle their naturally occurring sexual interest, or by leading an underground sex life.

The hopeful result is that over the past years the science of sex therapy has developed to include a wide range of treatments that can result in resolving the sexual problems that can trouble relationships. The science of sex therapy is still in its early days, but it is developing rapidly throughout the world.

Achieving Intimacy

One of the most important factors in the successful expression of sexuality between two people is communication—the ability to talk with the other person about sex in simple but honest language. This ability is closely related to the capacity the two people involved have for intimacy.

What is intimacy? It comes from the wish—the decision—of two people to form a strong, long-lasting, close relationship. One can certainly have an intimate relationship without ever having, or even thinking about having, sex as part of it. But it is hard to think of the reverse, that is, of any sexual relationship that will be long-lasting without the balance and support that true intimacy can give it. What then is intimacy? It is closeness. It comes from a Latin word meaning the highest degree of withinness.

Intimacy is the most important quality in a major life relationship. Most people cannot achieve true intimacy with more than a small number of people, for intimacy requires time, a good amount of time, as its first ingredient. Intimacy doesn't happen over a cup of tea, or overnight. The second ingredient for intimacy must be mutuality, that is, the desire of each person for intimacy with the other. The third factor is reciprocity, which has to do with exchange and commitment. Eventually both must want intimacy with each other equally.

And true intimacy cannot be achieved without trust, a most delicate and vital factor. Two individuals take many steps toward trust in each other, every step almost inevitably involving small revelations as each one opens his or her innermost self to the other and tests the safety of that opening. Virginia Johnson, of the famous Masters and Johnson team, has called this process "the exchange of vulnerabilities," meaning that by revealing themselves to each other the two partners are opening themselves up to the real possibility of being hurt, scorned, or rejected. Successive experiences of openness safely engaged in serve to build up the trust to its ultimate expression, which is open and free delight in one another. And this, to us, has to be the ultimate meaning of the word intimacy, for when two people delight each other, and delight in each other, in an atmosphere of security based on mutuality, reciprocity, and total trust each in the other, whatever their age or sex or relationship, this is surely the kind of relationship that every human being seeks, even if it does not involve physical sex.

We hope this chapter has helped you to a better understanding of highly varied aspects of human sexuality, and the way erotic sex can fit into a relationship. Understanding this expression of sexuality, in ourselves first and then in our children, can help all of us to accept and learn how to use it responsibly, appropriately, and with fulfillment in our lives, and to put our children on the road to doing the same thing. Ignoring it, repressing it, punishing it, fearing it—these negative attitudes do just the opposite by imprisoning us in walls of frustration, despair, and aloneness. We should not be afraid of erotic sex in ourselves or in our children, but instead learn how to treat it with dignity, honor, and responsibility—and with joy.

3
How Human Beings Have Children

The Human Reproductive Systems

At this point we come back to the distinction made in Chapter 2 between two systems in human beings, the *reproductive system* and the *sexual response system.* This distinction may surprise you, for it is not commonly made. Most people think, simply, "Sex—yes, that has to do with having children. Oh, and it also involves a lot of feelings." Of course, the reproductive and the sexual systems are closely related to each other in the working of our bodies, minds, and feelings, but they are not the same.

As we grow up, our reproductive system—the system that enables us to become mothers or fathers—generally does not begin to function until somewhere in our teens. Assuming we have led relatively healthy lives, it develops almost automatically. Its schedule of development, although different for each of us, is quite straightforward and very little affected by what we think, learn, or do. We automatically become capable of reproducing.

The Reproductive Systems

Human life results almost always from sexual intercourse between a male and a female. During intercourse, or coitus, the male ejaculates millions of sperm cells from his penis into the upper part of the vagina of the female. These sperm travel up the reproductive tract of the female. If they meet an egg cell, which has been released from one of the female's two ovaries, several sperm immediately surround the egg cell, the *ovum,* trying to penetrate its wall. One sperm, and only one, enters the egg, and this results in an instantaneous chemical reaction so that the cell wall shuts out all other sperm. About 266 days later, if all goes normally, the two joined cells have multiplied, by division, into some 200 billion cells, and a baby is born.

That, in simplest terms, is the story of how human beings beget children. But the full story is much more complex and very interesting.

The major basic difference between male and female, between the two *genders,* is that the male can ejaculate and can impregnate the female, while the female is the one who can be impregnated. Four other things the female can do that the male cannot are: menstruate, gestate (develop a life inside her), give birth, and lactate (give milk). Aside from these differences, males and females are capable of sharing each other's tasks and functions and feelings and exchanging roles freely—if they wish to and if society, that is, other people, allows them to.

THE MALE REPRODUCTIVE ORGANS

The reproductive organs of a male (see the illustration on page 34) consist of a remarkable and intricate system of glands, tubes, containers, valves, and muscles that work together to produce sperm, to store it until needed, and then to deliver it into the female's body. A man's most obvious reproductive organ—which is also his sexual organ—is his *penis.* Another word for penis is *phallus,* from the Greek. When limp (or flaccid), a grown man's penis is about the length of a finger but somewhat thicker. When erect, the penis increases greatly in size and somewhat in diameter and stands stiffly up and out from the body. An erect penis is usually six inches or more in length. When it becomes erect, a small limp penis increases proportionately more in size than a large limp penis, so that erection is a great equalizer of penis size. Except for obvious and rare abnormalities, penises of any size work perfectly well in performing their reproductive function. And there is no relationship between the size of the penis and body build, race, or reproductive power.

The penis is composed mostly of spongy tissue containing many small blood vessels and nerves. (It contains no bone, unlike the penises of some other male mammals, such as dogs.) A small tube, the *urethra,* runs the length of the penis and functions as a passageway to empty urine from the bladder and also as a passageway for the ejaculation of

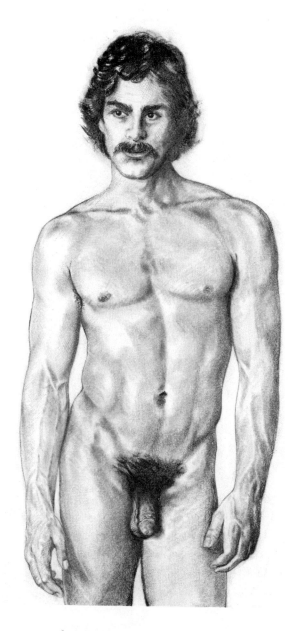

Male figure

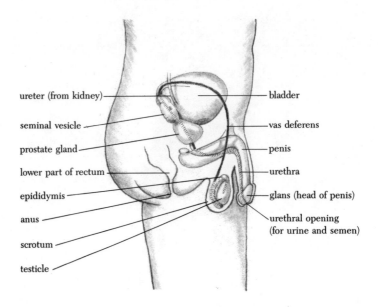

ureter (from kidney)
seminal vesicle
prostate gland
lower part of rectum
epididymis
anus
scrotum
testicle

bladder
vas deferens
penis
urethra
glans (head of penis)
urethral opening
(for urine and semen)

Male genito-urinary system (with anus and lower rectum)

semen, which contains the sperm. Urine and semen cannot use this passage at the same time—they cannot get mixed together—because when a man is about to ejaculate, a valve automatically closes off the connection with the bladder.

At the end of the penis is the head, or *glans,* which is its most sensitive part because it is supplied with many nerves. The glans is covered by a loose sheath of skin, the *foreskin.* When the penis becomes erect, the foreskin is retracted, exposing the glans. The foreskin can be pushed back from the glans, making it possible to clean underneath it. It is necessary to clean underneath the foreskin because small glands near the end of the penis produce a cheesy substance called *smegma.* No one knows what smegma is for, but it has a certain odor that can be unpleasant when too much is allowed to collect under the foreskin. (Similar glands in females also produce smegma around the clitoris, the corresponding female organ for sexual pleasure.)

In the United States, many male infants have the foreskin removed in the hospital on the second day after birth by means of a surgical operation called *circumcision* (cutting around). The doctor pulls the foreskin out in front of the penis and neatly cuts off part of it with a special device. Those who advocate circumcision say that it promotes cleanliness. Opponents are against the pain endured by the baby and the

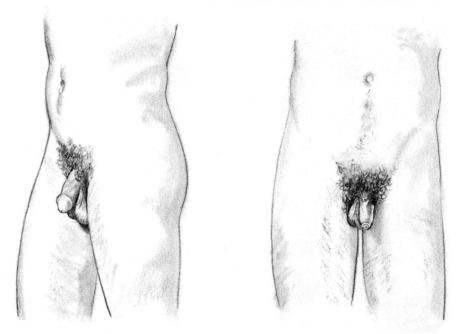

Left, circumcised penis; *right,* uncircumcised penis

occasional accidents related to circumcision. Despite various beliefs to the contrary, there is no evidence that circumcised males are any more or any less responsive sexually than uncircumcised ones, or that circumcision affects reproduction. Today most doctors and the American Academy of Pediatrics think that it is better to leave the penis uncircumcised, unless, of course, circumcision is required by the parents' religion.

Under a man's penis hangs a sac of loose, crinkly skin called the *scrotum.* The scrotum is divided into two compartments, each of which contains a *testicle,* an *epididymis,* and the lower part of the *vas deferens,* all of which we shall explain below. The scrotal covering also contains muscles that contract when cold, thus pulling the testicles up nearer the body. These muscles work involuntarily and operate like a sort of thermostat to keep the testicles at just the right temperature—lower than that inside the body, but not too much lower—for the manufacture of sperm. Generally, a man's left testicle hangs down slightly lower than his right, although both are the same size.

The two *testicles*—also called *testes* (*testis* being the singular), and a number of less formal terms—are the sperm-makers. They are oval-shaped and approximately 1½ to 2 inches long in a grown man, about the size of a plum. Each testicle contains perhaps 270 yards—over one-eighth of a mile—of threadlike, coiled-up tubules (tiny tubes) in

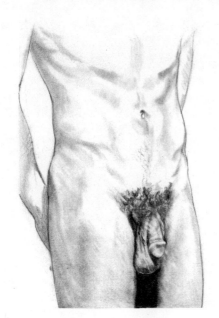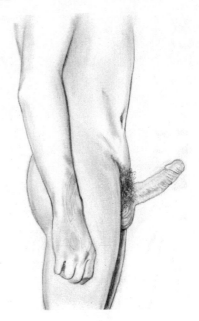

The penis when limp and when erect

which sperm are continuously made after a boy has reached puberty. These sperm pass into the *epididymis,* another collection of tubules, in which they mature as they pass through and on into the *vas deferens.*

Sperm are the male reproductive cells. The scientific words for them are *spermatozoon* (singular) and *spermatozoa* (plural). Sperm are invisible to the human eye, except under a microscope, a single sperm being about as long as two-thirds the thickness of an average human hair. A sperm is shaped somewhat like a tadpole, with a tail that lashes about and enables it to swim along. If one could line up a number of sperm head to tail, it would take five hundred of them to make an inch. Yet, small as they are, each sperm contains all that is needed to unite with an egg in a woman and start a baby.

We now come to that part of the male reproductive system which might be called "storage and delivery." Once manufactured and matured, the sperm pass along the duct known as the vas deferens and are stored there near the openings of the *seminal vesicles,* two small pouches well inside the man's body (see drawing on page 34). Here they remain quite inactive until they are ejaculated, when the seminal vesicles release a fluid which activates the sperm. At the time of ejaculation, a thick, milky fluid secreted by the *prostate gland* is also added. This mixture of sperm and fluid is then called *semen.* The semen nourishes the sperm and keeps them alive while they are in the vagina until a number of them find their way into the cervix and then upward toward an ovum.

The *prostate gland,* which lies just below the bladder, is a most important part of the delivery system for the sperm. It manufactures the milky part of the semen, of which the sperm form only a minute portion of the volume. When a man becomes sexually excited, and his erect penis is ready for *orgasm* (see pages 15 and 245), the muscles of the prostate and other muscles near it contract in a series of quick spasms that propel the semen down the urethra and *ejaculate* it out of the opening at the tip of the penis. These spasms of ejaculation—that is, when the male has an orgasm, or "comes"—are highly pleasurable.

THE FEMALE REPRODUCTIVE ORGANS

We said that the man's most obvious reproductive organ is his penis. The organ of the female that most nearly corresponds to the penis is the *clitoris,* which, although small, contains a concentration of sensitive nerves almost exactly like those in the head of the penis. However, the clitoris is not concerned with the process of reproduction and is not, therefore, considered a part of the female reproductive system. It is, however, as we have said, a very important part of a female's sexual response system.

A woman's primary reproductive organs are her *ovaries,* which correspond to the testicles in the man. The two ovaries, each the shape of a flattened oval and about 1½ to 2 inches long, lie inside the lower part of the abdomen, one on each side (see the drawing on page 39). When a girl is born, her ovaries already contain about 400,000 immature eggs, or *ova.* The ovaries do not manufacture ova, but rather store them ready to bring to maturity after *puberty.* That's when the ova start maturing, usually one ovum each month, roughly halfway between two menstrual periods. (See the picture on page 44.) However, the time intervals differ with different women, ranging from twenty-one to thirty-eight days. They may also vary in an individual woman, depending upon particular circumstances in her life.

The ovum matures within a little saclike bubble on the surface of the ovary. The wall of this sac gradually becomes thinner, and the sac contains an increasing amount of fluid surrounding the ovum. During the process called *ovulation,* an opening is created in the sac, so that

Female figure

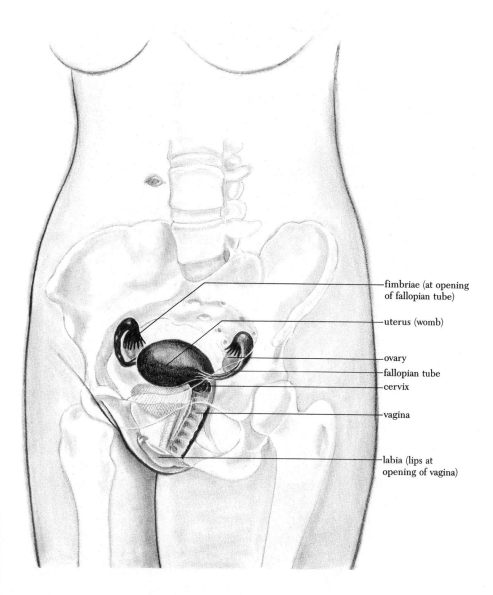

fimbriae (at opening
of fallopian tube)

uterus (womb)

ovary
fallopian tube
cervix

vagina

labia (lips at
opening of vagina)

Female reproductive system

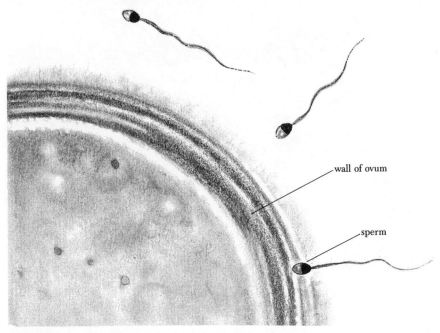

Moment of fertilization

the ovum and fluid are expelled. Some women can feel a slight twinge about the time this happens, although the twinge may occur as long as one day before or one day after the actual ovulation, or may never be felt at all. It is therefore not a reliable indicator of the moment of ovulation. When the egg is released, it is transported along with its fluid and surrounding cells into the opening at the end of the *fallopian tube,* assisted in its journey by the motion of waving fingerlike threads (*fimbriae*) at the opening of the tube. As the ovum is thus picked up, it is moved down the tube toward the uterus, propelled by the action of minute hairlike *cilia,* which wave downward toward the uterus. Whether it is fertilized or not, the ovum is retained within the fallopian tube for approximately three days, after which it is delivered into the uterus. If the ovum has not been fertilized, it begins to disintegrate in the uterus and soon disappears. (The human ovum is much smaller than the period at the end of this sentence. It would take two hundred eggs side by side to cover an inch. However, compared to a sperm, the egg is a giant (see the picture on this page).

In preparation for the possible arrival of a fertilized egg—called a *zygote*—the uterus has been developing, over a period of about two weeks, a thick, soft, velvety lining, the *endometrium,* which is made up

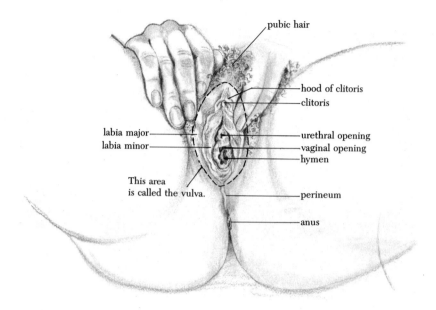

pubic hair

hood of clitoris
clitoris

labia major
labia minor

urethral opening
vaginal opening
hymen

This area
is called the vulva.

perineum

anus

Female genital area

mostly of blood vessels. In this lining the zygote can be imbedded and continue its growth. If no egg is fertilized, the uterus sheds its lining in the process called *menstruation.*

If an egg encounters sperm in the tube, it probably will be fertilized. Then it continues down the fallopian tube, its cells dividing rapidly all the while, so that by the time it has been floated down and into the *uterus* (or *womb*) it has divided several times and contains between eight and sixteen cells. The uterus is an amazing organ about the size and shape of a small pear, some 3 inches long in a woman who has not had children. It is strongly muscular, yet stretchable. In the lining of the uterus the fertilized egg becomes implanted and will grow into a baby. As the baby grows, so will the uterus to accommodate it within its strong muscular walls. These muscles, aided by the muscles of the abdomen, will not only protect the baby but will later do the work—the labor—of pushing the baby out through the birth canal (vagina) and into the world.

The vagina actually belongs to both the reproductive system and the sexual response system. It is the place where the penis deposits the sperm during sexual intercourse; it is the main passage through which the baby passes when it is born; and it is the passage for the menstrual

Different types of hymen

flow. The outer opening of the vagina is not a visible hole and can be seen only when the lips of the vulva are parted. (See illustration on page 41.) The entrance to the vagina of a woman before she has had intercourse is usually partly closed by a membrane called the *hymen*. (See illustration on this page.) No one knows of any particular use for the hymen. In most women it is quite delicate; in a few it is rather tough. In some cases the hymen has only a small opening, which permits the exit of the menstrual flow; in other cases there are a number of openings, either large or small; in still others there is no hymen at all. Many people mistakenly believe it is possible to tell whether or not a woman is a virgin (one who has not had sexual intercourse) by whether her hymen is unbroken or broken. If it is unbroken, yes, she is a virgin, but if it is broken, no one can say (except the woman herself), for in many girls an ample opening develops quite naturally, or the hymen may have been almost entirely absent even at birth. Also, using a tampon during menstruation may enlarge to some degree the opening in the hymen of a woman who is a virgin, although the largest tampons are smaller than an erect penis. With the help of a hand mirror and a flashlight, girls and women can easily examine and identify for themselves all the external organs we have mentioned, and it is helpful for them to become acquainted with their bodies in this way.

The vagina most of the time is a soft tube about 3 or 4 inches long that, except when it is being used as a passageway, is rather like a collapsed balloon. Its inner lining is soft and moist, much like the lining of a person's mouth. Most of its length it is not sensitive to touch, but the outer end—the area surrounding the opening—is sensitive and excitable. When a woman is sexually aroused, the walls of her vagina produce a slippery fluid that makes it easy for an erect penis to enter.

At the upper end of the vagina is the *cervix,* or neck of the uterus, the passage into the uterus. This passage is not much larger than the lead of a pencil and is called the *cervical canal.* It is large enough for thousands of sperm to pass through at each ejaculation.

Menstruation

If, as is usually the case, no egg has been fertilized and become implanted in the lining of the wall of the uterus (the endometrium), that lining is no longer needed and is shed, or discarded. This process is called menstruation. Many women, when they menstruate, say they are "having their period." The menstrual flow lasts from three to six days. It is not bleeding in the ordinary sense of the word, although the flow is red and contains blood and tissue, including minute blood vessels. Ordinarily, menstruation does not weaken a woman, for it merely discards material that her body has already supplied but that is no longer needed. Menstruation usually occurs at four-week intervals, but this can vary from three to five weeks or more.

During menstruation a woman needs to wear some disposable absorbent material to collect the menstrual flow. One such device is a pad or napkin that is held in place against the opening of the vagina by an elastic panty, a belt, or a sticky backing that makes it cling to a panty. (See the drawing on page 45.) Another menstrual aid is a tampon or insert made of absorbent material shaped into a small roll that can be easily inserted into the vagina to absorb the flow. The use of tampons was linked in 1980 to a rare disease, toxic shock syndrome. (TSS). To avoid TSS, women should: change tampons every four to six hours; wash their hands before changing tampons; use the inserter barrel if one comes with the tampon rather than inserting it with the fingers; and

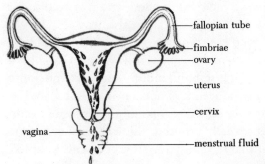

Day 1, menstruation begins.

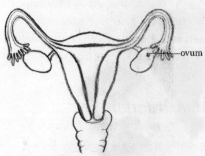

Approximate days 8 – 9, egg sac starts
to grow and **uterine wall** to build up.

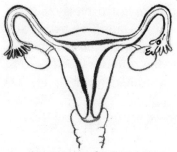

Approximate days 14 – 15,
ovulation occurs.

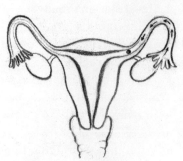

Approximate days 19 – 20,
ovum about to enter uterus, building
of uterine wall now completed.

The menstrual cycle.
Note: The time intervals differ with different women.

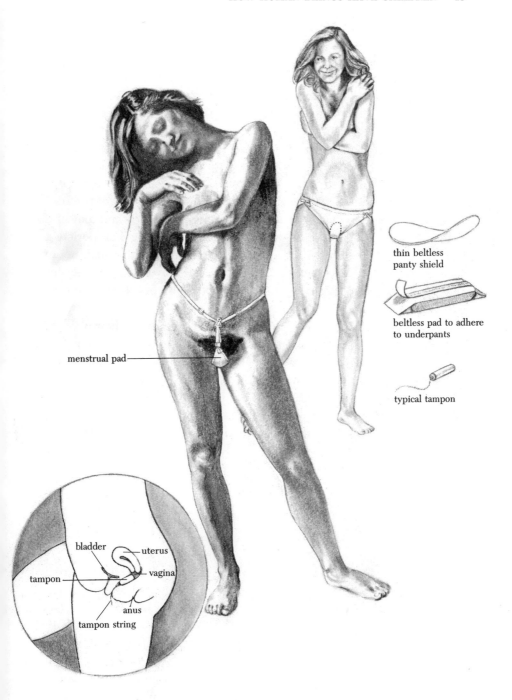

thin beltless
panty shield

beltless pad to adhere
to underpants

typical tampon

menstrual pad

bladder   uterus

tampon   vagina

anus

tampon string

Menstrual aids

wear a menstrual pad at night instead of using a tampon. Also, a tampon-free interval every day is a good practice.

Some women find the few days before and during menstruation somewhat uncomfortable. A common term for this condition is *premenstrual syndrome* (PMS). Part of the discomfort may be caused by congestion of the blood vessels in and around the uterus before the flow begins; part by the contraction of the uterine muscles to discard the lining, which may be felt as pains or aches in the lower back; part by a tendency in some women to accumulate fluids in the tissues, which gives a heavy feeling to the body; and part by the chemical changes in the woman's body as the glands of her ovaries secrete less of the hormones that prepared her uterus for a possible pregnancy and may also have given her a feeling of well-being. Thus, during her period a woman may feel edgy and may tire more readily than usual. Some women still call menstruation "the curse." If a woman experiences nausea, vomiting, or severe cramps, or if she feels very depressed during menstruation, she should consult her doctor.

Today's girls and women lead their usual lives during their periods. With the modern methods of protection against the flow now available, there is no reason why they should not participate in all sports and other activities, including swimming.

When a woman menstruates, it is a clear sign that she is not pregnant. On the other hand, if she does not menstruate within a week or two of her usual time, and if she has been having sexual intercourse, this is a sign that she may be pregnant, and she will want to check with a doctor or clinic to find out for sure. (Other signs of possible pregnancy are discussed later in this chapter.)

The Puberty Timetable

How can a girl know when she is about to have her first menstrual period, or a boy when he will have his first ejaculation of semen? When will they reach *puberty*, as it is called? Usually, girls and boys are very much interested in knowing this, and some are quite worried about it. Parents ought to be aware of this concern and anticipate it by providing full information.

Perhaps the most important point to make is that there is tremendous variation in the ages at which people reach puberty; there is no single "right" or "proper" age. Further, there is no relationship between people's ability to respond sexually and the age at which they first menstruate or ejaculate.

BOYS

In general, boys have their first ejaculation quite some time before they appear to be "men." This first ejaculation announces that a boy has arrived at puberty, that he is capable of making a female pregnant. Although, in general, boys' physical development comes about two years later than that of girls, the average age of first ejaculation is only about six months to a year later than that for first menstruation in girls. Despite the general impression one gets, based on body shape and size, that boys are about two years behind girls in reaching full physical maturity, in fact, they are much less far behind in their capacity to reproduce.

Usually the first stirrings of puberty and the beginnings of adolescence are marked by the start of a spurt in growth. The average male begins his growth spurt at about age 12½ and finishes it at age 16, with the fastest rate of growth coming, on the average, around age 14. However, the age *range* for the *start* of the growth spurt is from 10½ to 16, while the age range for its completion is 13½ to 17½. Many perfectly healthy individuals fall outside these typical ranges, so that some boys actually complete their growth spurts before others have even begun theirs. In a single year of his growth spurt, a boy may become 2½ to 5 inches taller. The upper-age ranges of the growth spurt do not indicate that a boy has reached his full height at these ages—only that his period of extra-rapid growth has ended. Usually, he will continue to grow for from two to four more years.

A boy may have been masturbating and experiencing orgasm for a number of years, even though his first ejaculation of semen will not occur until his growth spurt, and he cannot predict exactly when that will be. On the average—but remember the great variation—it comes about a year after his penis and testicles have noticeably started to grow and at about the time that his growth spurt peaks. A fairly reliable sign of approaching ejaculation is the appearance, just above the penis, of pubic hair, at first downy but gradually becoming darker and coarser. Usually somewhat later, hair begins to grow under the arms. About three to four months after the first *curly* pubic hair appears, the first seminal ejaculation will probably happen—perhaps in a "wet dream" (nocturnal emission), perhaps in masturbation; there are great varia-

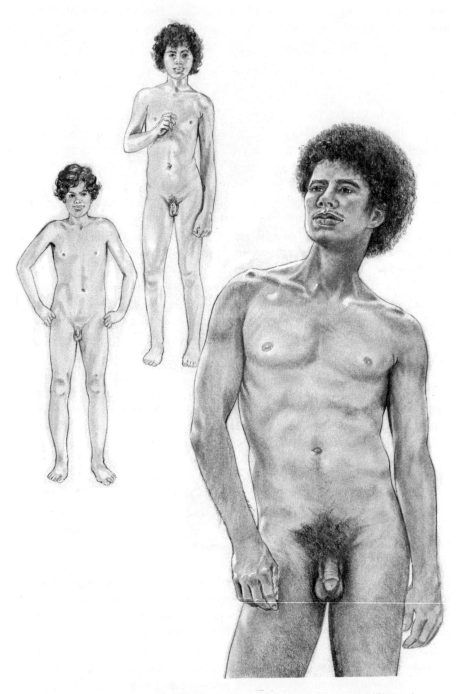

Three males: *left to right,* prepuberty, early puberty, postpuberty

Three adolescent males, same age, different stages of growth

tions. The change of voice in early adolescence generally begins to be noticeable a few months *after* the first ejaculation. This change, a part of the growth spurt, is caused by a rather rapid growth in the size of the larynx (voice box).

Two sources of embarrassment to many boys during their adolescence are *acne* and temporary enlargement of the breasts. Acne is a skin condition, especially of the face, that causes pimples, often rather deep ones, to form when the skin begins to secrete increased amounts of an oily substance which clogs the pores. (Acne occurs in some girls, too, but usually not nearly so severely as in boys.) Temporary enlargement of the breasts occurs in about 80 percent of boys during puberty. It is probably caused by a very small amount of female sex hormones, normally produced by the testicles, and it soon disappears as the body adjusts to the changes of adolescence.

It is perfectly normal for a boy to reach puberty as early as age 10 or 11 or as late as 15 or 16. The drawings on page 49 illustrate the differences in normal development.

GIRLS

Girls also experience an adolescent growth spurt, usually—but not always—about two years before boys. On the average it begins at age 10½ and ends at age 14. Generally, a girl's first menstruation (called *menarche*) comes about three-quarters of the way through her growth spurt, not, as in boys, at its apex. There is an age range of three to five years in the time girls reach the apex, and, as with boys, some girls will have completed their spurt before others have started theirs. The drawings on page 52 illustrate how great the physical differences are and how misleading it is to make generalizations about the rate and stages of adolescent physical development.

On the average—and remember that few people are exactly at the average—a girl's breasts begin to bud about three to four years before menarche and become noticeable two to three years before. About one and a half to two and a half years before, pubic hair appears above her genitals, and underarm hair appears about six months before.

A girl's first menstruation is the sign that she has arrived at puberty, that she might be capable of pregnancy. Even though in many girls there is a gap of several months to more than a year between first menstruation and first ovulation, it is impossible to tell which girls have this gap. In fact, some girls may first ovulate even *before* they menstru-

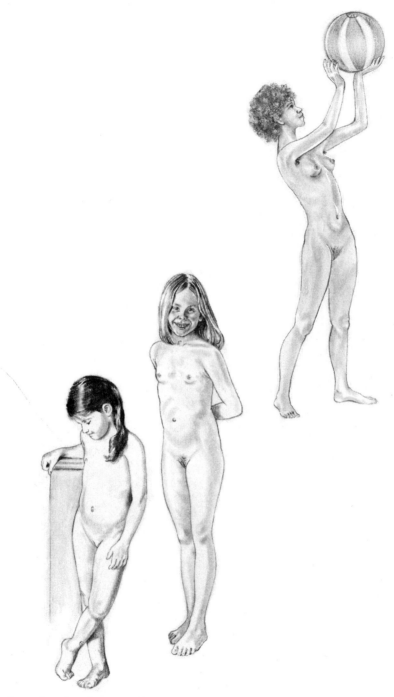

Three females: *left to right*, prepuberty, early puberty, postpuberty

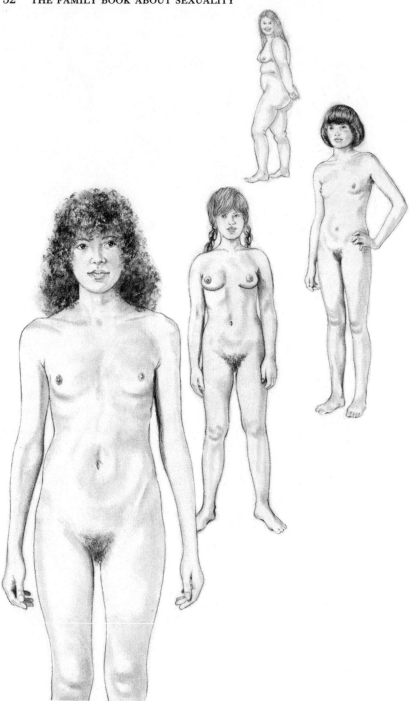

Four adolescent females, same age, different stages of growth

ate, so that it is entirely possible for a sexually active girl to become pregnant before her first menstruation. Once a girl has ovulated she is thereafter fertile.

The normal range for menarche, the arrival at puberty, is from age 10 to 16.

Sexual Intercourse

A new human life can be started by the joining of a fertile male and a fertile female in *sexual intercourse.* Another standard word for this act is *coitus.* In animals it is called copulation—mounting or covering, in farm language. In sexual intercourse, the erect penis of the man enters the vagina of the woman and, after a variable period of time involving various movements, generally pleasurable to both, the man ejaculates semen into the upper end of the vagina. One ejaculation usually contains about a teaspoonful of semen. This includes some 200 million to 400 million sperm, which are only a minute proportion of the volume of the semen.

Some of these millions of sperm enter the cervical canal and the uterus. The notion of many people that sperm have a sense of purpose and swim steadily toward their goal, the unfertilized egg, is a false one. Once sperm are ejaculated, their swimming motion is quite random, but it is somewhat guided by tubelike formations in the cervical mucus and by muscular contractions of the uterus. When some of the sperm reach the entrance to the fallopian tubes, they enter and move through the tubes, on out the other end, and into the abdominal cavity. Their movement up the tubes is caused partly by their own swimming action, partly by the direction given by the mucus, and partly by contracting movements of the tubes themselves (called peristalsis). Sperm have been detected in the fallopian tubes within five minutes after ejaculation, and generally, from that point on, several sperm are passing through the tubes at any given time, over a period of two to three days, in some cases as many as five, ready to fertilize an egg that may be on its way down. The whole matter of how the egg is moved down the tube and how sperm pass into and up through the tubes is a complicated one, not entirely understood. But it works. An egg gets fertilized and begins the process of multiplying and dividing which, if nothing interferes with it, will eventually result in a baby.

Of course, there is much more to sexual intercourse than we have described here, as you saw in Chapter 2 on the sexual response systems.

Just remember: "Penises and vaginas do not love each other; only people can do that."

Pregnancy

Once an egg is fertilized, the woman is pregnant and the lining of her uterus is needed; therefore she does not menstruate again until the pregnancy is over. Missing her period is one of the early signs that a woman can expect a baby, although one missed period is not a totally accurate sign, for some women occasionally skip a period without being pregnant. However, ten days to two weeks after her usual time for menstruation has passed, a woman who has been sexually active will want to know for sure if she is pregnant, and a doctor or technician can tell by any one of several tests of her blood or urine.

At-home pregnancy test kits can be bought at any drugstore for about $12 to $18. They test the urine and are very accurate, particularly when the result is positive—that is, when it shows pregnancy. Occasionally, however, the test kit result is a "false negative"—it shows no pregnancy even though the woman is actually pregnant. Therefore, it is important for the woman to repeat the test in one week. To repeat the test, a "double" kit can be used. Such kits are available in the same price range. Kit instructions are complicated and must be followed precisely. If the test shows positive, the woman should go to her doctor or to a clinic for evaluation and advice and, of course, talk with her partner.

There are early signs of pregnancy that the woman herself can notice. They are enlargement and tenderness of the breasts; "morning sickness," a feeling of nausea or aversion to food that some women experience during the first six weeks, most often in the morning; the need to urinate more frequently than usual; and a sense of fatigue and a need to sleep more than usual.

SEXUAL INTERCOURSE DURING PREGNANCY

While she is pregnant, a woman's ovaries produce no more mature eggs. Thus, when she has sexual intercourse there is no chance of starting another baby. Under normal circumstances, both man and woman can certainly enjoy intercourse during the pregnancy. The feelings of closeness and pleasure that sexual intercourse provides are just as important—perhaps even more so—during pregnancy as at other times. It is not true that the motions of intercourse or of orgasm will harm the developing baby or cause a miscarriage. However, because of a possible link between infections and intercourse in the last month of pregnancy, sexual relations toward the end of the period of gestation should be discussed with the obstetrician. Of course, if a woman should ever experience pain or bleeding during pregnancy she should consult her doctor at once. Intercourse may be resumed very soon after childbirth, whenever all bleeding has ceased—and if it does not cause the mother discomfort—usually after four to six weeks.

CARE DURING PREGNANCY

When a woman realizes she is pregnant, or thinks she may be pregnant, she should be in touch with a doctor regularly to be sure that everything is going all right and to get advice on such matters as diet.

In general, whatever makes a pregnant woman healthy is likely to improve the health of her baby, and whatever is damaging to her health may endanger the baby. That is why it is important for a pregnant woman to be constantly under the care of a doctor and to tell him or her everything about her food and drug or medication habits. Even when the pregnant woman suffers from poor health, however, in the vast majority of cases her baby is born healthy.

More and more women are participating in classes and groups to help them enjoy their pregnancies and to prepare themselves for childbirth. Fathers often join the classes so that the pregnancy and birth can become a closely shared experience for the couple.

TOBACCO, DRUGS, AND ALCOHOL
DURING PREGNANCY

Whatever a pregnant woman takes into her system will have some effect on the life growing within her. The food she eats nourishes both her and the baby. There is much study now under way to determine the effects of substances other than food taken into the expectant mother's system.

It has been observed that when a mother smokes, the fetus

becomes more active and its heartbeat speeds up. Mothers who smoke give birth, on the average, to somewhat smaller babies than those who do not, and the babies' chances of survival are slightly decreased. Marijuana has a temporary effect on the fetus, but as yet no known harmful one. Heavy drugs, especially cocaine and heroin, are very injurious to the baby. If the mother is addicted, the baby will be born an addict and suffer the same severe withdrawal symptoms that an adult addict suffers when suddenly taken off the drug. Other drugs—even those that are commonly obtained without a prescription—can also have major effects. No pregnant woman should use any drug or medicine at all without the advice of her doctor.

As for alcohol, when the mother drinks even a very small amount, the baby's movements inside the uterus are slowed down while the alcohol is in the mother's bloodstream, but if the mother drinks more than just a small amount, the chances of her having a severely defective baby are much higher than normal. Some babies of alcoholic mothers are born with a disorder called fetal alcohol syndrome, which causes fetal deformation and mental retardation.

From Fertilization to Birth

The average length of time from fertilization until birth is about 266 days, a little less than nine months. The length of time from the last menstrual period is 280 days, a bit over nine months. In general, we divide the period of pregnancy into three *trimesters,* each about three months long.

From the beginning of pregnancy until its eighth week, the future baby is known as an *embryo,* after which it is called a *fetus.* It gets its nourishment through a thick, disk-shaped collection of very fine blood vessels and tissue, the *placenta,* to which it is connected by a long, ropelike cord, the *umbilical cord.* The minute blood vessels of the placenta grow outward to lie alongside those of the mother's uterine lining, her *endometrium.* Through the very thin walls of both sets of blood vessels, an exchange occurs: nutritional elements and oxygen pass from the bloodstream of the mother to the bloodstream of the growing baby; waste materials from the baby pass the other way, from baby to mother, whose kidneys then excrete them. Food and oxygen are carried to the baby, and waste is carried from the baby, through the umbilical blood vessels. The embryo makes its own blood, which never mixes with the blood of the mother and may be of a different blood type.

THE FIRST TRIMESTER (ABOUT WEEKS 1–13)

At first, the human embryo resembles the embryos of other animals. For a short time it has what look like the beginnings of gills, as in fish embryos, and later what appears to be a tail. But these are not real gills or a real tail, and they turn into real parts of the baby. Even later its body is covered with fine, downy hair, which it soon loses.

At *four weeks* the embryo is about ¼-inch long. It has lost its "gills" but still has its "tail," and an ordinary observer would not be able to distinguish it from the embryo of a fish, turtle, chicken, cat, rabbit, or dog. At as early as six weeks, brain waves have been recorded in a human embryo.

At *nine weeks* the fetus has grown to 1½ inches in length and weighs only about ¹⁄₂₀ of an ounce. To reach an average birth weight only seven months later, it will have to grow about 2,400 times heavier. As you can see from the picture on page 58, the fetus has a large head, and fingers and toes are starting to appear. The head contains the beginnings of eyes, ears, nose, and mouth, and the heart is pumping blood through the tiny body. The umbilical cord is still connected to the placenta, which has by this time grown into the muscular wall of the uterus. The reproductive system of the fetus has now been developing for about three or four weeks. By the ninth week, if one were able to examine the fetus with a microscope, it would be possible to tell whether these beginnings would turn out to be testicles or ovaries.

By *twelve weeks* the fetus has made a great spurt of growth and is now about 4 inches long, but weighs only ⅓ ounce—about ¹⁄₅₀ pound. The beginnings of the testicles or ovaries have now grown larger and have moved lower in the body of the fetus, but not to their final positions. The penis of a male fetus and the clitoris of a female fetus are not distinguishable; they look very much alike at this stage.

THE SECOND TRIMESTER (ABOUT WEEKS 14–25)

By *sixteen to seventeen* weeks the fetus has grown to be 7 or 8 inches long and weighs ⅓ pound. Its bones have begun to develop, and its arms and legs can move. The mother may now be able to feel the first faint flutter of activity inside her womb, called "quickening," although the fetus has been moving, unfelt, for some weeks prior to this. The

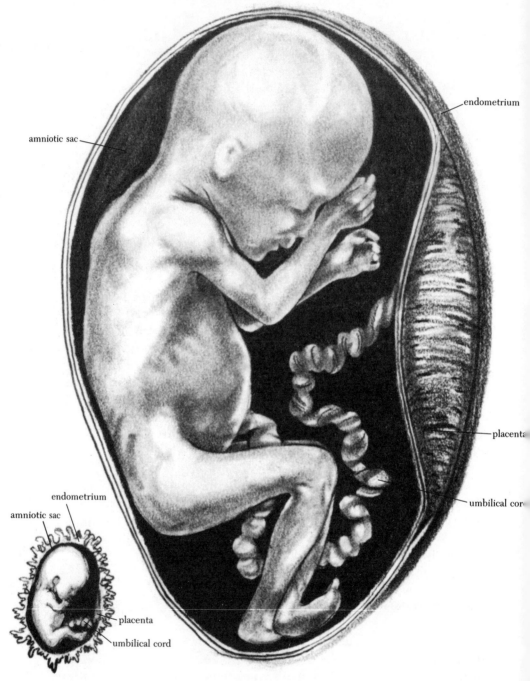

endometrium

amniotic sac

placenta

umbilical cord

endometrium

amniotic sac

placenta

umbilical cord

at nine weeks

at five months

Actual size of fetus at two stages

picture on page 58 shows a five-month-old fetus, umbilically attached to its placenta and floating in fluid inside the *amniotic sac,* to cushion it from bumps. Notice that by now it looks more like a skinny baby with fairly well-developed hands and feet and an oversized head.

At *twenty-one weeks* the fetus would be about 10 inches long if its curled-up legs were stretched out straight. It weighs about ¾ pound and is covered with downy hair. (No one knows why it develops body hair at this stage, only to lose it about a month later.)

At *twenty-five weeks,* the fetus is 12 inches long and weighs about 1¼ pounds—still quite thin, not yet having begun to store up body fat. (It is losing its body hair, which stays floating around in the amniotic fluid until expelled during the birth process.)

If the fetus should be born, or delivered, at the end of the second trimester, it would have only a slight chance (perhaps 10 percent) of survival, if given heroic care for many weeks by doctors and nurses. By week 29 or 30, the chances will have risen to over 80 percent. As the fetus develops through the third trimester, its chances of surviving increase steadily. Medical technology has, over the years, been able to lower the age of viability—the age at which a fetus is likely to be born alive. For it just to be born alive, however, does not always mean that it will stay alive or have all its systems functioning normally.

THE THIRD TRIMESTER (ABOUT WEEKS 26–38)

At twenty-nine weeks the fetus is about 14 inches long and probably weighs over 2 pounds. The body hair is gone. In the next two months the fetus will have to increase its weight three or four times to reach the average birth weight. Around this time the testicles of the male fetus have, in almost every case, descended into the scrotum, and the penis is having periodic erections.

During weeks *thirty to thirty-eight,* the eighth and ninth months, the fetus grows rapidly to an average weight of 7½ pounds and, at the end of the 266-day gestation period, perhaps a few days earlier, perhaps a few days later, it is full-term and ready to be born.

In the last trimester of pregnancy things get a bit crowded inside the mother's abdomen as the baby and the uterus expand and press upon the other organs (see the drawing on page 60). At this time an expectant mother urinates more often than usual and may want to eat smaller, more frequent meals.

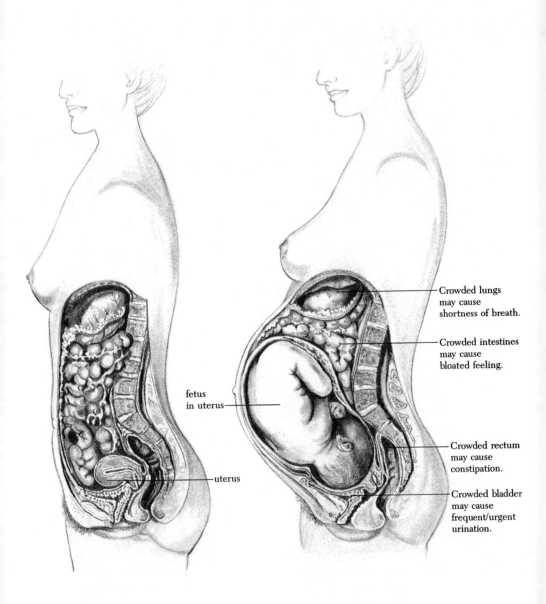

fetus
in uterus

uterus

Crowded lungs
may cause
shortness of breath.

Crowded intestines
may cause
bloated feeling.

Crowded rectum
may cause
constipation.

Crowded bladder
may cause
frequent/urgent
urination.

Effect of pregnancy on body organs: *left,* normal position; *right,* at ninth month
of pregnancy

Childbirth

For most of the hundreds of thousands of years that human beings have been reproducing their kind, childbirth was looked upon as a natural phenomenon, experienced without special help, except for that given by other women. Often childbirth was a quite casual event, with only a brief interruption of the mother's daily life. But during this long period of prehistory and history, the numbers of infants dying at birth or shortly afterward (the infant mortality rate) was very high.

Until about 150 years ago, babies in the Western world were usually born at home, often with the help of a specially trained woman called a *midwife*. While certainly not a physician, the midwife knew how to help a mother have a delivery that was more comfortable and safe than if no experienced person were present. Beginning in the early eighteenth century and until very recently, the conduct of childbirth has been more and more taken over by male doctors and surgeons. It has become more of a medical process than a natural one, with women having their babies in hospitals rather than at home, and with emphasis on anesthetics, surgical instruments such as forceps, and a team of medical technicians assisting. Until recently, husbands were rarely allowed to be present.

The development of the specialty of *obstetrics* (an *obstetrician* is a doctor who specializes in childbirth), with its highly developed procedures and its emphasis on sterile conditions and anesthetics, rapidly reduced the infant and maternal mortality rates. But it also took childbirth out of the home and out of the context of the family, and it may have encouraged the notion that pregnancy and giving birth were more medical problems to be dealt with by doctors than natural parts of ongoing family life. Mothers tended to become isolated from the process of birth (during it they were often made unconscious, or nearly so, by anesthesia) and were physically separated from their babies during their stay at the hospital, except for nursing time. As for fathers, they were considered to have done their part nine months earlier and were not welcome either as observers or as participants in the process of birth; fathers were often not even permitted to hold their babies in the hospital.

Today, however, there is a growing conviction on the part of mothers, fathers, and many doctors and nurses—and the midwives who have again become part of the birth team—that childbirth can and should be made less clinical and more natural; that, if they wish, mothers should be awake and aware during childbirth; that husbands (again, if they wish) should be included in the preparation for childbirth and be present with their wives, helping them during the birth itself; and that babies should room in with their mothers much of the time they are in the hospital, rather than being whisked off to the hospital nursery for most of the time. Some parents are now even deciding to have their babies born at home, with a midwife attending. If that is their choice, they should make sure that medical help will be available in case of complications.

Preparation for childbirth according to a "natural" way involves teaching a prospective mother and father exactly how childbirth works, what the mother's body will be doing during the birth, and how she can relax and cooperate with the actual processes of labor and delivery and in fact enjoy the whole experience, the hard work, and especially the product—a new baby—from the very instant of his or her birth.

THE PROCESS OF CHILDBIRTH

The mother's first signal that the time for childbirth has come is usually the start of contractions of the strong muscles of the uterus, accompanied by a dull ache across the lower back or a sensation of tightening as the contractions increase in power. At first these contractions are spaced perhaps fifteen minutes to half an hour apart, but when they begin to come regularly every five to ten minutes, the mother should be taken to the hospital, or the doctor or midwife who will help her with the birth should be called in.

The muscular contractions are called *labor,* and a woman who is about to bear a child is said to be *in labor.* There is no doubt that giving birth to a child is usually hard work. It can also be very painful over a short period of time, but much of the discomfort in a normal birth can be avoided by the expectant mother who has conditioned her body for childbirth and who understands so well what is happening during the birth that she can help guide the process.

The normal pain of a woman in childbirth is caused by the aching of the powerful muscles that work to push out the baby. Many women prefer to have an anesthetic, which relieves the pain. Other women would rather be fully conscious while bearing a child, with only a mild anesthetic or none at all. But understanding what the experience of childbirth involves tends to relieve fear and anxiety, and it is this that helps to relax the muscles around the vagina, and particularly the cervix, which must dilate, or stretch, to permit passage of the baby. Understanding the process and learning how to cooperate in it can make the mother more relaxed, which increases the ease of the birth and may help speed the arrival of the baby.

Labor in childbirth is divided into three stages. The *first stage* extends from the time when contractions become regular until the cervix is well opened—dilated—about 4 inches. The first stage of labor is the longest, lasting on the average about fifteen hours for a first pregnancy and perhaps four to eight hours or even less in subsequent ones. There is a great variation in the duration of labor, some babies taking a full day or more to be born, others coming in a few hours or even minutes.

The *second stage* of labor extends from the time of full dilation of the cervix until the baby is born. It lasts anywhere from a few minutes to a few hours. Usually, early in the first stage of labor, the covering membranes that have enclosed the baby in the womb break by themselves, and the amniotic fluid they contained, which had acted as a cushion for the baby, flows out through the vagina and helps to lubricate it. Sometimes labor is progressing well into the second stage but the membranes haven't broken by themselves. In such cases the doctor may use a device that painlessly pinches an opening in the membranes so that the fluid will come out and the period of labor be shortened. After this "rush of waters," as it is called, and once the baby's head has passed the cervix, the baby is fairly quickly pushed down through the vagina and out into the world by a series of hard contractions of the mother's uterus and abdominal muscles. The baby's head generally comes first; it is usually a tight fit, but the bones of the head are compressible enough to be undamaged. The head serves well as a kind of wedge to open the way for the rest of the body. The doctor or midwife is waiting to guide the head gently as it emerges and to help the baby come out easily as the birth is completed. The birth attendant then lays the baby on the mother's abdomen where she can see it and, after a minute or so, ties and cuts the umbilical cord about 2 inches from where it is attached on the baby's belly. This is painless, since the cord contains no nerves. (A person's navel, or belly button, is the small scar that shows where the cord was attached.)

The *third stage* of labor, which is usually over within fifteen minutes, follows the birth. The uterus goes on contracting, but less vigorously, as the placenta slowly separates from the wall of the uterus where it has been attached and is passed out. After the doctor has examined this *afterbirth*, it is disposed of.

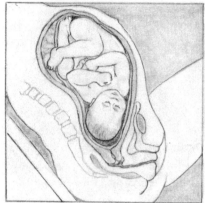

1. Birth process begins.

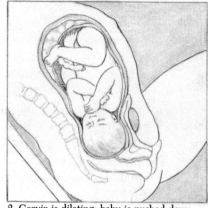

2. Cervix is dilating; baby is pushed down.

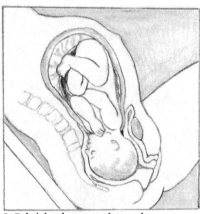

3. Baby's head enters pelvic outlet.

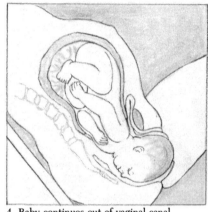

4. Baby continues out of vaginal canal.

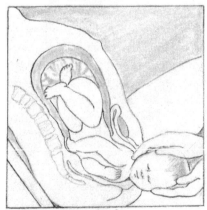

5. Birth nearly completed.

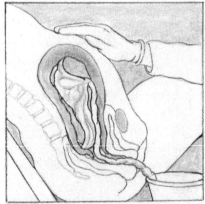

6. Some minutes after birth, contractions squeeze placenta, making it fall away from lining of uterus and be expelled.

Childbirth, internal view

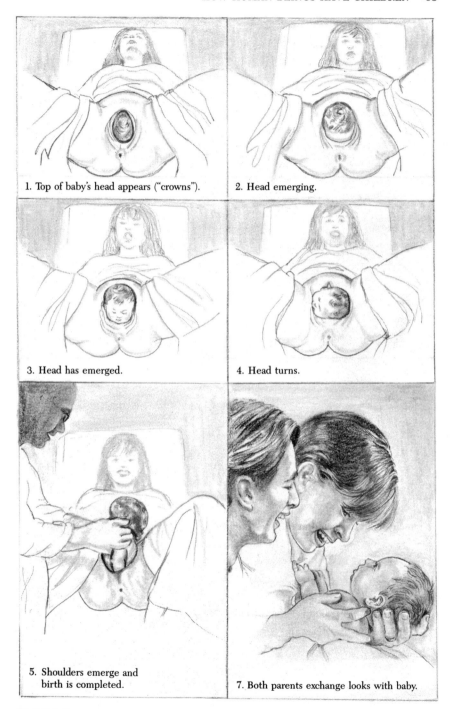

1. Top of baby's head appears ("crowns").

2. Head emerging.

3. Head has emerged.

4. Head turns.

5. Shoulders emerge and birth is completed.

7. Both parents exchange looks with baby.

Childbirth

In about one birth in five, the baby's head may be too large to pass through the mother's pelvic opening, or the baby may be in such a position that a normal birth would be difficult or dangerous. In such cases, the baby is delivered by what is called a *cesarean section* (named for Julius Caesar, who was supposed to have been born this way). The doctor makes a surgical incision in the abdominal wall and the uterus, lifts the baby out, and carefully sews up the opening. Some mothers have several children by cesarean, and their babies are just as healthy as those born in the usual way. It is especially important for the mother-infant bonding to let the mother have time with her baby as soon as possible after delivery (see Chapter 2) in the case of cesarean birth.

Newborn Babies

At birth, babies are on their own for the first time, and their first task is to start breathing—something they did not need to and could not do floating in amniotic fluid inside the uterus (although fetuses do perform breathing actions even when they are thus immersed). Usually the doctor or midwife suctions out the baby's nose and throat with a rubber bulb syringe or suction machine, to clear out any fluid or mucus that might interfere with the start of breathing. After its first breath or two, the baby is likely to utter a small, high cry, which is a delightful sound to the mother and all others present.

Many people, having seen babies a few weeks old or more and knowing how cute and pretty they look, are a bit disappointed and even shocked when they see a new one. A newborn baby is usually not at all beautiful or even cute. It is wrinkly, splotchy, and often quite red. The face may be swollen and look troubled, stupid, or even worn out. In general, the baby doesn't appear to be much of an addition to the world. One must remember that the process of getting born can sometimes be quite hard on a baby, who has been subjected to some strong pushing around. The baby's color will soon become normal, however, and his or her skin will look better before long. In less than a month he or she will be a cute and desirable-looking baby; every day after birth seems to work wonders.

Newborns can see enough to tell light from dark, but things are blurry to them at first, until their eyes learn to focus. Babies can taste, and they can feel pain and pressure. They do not like loud noises or the sensation of falling. They quickly learn that the way to get what they need is to cry. Many babies do a lot of crying during the first month, whether they need something or not.

One activity newborns do very well is sucking. They have very strong sucking muscles and a little pad of fat in each cheek to help out. A baby's head will turn to suck on anything that touches his or her face near the mouth. The mother has just the right equipment for the baby to suck on: at the tip of each breast is a nipple, and within the breasts are the glands that manufacture milk, and a network of small tubes that bring the milk to the nipple whenever the baby sucks.

For the first day or two after the birth, the fluid from the mother's breasts, called colostrum, is slight in amount, yellowish, and watery. Even though it contains little nourishment, it is important to the baby's health because it contains special and important substances that give the baby temporary protection from infections to which it may now be exposed—at least until its own immune system develops. The baby's sucking stimulates the breast glands to make milk. Milk from the mother's breast is a perfect food for the human baby because it is clean, safe, at no cost, easily digestible, always just the right temperature and always available, with just the right proportions of protein, fats, carbohydrates, minerals, and vitamins.

One of the most important things in people's lives, especially when they are infants, is being held close by those who love them. It makes them feel warm and secure and helps build a foundation of emotional strength. Many mothers get great pleasure from the experience of breastfeeding their babies, just because of the close link it gives them with their child. Many mothers also find that it can be somewhat sexually arousing, and they may feel frightened of and even guilty about this. Being aroused in this way by nursing is a quite normal reaction of pleasure, and there is no need for fright or guilt.

Many mothers do not wish to, or are not able to, breastfeed their babies. There is no reason for them to feel distressed about this, even though they are missing what might be a great joy. Babies fed from a bottle and rubber nipple with the modern formulas that are very similar to breast milk grow to be as sturdy and healthy as breastfed babies. But the mother and father of the bottle-fed baby must be especially aware of the importance of body contact during the first year and hold the baby in their arms lovingly while the child has his or her bottle, taking plenty of time and allowing bare-skin contact and gentle stroking of the baby's body.

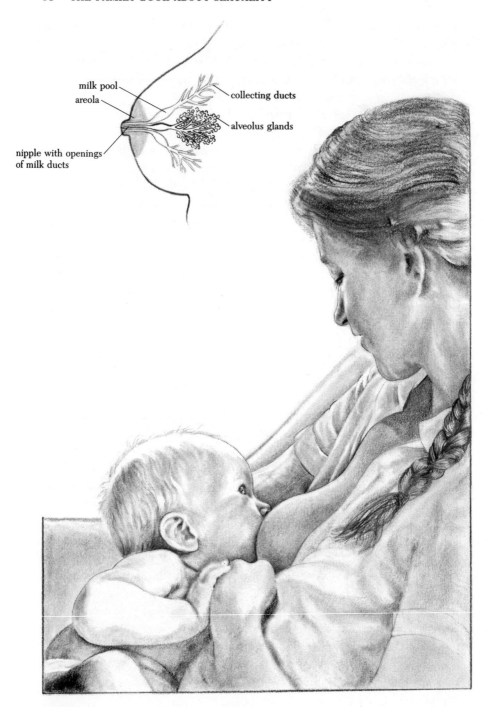

Breastfeeding; *inset,* diagram of breast

Twins and Other Multiple Births

One birth in every ninety or so produces twins, and one in seven or eight thousand produces triplets. Multiple births come about in one of two ways. In the first, a single egg is fertilized by a single sperm in the usual manner; then the zygote splits into two or three parts, each of which forms an embryo that develops independently. Babies formed this way are termed *identical twins* or *triplets,* and since a single sperm with either an X or a Y chromosome fertilized the egg, these babies are always of the same sex (all boys or all girls). They share one placenta and, with exactly the same genetic inheritance, they usually look almost exactly alike.

In the second way that multiple births occur, two or more eggs are ovulated at about the same time, whether from one or both ovaries, and each is fertilized by a different sperm. These babies are called *fraternal* (the word means like brothers or sisters), and are no more likely to resemble each other than any other brothers or sisters in a family, except, of course, they are born at one time. They may be of the same sex or different sexes.

Identical twins get their nourishment from a single placenta, but each fraternal twin has his or her own placenta. (See the drawing on page 70.) Twins are likely to weigh less than single babies.

Triplets, quadruplets, and quintuplets—the latter two being very rare—usually develop from more than one egg. They can be combinations of identical and fraternal or all fraternal. Even more rarely do they come as a result of one fertilized egg splitting apart a number of times. (In recent years, there has been an increase in the number of multiple births as a result of the use of certain fertility drugs by women who are otherwise unable to become pregnant. These drugs can occasionally cause the release of several ova, and the babies born are always fraternal siblings, not identical ones.)

Menopause

Usually between the ages of forty-five and fifty-five a woman stops menstruating. This is not a single, sudden event but a process lasting several months or years, called *menopause* (sometimes "change of life"). At the end of the process, a woman's ovaries will no longer release eggs and she can no longer become pregnant. This can, but need not,

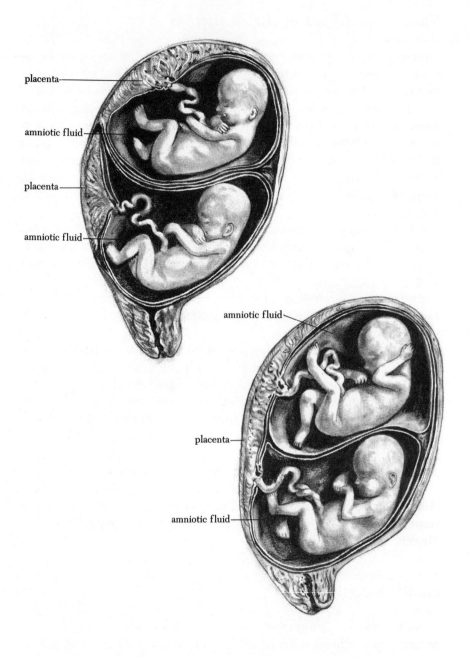

The two types of twins: *left,* fraternal, developed from two eggs, each with its own placenta—sexes may differ; *right,* identical, developed from one egg, sharing a single placenta—both are always of the same sex

be a difficult time for a woman, involving as it does a number of hormonal and psychological changes and adjustments. But menopause does not mean that a woman's sexual response system has stopped functioning, only her reproductive system. Her sexual life can and should remain just the same after menopause as before—and often even better, since there are no more worries about an unwanted pregnancy.

Many women fear menopause because they have heard tales from their mothers' or grandmothers' generations about hot flashes, weakness, and so forth. Generally speaking, attitudes today about menopause are different, so that psychologically a woman understands that it is not to be feared but simply dealt with matter-of-factly. Her periods have stopped. If they had been profuse she may have been anemic, but after menopause she will not be. And she no longer has to deal with menstruation; if she and her husband go on an extended trip she can leave sanitary napkins or tampons and contraceptive measures at home, never to be needed again. For many women this brings on feelings of well-being and a renewed sense of vitality and, often, romance and capacity for sexual enjoyment.

Some women may not be so fortunate. They may have wanted children and had none, or not as many as they would have liked, and thus feel depressed at being confronted by the end of any prospect of having babies. The family and the husband can be helpful by not belittling her feelings and by showing her extra tender concern and affection. A physician may also be helpful by providing mild antidepressants. Change of pace such as a trip is very often helpful, as can be the arrival of grandchildren. In any case, the woman should always bear in mind that whatever sexual life she enjoyed previously, she can enjoy undiminished, or even enhanced, for the rest of her life.

If the physical symptoms of menopause are bothersome, a woman's doctor may prescribe estrogen replacement therapy (ERT). And today most doctors, including a panel of experts at the National Institutes of Health, and the American College of Obstetricians and Gynecologists, endorse ERT, not just for a brief period after menopause, but for the rest of a woman's life. Estrogen replacement prevents the condition called osteoporosis, a softening and weakening of the bones which may cause women to fall and severely damage their bodies, and may cause a "widow's hump," which in turn can bring trouble with heart or lungs or circulation. Estrogen replacement also relieves a feeling of weakness and dryness of the vagina, with consequent effects on the sexual life.

With men, there is no such physical phenomenon as menopause. Some men, at about age fifty or so, begin to reassess their lives and perhaps find them wanting. This is a psychological depression that can be recognized and, again, helped by a loving family, and sometimes by a physician.

A Word About Heredity

The subject of human heredity, by which each of us inherits traits and characteristics from both parents, is too complicated to discuss fully in this book. But everyone should know that in each human egg cell and each human sperm cell are twenty-three minute bodies called *chromosomes,* which determine the heredity of the life that is begun when egg and sperm unite. These forty-six chromosomes (twenty-three pairs) contain an extremely detailed and complicated code of instructions, called *genes* (from which word comes the adjective *genetic,* meaning "having to do with inherited characteristics"). Among the thousands of traits programmed by the chromosomes in the developing embryo are the color of the skin, eyes, and hair; the shape of the face and the other parts of the body; eventual height and body build; and the potential intelligence—all the inborn things that make each individual different from any other. All people carry traits inherited from their mother and father and through them from previous generations on both sides.

GENDER AND HEREDITY

One important factor is not inherited: *gender*—whether a baby is male or female. As we noted before, this is determined by the sex chromosome in the sperm. There are two types of sperm: those that carry a Y chromosome which, when it pairs with the X chromosome of an ovum, will produce a male baby (XY); and those that carry an X chromosome, which will produce a female baby (XX). The sex, or gender, of a child is determined by the sperm at the moment of fertilization, and nothing that happens after that instant can change it.

NATURE AND NURTURE

Although a person's gender is determined at the moment of fertilization, how people *feel* about their gender depends on how they are treated after birth. Let us look more closely at what else besides gender comes to us inherently at birth (we'll call this our *nature*) and also at the experiences and treatment we receive after birth (we'll call this our *nurture*). We must begin with conception.

When the egg and the sperm fuse at the moment of fertilization, their chromosomes mingle, and the single cell formed by the fusion immediately begins the division that will take the rapidly multiplying cells through a number of complex processes and end 266 or so days later in the birth of a baby. The new human being just formed is alive and growing, but it is not yet the entity it will appear to be perhaps ten weeks later in the pregnancy, and it will not be capable of independent life outside the mother until, at the earliest, about the twenty-fourth week. Even if born at the end of the usual nine months, it is far from being able to live independently. It will for some time need a very complex support and nurture system called a mother!

Fertilization marks the beginning of an individual who will be born unique. This means, except for identical twins, that no other human being has ever existed, or can ever exist, who will have *exactly* that particular combination of forty-six chromosomes, each one bearing a thousand or more genes in all their particular myriads of combinations, complexities, and possibilities for interaction. So one of the most diffi-cult and yet fascinating questions that scientists have had to grapple with since the development of our knowledge about how heredity works is: How much weight should be given to the many various forces acting upon the individual after birth? The "nature versus nurture" question is one that has engaged the attention and motivated the re-search of scientists for some time, both scientists in the field of genetics (the study of inherited characteristics) and scientists in the somewhat newer field of human behavior (sociologists, psychologists, anthropolo-gists). Right now, there seems to be a tentative meeting of minds that can be stated like this: There is no way known at present to alter the heredity of individuals. There are, however, many ways in which the nurture (environment) of individuals acts upon their particular combi-nation of inherited traits and brings about specific results. For example:

A child is born to parents who are of average intelligence. One parent is quick to feel things—to be angry, to be irritated, to pass judgment, to make decisions, to accept new ideas, to move into action. The other parent is deliberate, thoughtful, considered, slow to accept ideas but persistent once action has been initiated. What effect will these two different people have upon the child born to them? There are many factors: Was the child wanted by one or both of the parents? Was a girl or boy wanted? What other children are there in the family? What is the professional and time involvement of each parent? Are the parents religious and do they agree about religion? What are the racial and national origin of the parents? Is there a larger family network, and what is it like? What is the immediate neighborhood?

You can see the infinite and bewildering number of possibilities that just these ordinary but often conflicting elements of *nurture* open up for influencing the *nature* of the child. How can we tell what might have been if one or more of the factors we have listed had been different? For example, would Hitler have grown up to be the cruel, ruthless dictator we knew if he had had a loving, caring father in his early life? Would Albert Einstein have been the scientist we knew if he had had parents who pushed and nagged him to finish his education—which he never did?

We can never know the answers. Some studies of identical twins (who always have exactly the same hereditary genes) who were separated very early and brought up quite differently without contact with each other seem to show how important *both* nature and nurture are for eventual outcomes. Right now, we have to accept nature as it comes, but nurture is so important that we can and must do something about making the child's upbringing as warm and beneficial as possible from birth onward.

4
Family Planning

If a woman had her first child at age sixteen and gave birth each year until she reached menopause at, say, age forty-six, she would have produced thirty children—more if some of the births had been of twins or triplets. Although having thirty children is possible, from every point of view it would be a disaster: for the mother, for the father or fathers, for the children, for the society, and for the world. If most women had thirty children, or even ten—in other words, if the birth rate were very high—the earth would quickly become so densely populated that poverty, overcrowding, misery, disease, starvation, and early death would become the normal expectation for almost everyone. This has actually been the case for some time in a number of countries.

Until very recently in the history of humankind, there have been no reliable means of *contraception,* that is, ways to prevent pregnancy. World population was kept low by high death rates. Many babies died in infancy, and most other people died young because there was no sanitation of water and milk and no effective medical science to cure diseases or to control plagues and epidemics. It was only after the beginning of this century that the world as a whole came to have a population problem, even though local areas might have suffered from overpopulation. However, in those countries in which modern medicine developed, and especially in those countries which enjoyed sanitation of waste disposal and of water and milk supplies, the death rates were sharply lowered, people lived longer, and a population explosion began. The people of many countries, especially those where most of the population is well-educated and prosperous, have learned to lower their birth rates. However, in less developed countries, the population explosion is a major problem.

Family Planning for Health Reasons

It is not only because of population difficulties that family planning must become a vital part of the health habits of every sexually active couple. One fact that many people ignore is the high risk that accompanies pregnancy in a teenage woman. The risk is not only to her health—and even to her life—but equally to the health of her baby after he or she is born.

The main cause for the higher health risk in this age group is that in our society the typical unmarried pregnant teenager does not, for a number of reasons, receive medical attention, nutritional advice, and general support equivalent to those given a typical, married pregnant woman. Many unmarried pregnant teenage girls hide their pregnancies for too long, and both they and their babies suffer. The babies are more likely to be born prematurely, and this results in a higher-than-normal rate of mental retardation, so that such babies are likely to be dependent for the rest of their lives either on their mothers and their families or on the state. But if a teenage woman is given good prenatal care, nutrition, and attention, her chances of having a healthy baby are as good as any other woman's.

Another fact is that the health risks to the mother and baby rise slightly in pregnancies after the age of forty. We should remember, also, that a mother who is dragged out with too many births too close together finds it difficult to be a good, nurturing mother to her children. When there are too many to feed, clothe, and be patient with, other troubles such as malnutrition, a higher rate of childhood and respiratory diseases, decreased ability to learn, and child abuse arise. Thus the need to have some kind of family planning for the sake of the health of the mother and the baby is vital for every couple to understand and for society to support.

A Couple's Decisions and Actions

Many people believe that the primary responsibility for family planning and for decisions about contraception and what method to use is the woman's. This is erroneous. The most successful users of family planning are those couples who decide together what method to use, and who practice it together. For instance, if the decision is for a condom, the couple can make its use a part of their lovemaking foreplay, with the woman taking responsibility for applying it as a loving and care-taking gesture on behalf of both. In the use of the diaphragm, if inter-course takes place more than once in the six-hour period following ejaculation the diaphragm must not be removed. Instead, with the diaphragm still in place, an injection of spermicidal cream or jelly should be made. Here again the couple can share in this responsibility, for the wife can load the applicator and leave it beside the bed, and the husband can inject it when it is needed.

But of all the decisions that must be made regarding family plan-ning, none is more important than the choice of method. A well-trained family-planning physician or a family-planning service in a good center will describe each method thoroughly for every couple, showing all the various chemicals and devices that are available for them to choose from. After this, the couple can have the time to discuss which method will best suit their particular needs. They can always begin with one method and, if it does not suit them, shift to another, until they find the method that they prefer. When people find the method they will use with the greatest degree of consistency, that is how the best rate of control of pregnancy can be achieved.

Methods of Contraception

Contraception, or birth control, is important not only from the point of view of world population but also from that of the individual family, whose future well-being may depend upon the ability of the parents to plan and have the number of children they want, when and how far apart they wish to have them. In fact, contraception is vitally important for everyone who is having sexual intercourse but does not wish to have a child as a result.

In general, we can say that today our knowledge of methods of birth control is adequate to keep the world's birth rate, the population of the world, and the number of children in any family, community, or group within desired limits and to protect those who wish to have intercourse without risk of pregnancy. What is not known as yet is how to get that knowledge to people who need to use these methods in such a way that they will be *motivated* to use them consistently.

The essential thing in preventing the conception of a child is to keep a live sperm cell from meeting a live egg cell and joining with and fertilizing it. Here are the principal methods of contraception.

METHODS THAT DO NOT REQUIRE A DOCTOR'S HELP

Abstinence

Abstinence means abstaining from—that is, not having—sexual intercourse. It is a widely used and totally effective method of birth control, for couples who are willing to forgo sexual intercourse.

Condoms

A condom (also called a rubber, prophylactic, safety, or sheath) is a thin rubber device shaped like the finger of a glove. It is placed over the penis after erection but before sexual intercourse, and it prevents the ejaculated semen from entering the vagina. Condoms are by far the most commonly used contraceptive device in the United States and can be bought by anyone at any drugstore without prescription. Condoms come in packages rolled and ready for use. Some contain a small amount of lubricant to make them easier to put on. There are a number of "ifs" involved in their successful use: if the condom is a new one, without pinholes; if the couple makes certain that the woman's vagina is not dry but is lubricated before insertion; if, when the condom is put on, about half an inch of space is left at the end to receive the semen; if the man carefully holds the condom in place with his fingers as he withdraws his penis *before* he loses his erection completely, so that no semen will spill out; and if there is no continuation of intercourse after the first ejaculation without changing condoms—then it is a highly effective method of contraception. If condoms are used hastily or inexpertly, or if they have been kept a long time so the rubber has deteriorated (or even a short time in the hot glove compartment of a car), they are not reliable. (The practice of using plastic sheeting like Saran Wrap as a sort of condom may be better than using nothing at all, but such sheeting is very unreliable, since it tears or comes off easily.)

Condoms are also quite (but not 100 percent) effective in reducing the spread of sexually transmitted diseases (venereal diseases) during sexual intercourse, provided there is no contact between the uncovered penis and the woman's genitals prior to penetration.

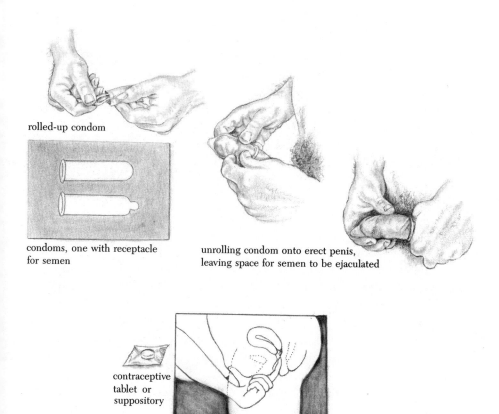

rolled-up condom

condoms, one with receptacle
for semen

unrolling condom onto erect penis,
leaving space for semen to be ejaculated

contraceptive
tablet or
suppository

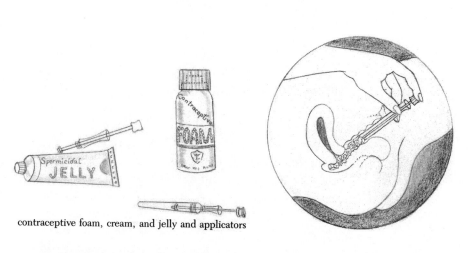

contraceptive foam, cream, and jelly and applicators

Contraceptives not requiring a doctor's help

Foams, Creams, Jellies

Sperm-killing chemicals can be bought without prescription at the drugstore and are available in various kinds of foams, creams, and jellies that the woman can place in her vagina before each act of intercourse. The foam is probably the most effective, but it is not as effective as the condom, the pill, the IUD (intrauterine device), or the diaphragm. Users should follow directions on the package exactly but also be skeptical of claims for effectiveness, which can be exaggerated.

Withdrawal

One of the oldest methods of birth control, and one that is still frequently used, is withdrawal. (The technical term is *coitus interruptus,* interrupted intercourse.) This requires the man, just before he ejaculates, to withdraw his penis from the woman's vagina and to ejaculate well away from the vaginal opening. Although the method is far more effective than using no method at all, it is not effective enough, because: (1) many men, at the height of sexual excitement and pleasure just before ejaculation, do not have the self-control to withdraw; (2) the pleasure of ejaculation is considerably reduced when ejaculation occurs outside the vagina; and (3) many men, before ejaculation, secrete a small amount of fluid containing enough sperm to cause pregnancy.

Combined Methods

A combination of two methods has, in practice, been found to have a higher effectiveness rate than either method used alone. Such a combination is possible in two ways: the use of the condom or of withdrawal, each with the addition of the vaginal foam. In the case of withdrawal, the chances of pregnancy are greatly reduced if the woman has, previous to intercourse, inserted a contraceptive foam, in case semen leaks before ejaculation or the man does not withdraw in time. The use of foam with the condom provides an even higher degree of freedom from pregnancy—probably as high as the pill or the IUD.

What must be remembered is that, as with all other methods, effectiveness depends very specifically on consistency of use. *If a hundred couples use the same method for a year, omission of the method, no matter how good it is, even once by five or ten couples, can result in several pregnancies among the hundred in the course of that year.*

METHODS THAT DO REQUIRE A DOCTOR'S PRESCRIPTION

The Pill

First put on the market in 1960 and steadily improved ever since, the birth control pill is the second most commonly used method of contraception in the Western world. The pill is taken by mouth and contains synthetic chemicals that resemble closely the two hormones (progesterone and estrogen) that prevent a pregnant woman from ovulating. With their use, no egg is released to be fertilized. Thus they induce a kind of chemical imitation of pregnancy.

Different brands and types of pills use different amounts and kinds of chemicals, and for each the directions are specific and should be followed *exactly*. In most cases, beginning on the fifth day after menstruation starts, the woman takes one pill a day for three weeks and then stops for a week, during which a vaginal flow very much like menstruation occurs. Taking a pill for one day or a few days is useless. If a woman forgets to take her pill for a single day, she should take the forgotten pill along with the scheduled one the very next day. If she forgets two or three days in succession, she definitely risks pregnancy and should immediately use a substitute method of contraception until a new pill cycle is begun—diaphragm and foam, or condom and foam, are suggested. Generally, the pills are sold in dispensers that make it as easy as possible to remember to take one each day; some dispensers contain seven placebo pills (pills containing no chemicals) for the fourth week, so that a woman does not break the habit of taking a pill every day, even during the week when her flow is occurring. When used properly, the pill is an almost 100 percent effective means of contraception.

Birth control pills are available only by prescription, and the prescribing doctor should explain all the possible side effects, such as nausea, weight gain, headaches, and increased vaginal discharge. Generally, these effects tend to disappear as women adjust after two or three months of use. Women with a history of blood clots may be advised by their physician against the pill, even though the increased danger of death by blood clot is slight—only one-eighteenth that of the danger of death from labor and childbirth.

In general, it is believed today that the pill should not be taken by women over the age of forty, because of possible increased rate of heart attacks. It should not be used by pregnant women or those who think

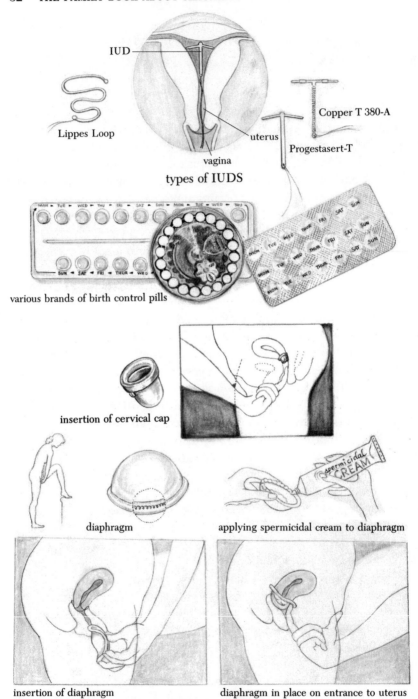

IUD

Lippes Loop

Copper T 380-A

uterus

Progestasert-T

vagina

types of IUDS

various brands of birth control pills

insertion of cervical cap

diaphragm

applying spermicidal cream to diaphragm

insertion of diaphragm

diaphragm in place on entrance to uterus

Contraceptives requiring a doctor's prescription

they may be pregnant, because of possible injury to the embryo or fetus (this is why they are always started at the end of a normal menstrual period). Very young women should avoid the pill also, because there are questions about the number of years it can safely be used. Smaller and smaller doses of the hormones in each pill are now being used, and a woman should ask her doctor all the questions that occur to her and follow the doctor's advice scrupulously.

There have recently been a considerable number of fears voiced concerning the connection between use of the pill and increased incidence of cancer. The facts are that the pill was introduced on an experimental basis in 1954 and for the succeeding six years was used by large numbers of women in clinical trials both in the United States and abroad. Since then, it has been used by millions of women. Thus far, careful studies show no relationship between cancer and the pill. There does, however, seem to be a relationship between age, the pill, and smoking. Women over forty who smoke do exhibit an increased rate of coronary disease and stroke when on the pill. It is likely that tobacco and the pill in some way reinforce each other's effects, whereas either alone has only a slight effect on the incidence of heart disease and stroke. This is also undoubtedly the case even in young women who smoke.

Intrauterine Device (IUD)

It has been known for centuries that placing a foreign object in the uterus of a female tends to prevent pregnancy. Arabs would prevent female camels used in desert caravans from becoming pregnant by placing a stone inside each one's uterus.

In recent years, plastic devices containing copper (the Copper-T and Copper-7) and plastic devices shaped as rings, coils, and loops have been developed. They are called intrauterine devices—IUDs—and they are inserted by a doctor or trained clinician into the flat, triangular cavity of a woman's uterus, where, by a process not fully understood, they seem to interfere in some way with implantation of the fertilized egg in the uterine lining or with the development of the embryo.

However, in 1974, it became evident that there were a number of very bad effects from women using the now-illegal IUD called the Dalkon Shield, and it was removed from the market. Since then, other widely used and effective IUDs, especially the Lippes Loop, have been the cause of vastly expensive litigation. Consequently, the drug companies decided to remove the devices from the market, not because of proven ill effects from properly used IUDs, but because of the legal costs. As David A. Grimes, M.D., Associate Editor of *Contraception—an International Journal,* wrote in July 1987, "The recent sad saga of IUDs in the United States has its origin in financial interests, not in the heart or mind. . . . We must reestablish science and humanism as the driving forces in reproductive medicine."

On page 82 are illustrations of three IUDs: the Lippes Loop, highly effective and available almost everywhere except in the U.S.A. (it is obtainable in Canada, Mexico, Great Britain, and Europe, for example); the Copper T 380-A, effective and available in the U.S.A.; and Progestasert-T, also effective and available in the U.S.A.

IUDs must be inserted and removed by doctors or well-trained clinicians at established contraceptive clinics (such as Planned Parenthood), and instructions for their use and about possible side effects must be carefully read. IUDs should not be used by women who are pregnant, who have multiple sex partners, who show signs of abnormal bleeding, who have any infections (until the infections are treated and cured), or who have or recently have had pelvic inflammatory disease (PID). Properly installed and used, IUDs are an excellent method of reversible sterilization. However, if a woman with an IUD experiences any unusual signs or symptoms (bleeding, pain during sex, cramping, a missed period, change of length of the IUD "tail" which hangs out of the cervical opening, etc.), she should consult a doctor or clinician at once.

The Diaphragm

A diaphragm is a round rubber cap, between 2 to 3 inches in diameter, which a woman places in the upper part of her vagina to wall off the cervix from the lower part, thus preventing sperm from entering. The diaphragm is obtained by prescription only because it must be specially fitted for size and shape by a doctor, who will then show the woman exactly how to place it correctly. It should always be used with a spermicidal cream or jelly, which creates a barrier that keeps sperm from the cervix and kills any sperm that might migrate around the edge of the diaphragm and thus reach the cervix. For the cream or jelly to be effective, the diaphragm should be in place not more than six hours before intercourse and should be left in place for at least six hours after the last ejaculation, but not for more than sixteen.

From time to time, a woman should have her doctor check the fit of her diaphragm. This is essential after she has given birth or if she has had a significant loss or gain of weight, for both events are likely to change the size of her vaginal canal and make refitting necessary. Especially vigorous intercourse, or intercourse positions resulting in especially deep penetration, are possible causes for displacement of the diaphragm—making use of the cream or jelly even more essential. The diaphragm is a very effective means of birth control if used with consistency and care.

The Cervical Cap

A cervical cap is somewhat like a diaphragm but is smaller, about 1 inch in diameter. It fits tightly but comfortably over the base of the cervix and blocks sperm from entering the uterus. It must be used with a spermicidal jelly. The cap can be inserted at the beginning of the day or evening and left in for as long as 48 hours, or it can be inserted just before intercourse. It should be left in place for at least 6 hours after intercourse. Cervical caps can be obtained by prescription only and must be fitted by a physician or clinical specialist.

Although the cervical cap has been used, mainly in Europe, since the mid-nineteenth century, it was approved only in 1988 by the U.S. Food and Drug Administration. Obviously, the cap should be used carefully according to the instructions. Its failure rate is about the same as that of the diaphragm. (See chart, page 91.)

Natural Family Planning Method

The natural family planning (NFP) method of birth control has evolved out of what was formerly called the "rhythm method." It is based on the regular, or rhythmical, nature of the menstrual cycle of most women most of the time. It involves *periodic abstinence,* that is, abstaining from sexual intercourse during the two or three days *after* ovulation, when there may be one or more live eggs in the fallopian tubes, and for two or three days *before* ovulation, since sperm can remain alive in the tubes or uterus and fertilize an egg on its way down.

The NFP method requires teaching women *fertility awareness,* that is, recognizing various signs and symptoms that indicate the days on which they may become pregnant. Learning this awareness is not nearly so simple as learning to use the pill, a diaphragm, or (for the man) a condom, but those who have developed the method report that in recent years a relatively high level of reliability can be attained if the teaching is skillful and the couple using the method does so with care and consistency. Although no drugs or devices are needed, it is important that a couple (especially the woman) considering using NFP be taught by a qualified specialist, either a doctor or a person or couple trained by doctors and experts and experienced in the successful use of NFP.

There are four methods a woman may use to determine which days in her cycle are fertile and which are "safe." Probably she will use two or more methods in combination.

The calendar method. This method, though still the one most widely used in natural family planning, is not the most satisfactory. It requires the woman to keep a continuous record of the length of her menstrual cycles over a period of six to nine months and then follow a formula to calculate her fertile days and her "safe" days. Here is the formula: subtract 18 from the number of days in the shortest menstrual cycle in the previous six to nine months (this represents the *earliest* day for the start of her fertile time) and 11 from the number of days in the longest menstrual cycle (this represents the *latest* day for the finish of her fertile time). For example, if, in the previous six to nine months her shortest menstrual cycle was 25 days and her longest was 30, the figures would be 7 (25 minus 18 equals 7) and 19 (30 minus 11 equals 19), which would indicate that, always considering Day 1 as the day she began to menstruate, she might be fertile from Day 7 until Day 19 and infertile from Days 1 to 6 and Day 20 on. Thus, she should consider Day 1 through Day 6 as "safe," then avoid intercourse between Days 7 and 19, and then consider Day 20 through to Day 6 of the *next* menstruation to be her "safe" days. This requires 12 days of voluntary abstinence.

The basal body temperature method. This method is based on the woman's taking her temperature every morning *before* she has gotten out of bed. She may do this rectally, vaginally, or orally, but it should always be done in the same way. This basal body temperature (BBT) is usually very slightly below normal during the week before ovulation but rises to very slightly above normal just before ovulation. When the temperature has remained relatively higher for three consecutive days, the "safe" days may have been considered to have begun. Convenient charts and instructions for taking and recording the BBT are available from most family-planning clinics.

The cervical mucus method. This method is based on the fact that just before ovulation most women show noticeable changes in the mucus discharged through the opening of the cervix (the *os*) and thence from the vagina. Usually the mucus is yellowish and rather thick, and the vagina quite dry (except when the woman is sexually aroused), but around the time of ovulation the mucus changes and becomes clearer and thinner, more like the white of a raw egg. Women can be taught to evaluate their vaginal discharge daily and thus to tell when ovulation is likely to occur.

The cervical os method. This method is based on changes in the position and texture of the opening (os) of a woman's cervix. Just before ovulation, the os retreats somewhat farther from the external opening of the vagina so that it is harder to reach, and at the same time it softens so that its texture is somewhat like that of the upper lip, whereas at other times the texture is more like that of the tip of the nose. By noticing these changes, the woman can tell when ovulation is about to occur.

When used together, the BBT, the mucus evaluation, and the cervical os methods are called the *sympto-thermic method,* and a woman who uses all three may achieve a fairly high rate of fertility control. However, the results of several studies of the effectiveness rates of NFP methods do not agree, ranging widely from 1.5 observed pregnancies per hundred woman-years to the very high rate of 33.

The NFP methods are considered to be "natural" and thus acceptable to those Roman Catholics whose beliefs do not permit them to use medical methods of conception control. Supporters of NFP, many of them not Catholics, point out that it avoids any possible dangers or discomforts that might result from chemicals or devices, that it "puts a woman in touch with her own body" in a way that is satisfying to her, that the periods of abstinence required increase the opportunities for better communication about sexual matters between partners, and that periodic abstinence may actually serve to enhance the pleasure of intercourse during the "safe" days. Those who do not support the method point out the complexity of the procedures involved and the low rate of reliability according to many studies, and maintain that with many couples the required period of abstinence may prove frustrating to the expression of sexual desire natural to intimate living.

Sterilization

An increasing number of men and women who are certain they want no (or no more) children choose to have themselves sterilized. There are two methods of sterilization.

Vasectomy for the man. Vasectomy involves removing a short section from each of the man's two vas deferens tubes (vasa deferentia) and cauterizing (burning out) the remaining ends. This is done in the doctor's office and requires only a local anesthetic and two tiny incisions in the scrotum. The sperm are thus prevented from reaching the seminal vesicles, and as a result the semen that is ejaculated does not contain any sperm. (Viable sperm may remain in the man's reproductive system for two or three months after the operation, however; the couple should therefore use another means of contraception during that time.) There is no noticeable reduction in the volume of semen ejaculated, since sperm make up only about one percent of the total amount. The blocked sperm are simply absorbed into the man's body and disappear. A vasectomy should be considered permanent, although modern microsurgical techniques sometimes succeed in reopening the vasa deferentia.

Tubal ligation for the woman. The tubal ligation method (commonly called "having your tubes tied") involves removing a short section of each fallopian tube so that egg cells cannot reach the uterus from the ovaries or be reached by sperm cells. A tubal ligation is now almost as simple an operation as a vasectomy, although it must be done in a hospital or a special clinic. A small incision is made in the navel (so that the scar will not be noticeable) and an instrument called a laparoscope is inserted. It enables the doctor to see the tubes by means of a miniature light and telescope and to cauterize a small section of each tube and seal off the ends. In most centers, laparoscopy is carried out under general anesthetic, although a local anesthetic may be used in places where general anesthetic is unavailable. Like the vasectomy, this operation should be considered permanent, for the possibilities for successfully reopening and rejoining the tubes are slim.

Neither a vasectomy nor a tubal ligation interferes with sexual pleasure, unless for some reason a person has some negative emotional reaction to the operation. Since sterilization makes it unnecessary to worry about pregnancy or planning for contraception, it can in effect increase the pleasure a couple experiences in intercourse.

"Morning-After" Contraception

When a woman has had unprotected sexual intercourse and then realizes that she may become pregnant and does not wish to do so, she has the possibility of taking a pill containing a massive dose of synthetic estrogen. This affects the hormones that are acting on the lining of the uterus and results in menstruation and the discharge of the embryo within three to four weeks. "Morning-after" contraception may cause nausea, vomiting, headache, and other symptoms. Although its success rate is very high, if it should not happen to succeed the changes are greatly increased that if the baby born is a girl she may develop cancer of the vagina when she is grown. Therefore, before a woman is given a "morning-after" pill she should make certain that she is not already carrying a baby started from earlier intercourse and that she is ready to accept a termination of her pregnancy by abortion in case the pill should fail.

METHODS *NOT* RECOMMENDED AT ALL

Douching

Douching as a contraceptive method involves squirting water or other liquid into the vagina immediately after the man ejaculates, the idea being to kill or wash away the sperm. Even if the woman runs from bed to bathroom, a douche is quite ineffective because sperm, when ejaculated, begin at once to move up the cervical canal and out of harm's way. There are a number of douching fluids sold in stores for which claims of contraceptive effectiveness are made or assumed by the user. But none of the douches work as a contraceptive. This method is therefore strongly advised against.

Urination After Intercourse

A method that some women use to attempt to kill the sperm is urination right after sexual intercourse. This is of no use whatsoever, because the vagina, into which the sperm are ejaculated, and the urethra, through which the urine passes, are entirely separate, even though their external openings are close to each other.

Suppositories

Many suppositories are advertised as contraceptives but are not very effective because body heat melts them into a liquid that may run out before or during intercourse. They are, however, better than no contraceptive at all.

Comparing the Effectiveness of Contraceptive Methods

Doctors and scientists are constantly working on improving methods and discovering new ways of preventing unwanted pregnancy. Some developments not yet perfected or officially approved are: birth control pills for males that would stop the production of sperm; small capsules that can be implanted under a woman's skin to release small doses of chemicals into her bloodstream and prevent pregnancy for periods of a year or longer; and methods for reversing sterilization operations in both men and women, so that a person could be sterilized and then de-sterilized. If ever perfected, some of the new methods may turn out to be more effective, more convenient and pleasant to use, less expensive, and less likely to have undesirable side effects than many of the contraceptive methods now available.

In addition to new methods, the old ones are being worked on steadily, and sometimes ways are found to make them more effective. Thus, the rates of effectiveness are likely to change from year to year. Before giving the latest figures available, we should point out that it is much easier to ask "How effective is my birth control method?" than it is to give the answer. Much depends on how carefully, competently, and consistently the method is used. For example, *theoretically* the pill is almost 100 percent effective, but *actually* from two to three women out of one hundred using the pill for a year will become pregnant. Why? Because of human error. The women forget to take their pill, despite forget-proof packaging. The table on page 91 gives the effectiveness rate actually observed for each method of contraception. The figures emphasize again how important it is to use all methods of contraception exactly according to directions and with care and consistency. Over a number of years of sexual activity, careless or occasional forgetting is likely to result in pregnancy.

We also want to emphasize that much wrong information about birth control methods is passed around, and many women get pregnant because they used a method that does not work or used a good method incorrectly. People planning to use a contraceptive method should make certain that it is approved by the medical profession and that the specific product used is approved for birth control by the United States Food and Drug Administration.

Getting Advice About Contraception

Any person of any age, married or unmarried, if he or she expects to have sexual intercourse and does not wish to cause pregnancy or become pregnant, should get the best possible advice about methods of contraception. Especially before beginning sexual activity, but also as

Number of pregnancies expected in 100 sexually active women during the first year of use of various methods of contraception, arranged in order from least to most effective method.

	Pregnancies observed in actual experience
No contraceptive at all	89
Spermicidal foam	21
Natural family planning	20
Cervical cap	18
Diaphragm	18
Withdrawal	18
Condom (without spermicides)	12
IUD (intrauterine device)	6
The pill	3
Tubal ligation	0.4
Vasectomy	0.15

Adapted from Robert A. Hatcher, M.D., et al., *Contraceptive Technology, 1988–1989,* 14th revised edition (New York: Irvington Publishers, 1988).

a person becomes more experienced, it is very helpful to seek advice (preferably together with one's partner) from a well-informed professional person.

FAMILY INFORMATION ABOUT CONTRACEPTION

We believe that it is best for children and their parents to be open with each other about matters of sexual information. Therefore, we hope that sharing this book will encourage parents and children, as well as husbands and wives and sexual partners, to talk openly together as each feels ready to do so. But, like it or not, it is a fact that many children do not want to or cannot bring themselves to talk with their parents about their sexual feelings, plans, or, in some cases, even the simple facts. Some parents are not available for such discussion, and many parents find it difficult—or impossible—to talk about such things with their children. We recognize these realities and we also recognize the strong need many people feel, even within the family (sometimes especially within the family) to have their privacy protected.

Thus, although we strongly favor family discussion, we are glad that there are organizations that have professionals available to whom young people can go to discuss sexual matters and from whom they can obtain information and needed products. These organizations, though they may strongly advise family discussion, will protect the privacy of those who come. It is legal in all states for such discussions to be kept private and for contraceptive information and materials, including whatever prescriptions are required, to be given to minors without the knowledge or consent of their parents.

There are many who feel that such discussion and provision of contraceptive materials to minors without the consent of parents is a threat to the strength and solidarity of the family. We know, however, that even among the members of many warm, loving families, in which there is generally a readiness to share and talk things over, the area of sex seems special and is particularly difficult to discuss. Therefore, parents or children should try not to feel threatened by discussions outside the family.

Some of the professionals and organizations available for confidential discussion and advice about contraception and all related questions are:

The family doctor. It should be remembered that many doctors have not been trained to discuss sexual questions with their patients, although an increasing number of medical schools and other medical organizations are now providing training in this field. Also, some doctors feel obligated to share with parents the matters that young people discuss with them.

Planned Parenthood. This organization has centers throughout the United States and the world where counseling is available, either individually or in groups, and where contraceptive materials and devices are obtainable and doctors are on hand to give prescriptions, advice, and instruction.

Family-planning clinics connected with hospitals. Here contraceptive information, services, and products are available.

Family-planning clinics of city, county, and state health departments. Here, too, contraceptive information, advice, services, and products are available. Look up the clinics in the telephone directory under "Health" or "Public Health," under the name of the city, county, or state.

Natural Family Planning. For Catholics and others who wish instruction in the natural family planning method, many dioceses of the Roman Catholic Church maintain a Family Life Bureau. Look it up in the telephone directory under "Diocese," "Archdiocese," or "Catholic Church," subheading "Family Life Bureau."

The family minister, priest, or rabbi. Increasing numbers of religious workers are receiving training in counseling on questions of sexual behavior. A minister, priest, or rabbi may be helpful in discussing with you the moral aspects of the choices you are making, but he or she is not qualified to give medical advice.

When Contraception Fails

It is a sad fact that for a variety of reasons—carelessness, ignorance, use of unreliable methods of contraception, or allowing one's reason and planning to be overcome by the feelings of the moment—millions of women of all ages, including very young girls, become pregnant each year and wish they had not. These women have a number of choices. One is to marry (this choice is rarely advised because almost all such marriages end in divorce); one is to carry their pregnancy through to term, have their baby, and keep it as a single parent; another is to have the baby and, if single, give it up for adoption; and yet another is to terminate the pregnancy by means of an abortion.

KEEPING THE BABY

For a woman who becomes pregnant when she did not choose to, the decision to give birth to the baby and keep it may be a hard one to make. She may feel unready for the responsibilities of parenthood; the father may not wish to help her, or, even if he does, if they are not committed to each other, she may not wish him to do so; her plans for education and career may be interrupted or even permanently changed; she may not be able to afford the costs of childbirth and, later, child care if she wishes or needs to go to work. Much, of course, depends on how much support she can count on from others, her family, the neighborhood, her friends, and various family-service agencies. Yet, despite the problems, many women choose to bear and keep their babies, and when they look back on the decision later, many but not all are glad, or cannot imagine having decided otherwise. Certainly, most women who find themselves pregnant not by choice will want to talk over their situation, and the future welfare of their prospective child, with other people whose opinion and experience they respect—with their family, possibly with an adviser from their church or synagogue, and probably with a professional counselor or social worker.

GIVING THE BABY UP FOR ADOPTION

Painful as it may be for a mother who has just given birth to a baby to which, during the nine months of pregnancy, she has usually become deeply attached emotionally, adoption is often the best solution for both mother and child. In most cases, the baby is given up almost immediately after birth, before mother and child develop an even stronger attachment to each other. It will be helpful for the mother, after the adoption, to talk over her feelings with a counselor.

When children are adopted, they have full legal rights as members of their adoptive family. Many children are adopted by relatives of their natural parents, such as an uncle and aunt, or grandparents. Most adoptions in the United States are arranged through licensed agencies, although quite a few others are worked out by physicians or lawyers. In most states, when the child is not already known by them, neither the adoptive parents nor the adopted child are permitted to know the identity of the natural parents, and the natural parents may not know who adopted their child. This is in order to avoid the stress and confusion that occur if a natural parent undergoes a change of mind and seeks to have the child returned.

In general, it can be said that adopted children have just about the same kind of chance of being brought up to lead happy, satisfying lives as do children brought up by their natural parents. Thus a mother can give up her child in the confidence that the child will have a good future, most likely a better one than could be provided for by a mother not well prepared to care for a child until he or she had grown up.

ABORTION

There are two kinds of abortion: spontaneous and induced. A *spontaneous abortion,* commonly called a miscarriage, occurs when the pregnant woman's uterus spontaneously (by itself) expels the embryo or fetus. About 10 to 15 percent of all pregnancies end in this way, most of them before the eleventh or twelfth week. About half the miscarried embryos are found to have one or more major defects. The signs of miscarriage are vaginal bleeding and pelvic cramps. If these occur and then the signs of pregnancy disappear, a woman can assume she has had a miscarriage. (Remember, an eight-week-old embryo is only an inch long and weighs about 2 grams—or $3/100$ of an ounce, about one-third the weight of a dime—so that the actual event of miscarriage is usually not very noticeable.) Some women believe that they can bring on a miscarriage by such activities as jumping up and down vigorously or falling down stairs, but all they are likely to do is hurt themselves, leaving the pregnancy undisturbed.

An *induced abortion* is one that is brought about intentionally. There are several methods for inducing abortion. Abortions performed during the first trimester of pregnancy (the first three months) are much simpler and safer than those performed later, although any abortion done by a qualified doctor in a well-equipped facility is quite safe, with a lower problem rate than childbirth itself. Two methods are commonly used during the first three months of a pregnancy: the vacuum aspiration method and the D & C.

Vacuum aspiration method. About 85 percent of all legal abortions performed in the United States today are done by the vacuum aspiration method, often called the suction method. First, in most cases, some dilatation (enlarging) of the cervical opening is done, under local anesthesia and with only slight discomfort. Then the doctor uses a suction curette, which is a small plastic tube attached by a rubber tube to a suction machine. The tip of the plastic tube is inserted through the cervical canal into the uterus and, working somewhat like a miniature vacuum cleaner, sucks out the embryo and other products of conception. The whole process usually takes only a few minutes, is quite inexpensive, and can be done in a clinic or hospital on an outpatient basis, so that after a short rest the woman can go home. If performed before the eighth week of pregnancy it is almost painless. Complications and aftereffects are rare if the procedure is competently done.

Dilation and curettage (D & C) method. Before the development of the vacuum method, the D & C method was very common. Now it is rarely used in the United States. It involves dilating the cervical opening by passing into it a series of dilators of larger and larger thickness, and then inserting a curette (which is simply a blunt scraper) with which the doctor scrapes out the contents of the uterus. The D & C takes somewhat longer than the suction method, involves considerably more discomfort, and must be done with care to avoid causing excessive bleeding of the uterus.

Saline injection method. After twelve weeks of pregnancy, neither the vacuum aspiration method nor the D & C can be performed safely. During the second trimester of pregnancy the most common method of performing abortions today is the saline injection. Under local anesthetic, a needle is inserted through the woman's abdomen into her uterus and about a cupful of amniotic fluid is removed; this fluid is replaced by an equal amount of a 20 percent salt solution. From 24 to 48 hours later, the uterus begins contracting and the woman miscarries spontaneously. Some doctors keep the patient in the hospital until the fetus is delivered; others permit her to go home, not to return until contractions have begun. The saline injection method does involve some dangers, such as hemorrhaging and infection. Therefore, close follow-up is important after the procedure is completed.

Prostaglandins method. The above methods all involve surgical procedures and cannot be done unless good equipment is available. But there is now a nonsurgical method that involves the use of prostaglandins. Many years ago it was observed that the injection of human semen into the uterus caused strong contractions of the uterine muscles. Later research showed that the chemical causing the contractions is produced by the prostate gland (hence the name), and techniques have now been developed to put fluid containing prostaglandins into the body of the pregnant woman, either by a catheter into her uterus, by a suppository placed in and absorbed from the vagina, or by intravenous injection. After a number of hours the woman aborts the fetus. Although the method has some uncomfortable side effects, it is approved by the Food and Drug Administration for use in second-trimester abortions.

Abortions, especially when performed early in pregnancy, are quite safe, simple, and inexpensive. (The death rate from legal abortions in the United States is about 1 in 100,000 abortions, a rate much lower than that from childbirth, which in itself is by no means a risky procedure under modern conditions.) But any woman considering an abortion should go only to a hospital or clinic registered for performing them, and the abortion should be performed only by a qualified medical doctor. The doctor will know which method is the best one to use, given the circumstances of the woman and the stage of the pregnancy. Information about where to go and how (and whether) to proceed can be obtained from Planned Parenthood, a city, county, or state public health clinic, or any hospital.

It is important that the woman considering an abortion be given ample opportunity to talk with a counselor about her situation and the choices she has. If the woman decides to proceed with an abortion, the counselor should explain exactly what it will involve. For many women, an abortion is a minor event, both physically and psychologically; for others it may have deeper effects than they expect, especially on their emotions, if they believe that their decision means they are responsible for terminating a human life and they feel guilty about this. It is therefore important that a woman also have a chance to talk about her feelings *after* the abortion has been performed. Of course, she should return to the hospital or clinic if she has any abnormal symptoms such as pain, fever, nausea, or bleeding following an abortion, or for further counseling.

ABORTION AND THE LAW

Before 1973 (before 1970 in New York State), performing an abortion was illegal in the United States except in cases where the life or health (or, in some situations, the welfare) of the mother was in jeopardy. And yet millions of abortions were performed illegally, often under very dangerous "back-alley" conditions, in which the life or future health of the mother was in great danger. Each year thousands of women died or were severely injured. When a procedure is illegal, it is of course impossible to regulate it by law, so people who are unscrupulous and unskilled often take over the business. Before legalized abortion, many women attempted to perform abortions on themselves by inserting a foreign object through the cervix into the uterus. Much suffering and many deaths were caused by such efforts, but those women who felt that, for whatever reason, they could not endure giving birth to and caring for a baby were apparently willing to risk their health and lives to avoid this. It has been pointed out by the medical and legal professions that, if abortion should be made illegal again, or very difficult or expensive to obtain, undoubtedly illegal "abortion mills" will again become common, with the same undesirable results as before.

In 1973 the United States Supreme Court ruled that no state could limit the right of a woman to have an abortion during the first trimester of her pregnancy. The court said that during the second trimester states might regulate medical practices (such as the licensing of physicians and the certification of hospitals and clinics to perform abortions), but that the right of a woman to have an abortion might not itself be limited. During the third trimester, the court said, states may prohibit abortions under conditions the states may determine, but they may not prohibit them if the health of the mother is endangered. The Supreme Court itself did not prohibit third-trimester abortions. The 1973 decision meant that it was now legal anywhere in the United States for a woman to have an abortion. A married woman did not need the consent of her husband, nor did a girl need the consent of her parents.

Since the Supreme Court decision, there have been major efforts by groups (often calling themselves "Pro-Life" or "Right-to-Life") to have the United States Constitution amended to prohibit abortion entirely and to affirm the right to life and protection under the law for the embryo from the moment of conception. (The Supreme Court decision stated that it was not competent to say when life begins and that thus a person's life should be considered as beginning at the moment of birth.) Opponents of abortion are also attempting to get Congress and various states to pass laws prohibiting the spending of public funds to perform abortions, although free medical care is, in other respects, available at low or no cost to people of limited means. Such laws would have the effect of making abortions available only to those able to pay for them.

ABORTION PRO AND CON

Many people have very strong opinions about the rightness or wrongness of abortion. In the Soviet Union, the countries of Eastern Europe, and Japan, abortion is probably the most common method of birth control. In these countries there are more abortions each year than there are live births. In Western European countries and North and South America, where the influence of the Christian religions and especially of the Catholic church is strong, there has always been vigorous opposition to abortion. Public-opinion polls differ on how widespread the opposition is; much depends on how the question is put.

Here is a summary of the views of those who oppose a woman's right to choose an abortion:

> From the moment of conception, the fertilized egg is an individual human life. The embryo as an individual life no more "belongs" to its mother or father than does a born child. It has its own unique genetic inheritance, and from the moment of conception its mother merely provides it with nourishment and a place to grow.
> Furthermore, this individual human life is harmless and innocent. We

have no right to kill it; to do so is murder. The baby growing inside the mother has a right to life as much as any other innocent human being, and it deserves the protection of the law. If we permit the killing of the most harmless human life with the greatest potential, there is nothing to stop us from taking other human lives—say, of unwanted children or of old people, or even of groups without whom we feel the world would be better off. If we oppose the killing of innocent human beings (which category does not necessarily include convicted criminals or enemies in war), we should oppose the killing of human life through abortion.

Those who favor a woman's right to choose an abortion express their views this way:

Every woman, as a matter of her right to the enjoyment of life, liberty, and privacy, should be free to determine whether and when to bear children. It is far better to end an unwanted pregnancy than to encourage the evils resulting from forced pregnancy and childbirth. Therefore, no matter what her age, a woman should, with the medical advice of a doctor, have the right to secure an abortion and to do so without being required to consult with or secure the permission of any other person. To require her to bear a child she does not want is not only unfair to her but may also work hardships on her family. Furthermore, it is unfair to the prospective child for it to be born unwanted, more likely than a wanted child to experience hardships, deprivation, and often even abuse after it is born. Every child should have the right to be born into circumstances in which it is likely to receive the physical and emotional support and love it will need for a healthy, happy life.

The argument that permitting the termination of pregnancy is murder or disrespectful of human life is unsound. An embryo or fetus is only an organism growing toward being a person, very different from a conscious, existing individual, born and actually living out in the world.

Certainly, no woman should be *required* to have an abortion, and the moral convictions of people opposing abortion should be respected. But it is also wrong for opponents of abortion to force their convictions on others by encouraging the passage of laws restricting the right of a woman to choose whether or not to have a baby. However, abortion should not be considered a primary means of birth control, only a back-up method, when other means of birth control fail or are not used.

It is interesting to note that after the court decisions permitting abortions were made, a good many physicians and nurses found themselves more deeply affected by what they came to see as the termination of human life than they had expected to be. In other words, they found that abortion was not a matter to be taken as lightly as some pro-abortion advocates seemed to think. Most doctors, however, feel that even though they themselves do not wish to perform abortions, they have an obligation to refer women desiring one to other physicians who will.

Human Beings as Decision-Making Animals

In this chapter we have been talking about control of the human reproductive system. In this connection, it is important to point out that while in most "lower" animals, sexual activity and reproductive activity are inseparable, in human beings they are merely closely related. The reproductive lives of most other animals are governed by factors over which they have no control: the seasons of the year, the cycles of their glands and organs, the state of their nutrition, and so forth.

Exceptions to this are some of the animals called primates. We human beings are primates; so, too, are our nearest animal relatives, the apes, such as the orangutan. Some primates may copulate frequently when there is no chance of conception.

Except for these primates, female animals will copulate only when they are in heat; that is, when they are ovulating and are ready to be fertilized. During the period of heat, female animals give forth certain scents and signs (such as a slight bloody discharge from the uterus) that inform the male they are ready. The male then becomes sexually aroused (he "ruts" or becomes "rutty"), and mating takes place. Only when the female is in heat is the male interested in her sexually. Any farm boy or girl, or any owner or observer of a female dog when she is in heat, will have a vivid idea of how automatic, compulsive, and cyclical the reproductive lives of animals are. Animals have no choices to make and take no responsibility for their sexual actions, and the same species behave the same way the world over. (There are exceptions, such as rabbits, which have no heat periods; they copulate first and *then* the female ovulates.)

In human females there is no such thing as a well-defined "heat." As we have explained, most women do not know when they are ovulating, and certainly a man cannot tell. Women do feel a greater desire for sexual activity at some times than at others, but not necessarily at the time when they are most likely to conceive. In the human male, there is no definite season when he is "rutty," although he too may feel more sexy at some times than at others.

Thus, human beings are unique among animals in being able to make conscious decisions about their sexual and reproductive behaviors. They have been endowed with the capacity to remember, to plan ahead, to make choices, and to learn from past experience in ways that will affect their futures, both sexually and reproductively. Human beings are responsible for how they will behave: they are taught, and they can learn.

5
Living Our Sexual Lives
Influences and Patterns
During the Life Cycle

Human sexuality infuses, and in turn is infused by, every part of life. Each person's sexuality at any given moment is based on the inherited endowments with which he or she entered the world. Added to these endowments are the effects of progressive sexual learning in early child-hood—or of lack of opportunity to learn—from parents or life experi-ences, about sexuality as part of life.

Just as we accept responsibility for developing the *bodies* of our children by providing good food and opportunities for exercise, and developing their *minds* by sending them to school, so should we also accept responsibility for the development of the third in the triad of human endowments—their *sexuality*. This means that we must be open to examining and reexamining our ideas about the nature of sexuality as it might or should be.

Sexual Programming Before Birth

In Chapter 1 we described how, when the sperm joins with the egg at the moment of fertilization, the sex chromosome of the sperm (X *or* Y), together with the sex chromosome of the egg (always X), make an embryo male (XY) or female (XX). Thus, gender is established right at the beginning of a new human life. The genetically coded message—*this is a female* or *this is a male*—has already been delivered, as part of the process of fertilization, to a developing group of cells thereby destined to become the sex glands: testes in the case of a male, ovaries in the case of a female. The following chain of events takes place during the first six weeks of the embryo's existence: The sex glands eventually produce either testosterone (male hormone) or estrogen (female hormone), which in turn assures the formation of the various sex and reproductive organs. The chain of events then extends to the development of those nerves that will be needed for the eventual functioning of the sex organs. The functioning of the sex organs is interrelated with the functioning of other body systems. For example, by the seventeenth week of gestation (about four months) the still-tiny male fetal sex organs have developed, along with the capability for periodic erection of the penis. This indicates that a network of connecting nerves between penis, spinal cord, and brain has developed to communicate the sensation of pleasure in erection and orgasm to the consciousness of the male—for without such consciousness there would be no sexual desire (though erection would continue automatically), no ejaculation, no mating, and therefore no procreation, and no continuation of the human species. In just the same way, nerve pathways and sex-center brain connections develop in the female, though as pointed out earlier, she need not experience pleasure in order to conceive.

Thus, the sex hormones assure that the right numbers and kinds of complex nerve circuits will, at the appropriate time of maturation, be built between the sex organs and the brain areas concerned with sex and procreation. Whether the hormones sensitize the male brain sex centers to function later in certain male ways or the female brain sex centers to function in certain female ways, is probable but not absolutely definite. Many researchers in the sexual sciences now believe that the hormones do influence the brain in this way.

Sexual Programming After Birth

Does the development of male or female anatomy, nerve pathways, and brain sex centers before birth guarantee development of matching male or female gender identity and behavior after birth and during growing up? Not necessarily. What it does guarantee is that the sexual systems of both genders will have been primed by the sex hormones so as to enable them to accept the process of sexualization that will begin at the moment of birth (see Chapter 1). This process must take place in the right way if a child is to reach the critical age, usually twenty-four to thirty-six months, with a correct sense of gender identity as indeed male or female. By five years of age the child should also be well on the way to understanding the kinds of behaviors and attitudes that go with being male or female in his or her society. In Chapter 1 we pointed out that in the years before kindergarten, parents or their substitutes play the major role in this process of sexualization. By then it is clear that the most powerful basic sex education of the child's whole life will already have taken place; it will continue to unfold from then on.

Facilitating Sexualization

The baby, whether boy or girl, can be said to come into the world with correct anatomic gender fixed, but with most of his or her sexual pages blank, so to speak, ready to be written on by life's learning experiences. At birth, the baby's anatomy announces his or her gender, and the sex pathways to and from his or her brain begin to be receptive to messages relating to that gender and to be resistant to messages that relate to the other gender. There are always two kinds of sexual messages received by the growing child from grownups. For a boy there are not only positive messages that convey "You are a boy," but also negative messages saying "You are not a girl, so you must not act like one." Such negative messages can actually imply that being a girl is a pretty poor thing to be.

For example, parents will praise a boy who is vigorous and assertive and toughly resists crying when he is hurt or upset. Or they may indicate that for him to behave in the opposite fashion—gently, sensitively, tearfully when feelings are hurt or injury occurs—is "too much like a girl, a sissy." Likewise, in the years before girls wore slacks or pants, mothers would keep telling their daughters to sit with their knees close together "like a little lady" and not to be boisterous or noisy or "bossy"—"too much like a boy."

Or, a mother trying to explain how babies are conceived and born might convey confusion, fear, or dislike for sex and the reproductive processes, unconsciously implying, "It was your father's fault we had you." This message would confuse a child not only about his or her own value but also about the relative values of males and females. A daughter who received this message might grow up to feel superior to males. She might then be even more confused if one of her parents intimated that he or she had been wishing for a boy baby before her birth; this would tend in turn to decrease the daughter's feelings of self-worth, and be difficult for her to harmonize with the feeling of being superior to males. Such variations in messages can be seen as a sure form of sex education that is confusing and potentially harmful.

Parents also need to be aware that no matter how hard they try to love all their children and treat them alike, it is unrealistic to ignore the many factors that make equality of upbringing unlikely. Being born into a family of two is bound to be different from being born into a family of three, four, or more.

What Is "Normal"?

There are so many factors in life that must and do vary that it is almost impossible to correctly apply the word *normal* to the word "sexuality." What does normal mean? Usual? Natural? Ordinary? As it ought to be? Or as someone who claims to be an expert says it should be? Actually, as regards sex, people may tend to call "normal" everything that they themselves do or feel or think, and to look upon as "abnormal" anything different that someone else does or feels or thinks about sex; they may even think of what someone else does sexually as a "deviation" or "perversion."

In its objective search for knowledge, science does not arrive at judgments in this way, for even in science the meaning of the word *normal* can vary. For instance, normal body temperature generally means 98.6 degrees F (37 degrees C). If we were to test body temperatures of one hundred people, most would probably show this to be their "norm," but there would always be a few whose temperatures might usually read as low as 98.4 or as high as 98.7 degrees—all "normal" for them. Or we might say that after childbirth the size of the uterus returns to "normal." Does this mean that its size was "abnormal" during pregnancy? No. For that period it was of normal size for each of the stages of pregnancy. Many times, a better word to use is "usual".

On the other hand, science today can say that masturbation not only is normal but is also the norm, for, as we have said, the facts now show that all mechanisms except consciousness about it are in place by the seventeenth week of gestation. Masturbation can therefore be scientifically regarded as normal and harmless, unless children are faulted for it. Such criticism can lead to a sense of shame and fear about anything having to do with sex. Research shows that there are far more people who have masturbated throughout or at some time in their lives than there are who have not.

But there are aspects of sexuality that scientific researchers and sexologists might properly consider to be "abnormal," in the sense that it is not behavior usual to most people: rigid compulsiveness about cleanliness, for instance, with constant washing of hands or genitals; or compulsiveness about refusing to appear nude before a partner; or compulsiveness about sexual intercourse always taking place in the dark. Here the "abnormality" is more of a "personality" problem than a sexual problem, but it can make spontaneous sex almost impossible to happen, and life difficult for both partners, even though they may be happy together in most other ways.

In the field of human sexuality, any behavior that cannot be related, however indirectly, to heterosexual intercourse is considered by some people to be a deviation from the "main" or "right" or "normal" way. However, to label a form of sexual behavior as *deviant* is dangerous, for many people would surely take this to mean wrong, harmful, or despicable. Unfortunately, for many people words like "deviant" and "deviation" have taken on such negative meanings. Thus, the terms "abnormal," "perversion," and "deviation" are no longer casually used by sexologists. These terms connote something "bad" or "sinful," and value judgments have no place in science except for acts that are damaging to others. That is why the preferred term for some forms of sexual behavior is now the nonjudgmental "variation."

There is no way to deal constructively with human sexuality as a vital force in the lives of all of us unless we develop some understanding of the full range of sexuality and sexual behaviors and place them in proper perspective. It is only in the past two or three decades that the kind of information in this book has been uncovered or verified by research, and many people are probably unaware of it or, more likely, do not choose to believe it. Once we find out more about various forms of sexual behavior and why or how some of these develop, we should be able to deal better and more constructively with our own sexual behavior and that of others, especially of those nearest to us.

Homosexuality

Homosexuality is a state of being in which a person prefers erotic satisfaction with a member of his or her own sex instead of with a member of the other sex. The prefix *homo-* comes from the Greek *homos* (the same), *not* from the Latin *homo* (man). A widely accepted word used to refer to homosexual people is *gay*. (A female homosexual has come to be referred to specifically as *lesbian*. The word comes from the

Greek island of Lesbos, in which women of ancient Greece formed a colony of females, all homosexual.)

Homosexuality (including lesbianism) remains a difficult subject for many people today to deal with, yet we cannot pretend it does not exist, even though only about five to ten of every hundred men and three to five of every hundred women are estimated to be exclusively homosexual. To insist on ignoring this six percent of the total population is unrealistic, especially when we accept—as we must if we are honest—that the state of being homosexual is in reality no more voluntary than is the state of being heterosexual. Put in another way, it would be as impossible for most homosexuals to decide to shed their homosexuality in favor of heterosexuality, as would be the opposite! Learning the "cause(s)" of heterosexuality will undoubtedly lead to discovering the same for homosexuality.

Both homosexuality and heterosexuality are, to the best of present knowledge, probably programmed in some way during gestation or the first five to seven years of life—or both. Those who have carried out a goodly amount of research in this field say honestly that the actual origins of heterosexuality and homosexuality still cannot be identified. Sexual orientation does not appear to be a matter of heredity, but neither has it been shown to be a matter of hormones—unless it should turn out to be something that happens before birth. If it were merely a matter of imitation, then there would be little or no homosexuality, because for centuries people who are homosexual have come almost entirely from heterosexual families. Research now shows that incidence of homosexuality among the children brought up by a homosexual parent is the same as or less than that among children coming from heterosexual backgrounds. (Such research is still in its beginnings, for until recently, a parent who admitted her or his homosexuality was rarely permitted to continue as a parent. Today, however, the courts are not compulsively taking children away from a parent specifically for that reason.)

It also remains important to distinguish between a fixed state of homosexuality and the homosexual behaviors that many children and young people experiment with as they grow up. Youthful experimentation with a person of the same sex and age does not mean that either will ultimately be homosexual. Homosexual experimentation is more likely to occur when heterosexual social opportunities are not there—for instance, in same-sex boarding schools, camps, reformatories, or prisons, in which young people and/or adults are segregated and meet socially only members of their own gender. This does not mean, how-

ever, that if both sexes were admitted to such one-sex institutions, all homosexuality would be eliminated. The percentage of people who are exclusively homosexual all of their lives would remain about the same.

Unless it is the result of predetermined homosexuality fixed from early childhood, the homosexual behavior that accompanies lack of opportunity for heterosexual relationships will almost undoubtedly revert to heterosexual behavior as soon as the opportunity arises. This has been found to be the case in prisons or the armed forces where some men or women who have no outlets for their heterosexually oriented mental, emotional, aggressive, spiritual, or sexual energies may become so desperate and lonely that homosexual behavior often occurs.

A question many people are curious about is: "What do homosexuals *do?*" Heterosexuals are so fixated on sexual activity only in terms of sexual intercourse in which a penis enters a vagina that it is hard for many to imagine anything different. Therefore a kind of folklore has grown up that suggests in hush-hush tones that homosexuals express their love for each other in all sorts of dark, mysterious, and ugly ways. Let's simply recognize that there are many ways by which human beings, whether heterosexual *or* homosexual, can and do express sexual love. Therefore, except for intercourse of penis with vagina, the ways in which homosexual men and women express their sexuality are essentially those by which millions of heterosexual couples also express theirs: The mouth, the vagina, the breasts, and the anus in women, and the mouth and anus in men, are body areas that homosexuals find just as pleasurable as heterosexuals do. The erotic aspects of skin-to-skin contacts are also similar.

There are some special problems that the homosexual faces, stemming mostly from the uninformed attitudes in the society-at-large. We'll illustrate by taking an extreme case. Suppose that heterosexuality were made illegal and labeled immoral and unnatural and that all heterosexuals were informed that they must immediately cease all lovemaking between the two sexes and begin making love only with people of the same sex. What would happen? Consternation would reign. Why? Simply because once the heterosexual "set" has been accepted in and by the self, no weight of law or fear of persecution, no persuasion or seduction, could succeed in making a heterosexual person *become* homosexual any more than the reverse. If a law were passed banning heterosexuality, heterosexuality would simply go underground—and this is exactly what has been happening with homosexuality throughout the ages in most cultures.

We have seen homosexuality declared totally immoral and sinful, and that means labeling human beings, who cannot possibly help the homosexuality that has been present from their earliest childhoods, as immoral and sinful. We hear of police harassing and spying on young teenagers as well as adults who are homosexual, trying to entrap these people into declaring themselves so they can be arrested or otherwise persecuted—although such incidents are less common than they were a few years ago.

In the United States today approximately 12 million men and women are exclusively homosexual, many of whom suffer from the effects of hostility, cruelty, isolation, and denial of their civil rights. Through the centuries this has tended to keep them underground, "in the closet," thus condemning many to lives of loneliness, fear, or furtive hiding, out of the mainstream of everyday life, especially in smaller towns where privacy is nonexistent. These are indeed problems, not only for the homosexual but also for the rest of the society, which permits and even at times encourages, to its own detriment, such unwarranted persecution.

Homosexuality is ceasing to be so much of a problem to our society as many people adjust to our present scientific understanding of that state of being. In a real sense, homosexuality might be compared to left-handedness. Not too long ago left-handed children were frequently branded and taunted and forced to "change." As a result, many of these children developed severe problems in reading or learning capacity. Research eventually established that, while in right-handed people the left side of the brain dominates, in left-handed people the right side of the brain dominates. Therefore, if we tried to force right-handed people to become left-handed, we would find them experiencing reading and learning problems too. Eventually we learned not to demand that left-handed children change, but simply to adjust to the fact that they are different. Our acceptance of that difference as "normal" for them is such that we even have left-handed scissors and can openers on the market. In other words, society has adjusted itself to accept that 10 percent of the population that is left-handed, rather than expecting left-handers to change in order to adjust to society.

Instead of trying to "cure" homosexuality, we must continue to educate society to the fact that until we learn how homosexuality occurs, homosexuals will certainly need our love and help in adjusting to homosexual life—just as heterosexuals often need help in adjusting to heterosexual life. This will enable society to provide such help for all who may need or want it.

Do we need to fear homosexuals? No. As a group, they tend per capita to be markedly less likely than heterosexuals to be violent, to be child molesters, to rape, or to kill. (Rape is almost always perpetrated by heterosexuals, against males as well as females.) Nor are homosexuals likely to try to "seduce" heterosexuals into becoming homosexual, because it would only be possible to "seduce" someone who was already programmed to be homosexual, or possibly to be bisexual and curious about a new experience. Hundreds of thousands of boys and girls must in the past have been exposed to people they did not recognize as homosexual—among clergy, teachers, pediatricians, scout leaders, youth leaders, and others, including their own or their friends' parents. These people have served as "role models" without any noticeable increase in homosexuality among the youths they worked or lived with.

Fears based not on fact but on ignorance and bigotry tend to be hysterically destructive to young people and to those who hold them. There is enough hatred and hysteria in the world without creating more.

The overwhelming majority of people are heterosexual, and most marry. For the same reasons (the longing to have their relationship formalized and socially accepted), many homosexuals in the United States seek "ceremonies of commitment" from official church bodies as a way for society to recognize their commitment. There are no laws permitting such unions, even though some state laws do not specify that marriage partners *must* be of different sexes. But there are places of worship that from time to time recognize a union of two gay people with an appropriate ceremony. Homosexuals are not a segregated group. They are among us and, like heterosexuals, they want and need the same things—companionship, love, success, creative work, fun, a home, friends, and *acceptance by the community*—regardless of orientation.

Almost all heterosexuals and homosexuals enjoy the same kinds of sexual activities. The person who is exclusively homosexual just accepts the fact that he or she cannot fall in love with and feel "turned on" by someone of the other sex, just as an exclusively heterosexual person cannot imagine falling in love with and feeling "turned on" by someone of the same sex. Parents of homosexual children need not ask themselves, "What did I do wrong?" That is not the right question. When they find out that one of their children is homosexual, nothing has changed and neither should the parents. Their question should be: "How can I do right?" The homosexual child is just as much in need of their love and caring and help—to become as good a human being as possible, as able to find love, companionship, fulfillment—as is a heterosexual child. Accepting these realities as rational brings a sigh of relief to countless people: one more thing we *don't* have to stew over!

In a report published a few years ago for study by the Catholic Theological Society of America, five Roman Catholic theologians and teachers made the following statement:

> Homosexuals have the same right to love, intimacy, and relationships as heterosexuals. Like heterosexuals, they are also bound to strive for the same ideals in their relationships, for creativity and integration. The norms governing the morality of homosexual activity are those that govern all sexual activity, and the norms governing sexual activity are those that govern all human ethical activity. It bears repeating, however, without provision, that where there is sincere affection, responsibility, and the germ of authentic human relationship—in other words, where there is love—God is surely present.

This statement, neither accepted nor rejected by the Catholic Theological Society of America, therefore speaks only for its five authors. But in speaking for themselves, they did provide us with guidelines with which many representatives of Protestant and Jewish faiths agree and observe in principle.

Bisexuality

We have talked about heterosexuality and/or homosexuality as states of being. In 1948, sex researcher Alfred Kinsey and his colleagues developed a scale of sexual experience, ranging from exclusively homosexual to exclusively heterosexual. (See the chart below.) We have been talking of the extremes at each end of this scale, with *0* the exclusive heterosexual, *6* the exclusive homosexual. In between are a series of scale marks

Kinsey Scale of Sexual Orientation

Heterosexual			*Bisexual*			*Homosexual*
0 ◄	—1—	—2—	—3—	—4—	—5—	► 6
100% Ht	A few Hs fantasies or experiences	More Ht than Hs		More Hs than Ht	A few Ht fantasies or experiences	100% Hs

From A. C. Kinsey et al., *Sexual Behavior in the Human Female* (Philadelphia: Saunders, 1953), p. 470.

in which *1* would be a person who has had some experience with homosexual behaviors but remained heterosexual in adult life, and *5* would be a person who had had some experience with heterosexual behavior growing up but remained homosexual in adult life. A *2* would be heterosexual by preference, but maintain some form of homosexual experience in adult life on a small scale; *4* would be the equivalent in the homosexual state. Point *3* on the scale would then be a person who is able to function comfortably either as homosexual or heterosexual, and today we are seeing more of this. We call it *bisexuality.*

Bisexual people can function in various ways: they can be married with children and carry on a full homosexual life in addition to the marriage, or they can live in a homosexual relationship and carry on an active heterosexual life as well. Or they can be bisexual in desire and attraction to other people, but choose to limit their sexual activity, say, to a single committed relationship. So far our society has not really recognized bisexuality because it has not been studied as fully as homosexuality. We know that bisexuality exists and that bisexuals are no more freaks than are homosexuals; they are merely human beings, like everyone else. Just as we now know much more about homosexuality than we ever did before, so too the growing research into bisexuality will help us more fully to understand all variations of sexual orientation.

Sexuality and "the Golden Years"

There are many potentially harmful myths about the effects of the aging process on sexual life. These myths can be harmful because believing them can actually make them happen. A letter one of us received from a sixty-year-old man described his worry because his erections were not as strong as they used to be. He wrote, "I often wake up at night with an erection, but as soon as I start worrying that it will go away, it does." That type of worry is the problem in a nutshell for many men, especially men over sixty. Male periodic erections during sleep are the rule and so is their loss due to interference in the sexual response process. There can be a variety of causes, including chronic anxiety. On awakening, that man should try simply to enjoy the erection, capitalizing on it by simple lovemaking or masturbation, for relaxed patience can be a positive step toward retaining or restoring capacity for sexual enjoyment.

As we age, how do our bodies and all their complex processes change? We tend to accept such changes, understanding, for instance, that whereas formerly we could run the length of an airport to make a plane, as we move past age fifty we are less able to do this; so we allow ourselves time for walking—briskly or temperately. Of course, females and males are different when it comes to aging, sexual performance, and sexual relationships. Furthermore, some women do not learn to experience orgasm until they are mature, sometimes not even until they are in their forties or fifties, so may not miss what they have not experienced. However, whatever the level of intensity of sexual experience women do reach at any age, whether it be from pleasuring by the self or by another, they tend to maintain that same level until well into their seventies and eighties. By contrast, males are at *their* peaks in their late teens and early twenties. Their capacity for erection is maintained, with a very gradual slowing, mostly of frequency, until the fifties or early sixties, when strength of erection may also be somewhat diminished. By the seventies, perhaps a quarter of males have noticed that their capacity for erection has much diminished or may even have ceased. This proportion increases with age, but some men remain sexually vigorous and capable even of impregnating into their eighties or even nineties.

With both women and men, the most important factors for retention of sexual capacity are desire and opportunity for regular sexual interchange with an interest*ed* and interest*ing* partner. In this connection, additional help can come from a zestful approach to life by both partners, so that if any inhibitions remain in either, both can help maintain sexual interest and response by finding new ways or new and different occasions or places for renewing their mutual sexual experiences. Thus masturbation, mutual hand-genital or oral-genital sex, or variations in position, can all be used to provide fresh feelings of interest and renewal, as can changes in locale: a different room or bed, in front of the glowing fireplace, in a hotel room or cruise ship cabin, or even under the stars in the fragrance of freshly cut hay!

Of course in the older age groups, long or chronic illnesses or conditions are more common than earlier, and these can interrupt one's sex life over long periods of time. An illness or surgery need not mean the end of sexual capability and enjoyment, however. The patient should ask his or her physician specific questions about the condition, for doctors have become increasingly sensitized to the way certain medications and/or prostate or other surgery can be sexually disturbing. In addition, sex counseling may be important. After a man has prostatic surgery, for example, sex counseling can assure the couple that the possible lost capacity for erection need not and should not interrupt other aspects of their sexual life together, because there are many, many ways of making love through shared experiences, touching, caressing, whispered words, and skillful use of lips and hands.

In women, hysterectomy, unless accompanied by very extensive removal affecting nerve connections in the pelvis, rarely influences post-surgery sexual enjoyment. Hormone replacement is today more and more often considered for women, and gynecologists and endocrinologists can advise on this. Many couples use artificial lubricants ("K-Y" or other greaseless creamy lotions, including an estrogen vaginal cream used in the clitoral area) if natural lubrication has been reduced, as frequently happens in absence of hormone therapy.

Family and social attitudes can play important roles. A critical attitude toward physical expression of sexuality among the elderly will be destructive of their peace of mind and sense of self-worth. It will also inhibit continued enjoyment of a valued sexual relationship that might add immeasurably to life's later chapters. Men and women should experience only dignity and pleasure in finding that they are not "dirty old men" or "dirty old women" but are simply sexually active older citizens—if they wish to be. Unfortunately, not all nursing homes have taken note of these findings, much less accepted and acted on them.

Separation, Divorce, Death—and Support Systems

Every relationship must end, for certain. And as time brings more and more intimate relationships between two people to a close (whether by divorce, separation, or death, the effects are much the same), the results are deep feelings of pain, loss, and confusion that can amount to genuine disorientation. The helping professions are needed to support individuals as they learn to live without the mutually dependent intimacy to which they are accustomed. In the case of death, the separation must be accepted as final, but acceptance is often difficult and the period of mourning and bereavement may be long. The same is equally true of separation by institutionalization or legal separation or divorce from a still-living partner. Here the sense of loss, mourning, or bereavement may be felt not so much for the person as for the relationship that had existed—or that might have been.

Going through such an experience of bereavement for whatever reason is easier if one has a strong sense of the self, of who and what one is. Also essential are love and support from close family members and unquestioning friends—what is often today called a support system.

Until we need a support system in the case of loss by death or by life processes, we may not realize how vital it can be to our ability to continue or to remold a life shattered by a severe loss. There are many people today who do not have such a support system—people who are alone or who do not have families that have learned how to coalesce themselves, their caring, and their concern into a system that can come to the aid of a member of the group who has been stricken in one way or another. Geographical distance is also a factor, but not the main preventative of such aid, for the telephone is there for lengthy, close conversations that can include such heartfelt remarks as "I love you," "I wish I were right there to hold you," or "I'm glad to hear your voice—it tells me that you're feeling better today than you were last week." These comments are particularly important because they mean that one is being kept track of as one moves along the path to recovery—whether from the death of a loved person, or from one's own illness.

When one is grief-stricken, strangers, no matter how kind, just cannot do as well. The greater the sense of loss over something that has been dear and familiar, the greater is the need for comfort, support, and strength from sources that are also dear and familiar, and have themselves known and cared about the lost one. Sometimes one can persuade oneself that a stranger is "the answer" to loneliness and despair, but this is rarely the case. Entering into new intimacy, especially sexual intimacy, too rapidly can be unwise and even dangerous, for if we do this we are really asking an unknown person to help handle suffering that can only be worked out by ourselves.

The question of sex itself inevitably intrudes, especially if one has become accustomed to a full, regular, and satisfying sex experience. Older women and men can both suffer cruelly from sexual deprivation, and if there is a haunting sense that this is unworthy or unbecoming, that at a given age one ought to be able to "sublimate," let it be remembered that the very ones who may be suggesting this are perhaps for the most part persons for whom the sex drive has not been a primary need.

The end of a relationship is a time when an already established sound understanding of and attitudes about the worth of self-pleasuring can stand in good stead. Our bodies are our own, are always with us, were made to serve us in many different ways in case of need. Masturbation and daydreaming are far safer than rushing into relationships with comparative strangers, who should not be enmeshed in our own slow movement toward recovery of our sense of wholeness and of self, until we become ready to develop another relationship. Deep feelings of need, sexual and otherwise, that spring out of a deep relationship, tend to match each other in intensity and power. These can help sustain in times of stress, whether there is the need to *receive* love and comfort from the support system, or the need to *give* love and comfort to a stricken one. The more one has invested in relationships for mutual giving, the more one has to give to others in their own crisis times.

6
Marriage

Marriage is something most people have; something most people want; something a great many people take for granted they will have; something a vast number of people consider to be the most wonderful thing they ever had; something some people would be better off never being involved in; something many people get out of after they're in; something others wish they could get out of but can't; something many people try a second time, usually more successfully than the first; something some people try even a third time or more; something many people don't *think* much about; and something most people do *feel* a lot about. In any case, marriage throughout the ages has been something very special in human life.

Marriage is not just the wedding, with the bride in white the center of attention. Nor is it an event that means romance will be the central force in two lives from that point on. For a great many men and women, romance can be a most important part of marriage and can help carry a couple through the difficult moments in living together. For others, a limited understanding of the part sex and romance play in marriage is likely to cause problems and disappointments. Too many people believe marriage is just a signal that they can at last have all the sex together they want and that the sexual part of their life together will always be perfect, without any effort on their part. They need to understand that romance is only a part of sex and that sex is only a part of romance.

About half the marriages that take place in the United States today will end in divorce, and the average length of a marriage is about seven years. These figures, of course, include marriages that last only a very short time and those that last for life, often many decades.

The Role of Childhood Experiences

Marriage affects lives so deeply that it is far more than a ceremony in which two people say, "I do"; the state says, "By this ceremony you are now legally bound to each other"; and the church or other religious body says, "By this ceremony you have now covenanted yourselves to each other in the eyes of God." In truth, the facts and conditions of a marriage begin not with the wedding itself but way back at those two moments when each partner was born, and they include all the moments in the lives of both since then.

From the time that the two people who will eventually marry each other come into this world, all kinds of things happen to each of them. These experiences will profoundly influence the kind of marriage relationship they will achieve. Thus it is worthwhile for people to look back at such experiences to try to see how they will—or do—affect the marriage relationship. Good experiences can be used positively, but experiences that were not so good must be understood so that a person can learn how to compensate for possible negative effects. It is important to learn how to change and adapt oneself, and how to grow in awareness and understanding—whether before marriage or within the marriage relationship—always bearing in mind that it takes two to make a marriage. There is no such thing as an uninvolved partner, inside or outside marriage. That is why marriage and sex counseling can generally succeed only when both husband and wife are in counseling, or therapy, together.

The Place of Sex in Marriage

Far more than a ceremony or a covenant, marriage is also far more than sex. Marriage means living together, growing together, building a relationship that is a source of strength for two people, not only a refuge *from* the world for them but also a springboard *into* the world. Intimacy—built on mutual need, mutual trust, between two people who are constantly saying, with or without words, "I need you, you are the most important person in the world to me"—is the ultimate refuge, the ultimate achievement of marriage. Love comes easily in this kind of intimacy, and so does sexual expression. Sex doesn't have to be constant fireworks with many orgasms. Although it can be, it can also be a loving, gentle experience that provides a kind of inner radiance for two lives, a warmth that others are aware of and that fully satisfies the partners.

Sex is only a part of marriage. For some couples, sex is perhaps the most vital part of their mutual need; for most it takes a lesser place; for still others it may be quite unimportant. But once mutual need and trust are firmly established for both, once lines of communication are opened up by talking and touching, the relationship is strong enough to stand the stresses that all living brings at one time or another.

Counteracting a Major Threat to Marriage

Among the many factors that threaten marriage today is the continuing pattern perpetuated by parents whose childhood experiences have not made them capable of achieving relationships that are giving, trusting, and intimate. These parents then have children, but they do not have the background to draw on to provide a good model for their children. Many efforts are being made to break into this self-perpetuating chain.

Besides psychotherapy for individual couples, there are groups of couples who help each other in the remembering and relearning process. These are known as marriage-encounter or marriage-enrichment groups, many of which are under religious auspices. All these groups take up, among other topics, the topic of sex. They provide information and encourage discussion so that members of the group can come to see that the physical sexual relationship can be a highly pleasurable and comforting part of life that can even be strengthened by discussion. All such groups should be carefully checked to ensure that their leaders are well-qualified people.

These groups also help people see that it is possible to change themselves and their lives for the better by being willing to remember and reexamine and evaluate all kinds of experiences, even those of earliest childhood and even—maybe especially—the most painful ones. When they are able to do this, with or without help, they can restructure their ways of relating to those who are most dear to them. Participation in such group experiences, by two people who can admit how important they are to each other even though they haven't been getting along well together, can serve to change the relationship so that a marriage that is hurting after ten, twenty, or more years can be salvaged.

More than being salvaged, such a marriage can be so strengthened and enriched that the two partners can find each other again—in a true sense fall in love again—and become for their children, their grandchildren, and all the members of their family, as well as for each other, sources of strength and joy and love.

But is marriage for everyone? Is marriage the only basis possible for the formation of a family? People used to think so, but today we are beginning to see a number of different kinds of "families." We talk about them in the next chapter, so right now is a good place to point out that everything in this chapter is as important for nonmarried people who have entered into a committed relationship to understand as it is for married couples.

7

The Family and Its Role
in the Development
of Sexuality

The family is certainly the oldest human institution and society's most basic unit. It has always been the principal means for protecting and training children and rearing them to maturity. In most parts of the world, it is still the principal way by which property can be cared for, improved or increased, and passed on to the next generation. At its best, the family provides steady love and caring for each of its members. The family can make possible, also, division of labor and pooling abilities and talents of its members so that the educational, social, and economic welfare of each one is promoted. And, as we have already suggested, it is the principal environment in which the sexuality of husband and wife finds intimate expression and in which the sexuality of the young, along with their minds and bodies, is first formed, to be guided and developed thereafter. Most of us, during our lifetimes, belong to at least two families, the one in which we were born and raised and the one which, usually with another person, we ourselves establish, by acts of love and intention.

The Family Today

In the United States, the most common as well as traditional definition of the family has been a married couple with children (the *nuclear family*). In another sense, family can also mean a group of people connected by ties of blood or marriage, such as one or more grandparents, cousins, aunts, uncles, nieces, nephews, in-laws, and so on (the *extended family*).

About two-thirds (67 percent) of the adults in the United States today live in arrangements that do not fit the traditional nuclear family pattern. These include couples without children or whose children have left home (36 percent); people living alone (24 percent); single parents with children (3 percent); and various sorts of extended families (4 percent). As the variety of family arrangements has increased over the past fifty or more years, the proportion of traditional nuclear families has decreased. Today, the most comprehensive and helpful definition of a family, one that respects different kinds of people who have chosen different patterns to establish and support a family lifestyle, is: *Two or more people who, regardless of gender, age (although one must be legally an adult), or marital status, elect to live together in commitment and trust in order to care for and about each other.* Even so, we should repeat, the most widely accepted definition of a family remains the one into which most people in our culture have fitted at some point in their lives: *A mother and a father and their growing offspring.*

One thing is certain: regardless of the pattern of the family, what is always required of its members is to learn how to live together. And, especially where there are children, another thing is certain: given that the family's primary functions are to house, nourish, clothe, educate, and protect its members, one additional function stands out—to teach its members how to give and how to receive love and how to support each other in mutual development and fulfillment. You can put figures and measurements to how well families carry out their practical functions, but no one has ever learned how to measure love, devotion, development, and fulfillment.

During thousands of years of human history, there have been relatively few options for family members: men did what was considered men's work, women did women's work, and children were trained to fit this pattern. In 1847 the British poet Alfred Tennyson described it this way:

> Man for the field and woman for the hearth;
> Man for the sword, and for the needle she;
> Man with the head, and woman with the heart;
> Man to command, and woman to obey;
> All else confusion.

Today, in many parts of the world, including our own country, there remains considerable support for this kind of division of labor and functions, because of the fear of "all else confusion."

But over the past century, new developments have led to revolutionary changes in family life: the invention of machines providing both men and women with more leisure time and tending to make less important the usually greater body size and muscular strength of men; the change in the nature of productive work, with less need for physical strength (of which the average man has more than the average woman) and more need for special skills and training (in which men and women are relatively equal), so that today men and women can be equally productive; and the discovery of reliable means of contraception so that, as women need no longer face unlimited childbearing and rearing, they can, if they wish or must, join the labor force.

In short, it is now possible for women and men, and girls and boys, to choose with equal freedom what they wish to do with their lives, and they now have the same freedom in choosing how they will express their sexuality and arrange their groupings, their marriages, and their families. With these new freedoms, for better or worse, it is now more possible to make decisions for oneself rather than have one's life pre-scribed by tradition or necessity. Some people welcome these changes, some are troubled by them, but all have no choice but to adapt to them, for they appear to be here to stay.

In the United States, because of these changes, for our satisfaction and happiness in family life we have come to place more importance on the love and companionship we choose and less on the blood rela-tionships and economic and physical necessities that once required us to stay together regardless of emotional needs and satisfactions.

Most people are now free to choose how, or even whether, to form a family, and, if they do form one, whether and when to add children to it, either natural or adopted. We have access to a vast range of ideas and information, and we see examples of all kinds of alternatives. We have fewer roots and we move around a lot. It is the exception to grow up in a single community surrounded by relatives and friends, younger and older, who grew up in the same community. More than half the women in our country are in the workforce, rather than home-bound, and children are at home alone more often than before, in the care of people other than their parents, or at school or at a day-care center.

Despite the wide acceptance of diverse patterns of family living there persists in the United States among many people a strong, deeply engrained sense of the "right" way for a family to be: the husband and father is "head" of the family and is the main breadwinner; the wife and mother takes care of everyone and is in charge of the home, except for major decisions; the two or three children, boys and girls, behave the way boy children and girl children are supposed to behave, which is not always "good" but is certainly not rebellious, except occasionally, when the boy children rebel more than the girl children.

That's the pattern still considered "typical" today by many middle-aged and older people, though not so much by younger people. Thus, as patterns have begun to vary and change has become more rapid, something of a gap has developed between generations, as has happened many times before. In the stable, unchanging, more isolated societies studied by many anthropologists, there exists little or no difference from generation to generation, but in our society—and in other developed countries today—such a gap is common. Furthermore, in countries now developing by rapid urbanization and efforts at industrialization, the communication gap between generations is becoming as marked as it is in the United States.

Parental Responsibilities

In spite of the influence parents can have on their children's development, there is no doubt that from the moment of birth, and even before, each child is his or her own being, a duplicate of no one else. Anyone who has had a number of children knows that from the very beginning some infants are placid and happy, some tense and irritable, some noisy, some quiet, some easy, some difficult. These qualities seem to be a part of the essential individuality of each child, not something conferred upon the child from outside. Thus, while parents do have a profound influence on their children, they do not form the basic stuff of the child.

Some parents make the mistake of feeling that they are responsible for everything their children are and everything their children do. They even try to live their lives for them. However, all that should be expected of parents is that they do their best with their children. While parents cannot live their children's lives for them, they can try to set good examples—without trying to masquerade as perfect. They can try to pass on to their children, as opportunities arise, the standards and values by which they live. The children think about these standards, try them out, reject them, return to them, discuss them with others; and all this helps young people mature.

Children will inevitably look outside the family for information, opinions, and experiences. Television, radio, movies, friends, books, magazines, visitors, and the like also reach them in their homes. Parents cannot and should not try to protect their children from outside influences, although they can rightly help to select the experiences their children will have. The main goal of parents should be to help their children equip themselves with information, with the capacity to reason about facts, with an awareness of where and when to make decisions, and with the ability to communicate, so that in the end the children learn to stand on their own. The age when, to a considerable degree, children must rely on themselves comes earlier than many of us think, in the middle and late teens. But even then the children must not be made to feel that their parents have abdicated their responsibilities, as did the teenage girl who told her friend, "My parents don't care what I do, as long as it doesn't come to their attention."

Single-Parent Families

Because one out of every two marriages in the United States ends in divorce or separation, a large percentage of children today spend some or all of their most formative years with only one parent, usually but not always the mother.

How does growing up in a single-parent family affect children? There is no simple answer. If the first six or eight years of a child's life have been spent with two parents who cared for and related closely to the child and to each other, much of the basic process of sexualization (gender identity, sex-role orientation, comfortable feelings about his or her body, sense of self-respect) has been accomplished. However, if the relationship between the parents has been hostile or distant, this is likely to leave a mark, but not necessarily an indelible one.

It is probably better for children to live with one loving parent than to live with two who are by daily example teaching poor human relationships. Children in a single-parent family have relationships with other families and other people who may be close to the parent. Thus there are many sources from which the children can learn about men and women, about what being "masculine" and being "feminine" can mean. With their own relatives, friends, and peers in the neighborhood and at school and, in turn, with their families, the lives of children with only one parent need not be narrow or restricted.

About three-quarters of divorced parents do remarry, and the process by which the parent develops a new relationship and then reenters marriage, while it may bring strains and fears and even jealousy, is observed and often participated in by the children involved, and they can learn from it.

When the single parent gives the children a sense of solid support and consistent love, and sees that they have opportunities to turn outward toward others for relationships and affection, a period of single parenting is not harmful. More depends on the quality of the children's relationships with the parents and others than on the number of parents. Healthy growth toward mature and responsible expression of sexuality can be fostered by many sources.

Sexual Feelings Between Parents and Children

Many a mother has experienced sexual arousal when breastfeeding her baby, and if this were understood by women as perfectly natural, it would not be so disturbing. Many mothers and fathers also feel turned on sexually by their own children after they outgrow babyhood, especially when the children reach the age of puberty or later, and these feelings are usually disturbing to the parents. Children, too, can have sexual feelings toward their parents. It is helpful for both parents and children to know that such feelings are common and, if they are managed reasonably, are nothing to be ashamed of. They certainly should not be allowed to interfere with spontaneous gestures of affection between fathers and daughters and mothers and sons.

Anyone who thinks about it knows that feelings can cause actions, and families and society will work better if people, whether children or adults, develop a sense of responsibility for their actions. But what of the feelings that lead to the actions? Are we responsible for them? Not directly. They occur as a result of our thoughts and how what happens to us affects our thoughts. However, our thoughts can be subconscious or even unconscious—often we don't even know we have them. But if we can talk and think together about them, and then reflect alone upon them, or as we are helped by counselors with special training, or by caring friends and teachers, it is often possible to bring our subconscious or unconscious thoughts into consciousness so that we can understand how they affect our feelings and actions. The best way to change the way we feel, if we need to do that, is to do something about how and what we think. We are not responsible for our feelings because we cannot control them, so we need not feel guilty about them. What we must be responsible for is our actions, because it is possible to learn how to manage actions in such a way that no one will be hurt.

In some families, strong feelings of sexual attraction between members lead to actual sexual activity. This is called *incest,* and we discuss it in Chapter 9, Sex and Sexual Problems, on pages 164–66.

The Parents' Sex Life

Another area about which many parents feel some guilt is their own sexual life with each other; they somehow don't want their children to know that it exists. It is true that most children don't particularly want to think about the lives of their own parents in sexual terms; most adolescents find it really hard to believe that their parents, much less their grandparents, actually have intercourse for enjoyment. In fact, quite a few children have the idea that their parents, if they have had three children, for example, have had intercourse only three times.

But there is no reason to conceal the fact that parents enjoy each other sexually. What a dismal impression of adult human sexuality some parents give by their asexual masquerade! This is not to say that parents should ever exhibit their sex lives to their children or discuss at the breakfast table how great (or otherwise) it was in bed last night. This would be harmful, artificial, and uncomfortable for everyone, for in our culture, intimate sexual activity is looked upon as a private matter, and children should learn this from the parents' example.

What if a child should happen upon his or her parents involved in sexual intercourse? The child is not likely to be adversely affected— unless the parents are upset and show it by such actions as slamming the door or shouting or scolding. The best way to handle the situation is to make clear that children should respect the parents' privacy, as parents respect the privacy of their children. Also, as soon as possible, it is important to tell the child that what he or she saw was an act of love, not an attack. (To a small child, intercourse can look like an attack of the father upon the mother.)

Adolescents and Growth Toward Independence

During puberty and on through adolescence, the need of children to establish independence from parents, even if well-managed, is likely to generate strains and stresses in family relationships. This is especially true when it comes to sexual matters. Parents feel they must protect the children from danger, while every child feels the need to be his or her own person, and is sometimes unaware of or unwilling to admit any need for protection.

It is important for parents to become aware that the period of

adolescence, which covers six to ten years, requires young persons to accomplish at least four major tasks of growth:

1. They must develop independence from their parents and learn to stand on their own—without rejecting the parents. This task requires mutual respect on the part of both the adolescents and the parents, a respect that is not always easy to come by, especially when the parents have a hard time letting go.

2. They must develop a strong and stable sense of who and what they are sexually: accepting their gender as male or female; understanding the appropriate gender role behavior and the actions, relationships, choices, and values that are consistently appropriate with this role and with the kind of person each one of them is; and coming to know for themselves where, how far, with whom, and under what circumstances they will go in testing and expressing their masculinity or femininity on the way to adult maturity.

3. They must meet expectations to complete their formal education and be ready to present themselves as educated people capable of living in a world in which being educated is highly important.

4. They must prepare for earning a living.

Frequently, at least in our society, the accomplishment of these four very large and difficult tasks causes rough periods of separation, or seeming alienation, from the family. Awkwardness, open conflict, and feelings of suffering and loss will be common on both sides. But the period of abrasive criticism and conflicting immediate objectives usually passes, especially if all sides can manage to deal openly and rationally with expressions of anger and frustration and have learned how to center these feelings upon situations ("I can't stand the way you are acting right now!") and not upon persons ("I can't stand *you!*").

Young adolescents are not children and not adults; they are people on the way to becoming adults. They wobble in and out of behavior that may appear inappropriately childish. When they feel most childlike, they come to parents (if parents are open and flexible) in need purely and simply of comfort, bolstering, a listening ear, a warm hug, and even advice. They are probably as surprised and confused by their swings of behavior as their parents are, but the waverings provide rich opportunities for communication and teaching.

As children grow through adolescence, influences outside the family become stronger. This represents a healthy centrifugal force, an increased interaction with peers, with other families, with the world outside. Young people at this stage are fortunate if they are encouraged to get to know and be on intimate terms with other families, so that they can learn from inside how other families work and how different kinds of people relate to each other. Also, your own family may find itself invaded by young people from elsewhere who find you and your family a source of strength, variety, and satisfaction of curiosity. Members of your own extended family—cousins, uncles, aunts, grandparents, family friends, and so forth—can also help provide a wide variety of people with whom your children can interact and learn, and from whom you as parent can also learn the various and changing ways of the world.

It is important that both parents and children accept adolescent sexual interests and urges as natural and good, while still agreeing on the need for limits to sexual behavior. As adolescents increase their capacity to take on responsibilities, the amount of freedom they are granted must increase. In this way they will gain the experience needed for maturity. The degree of maturity they can reach must serve to arm them for the time when the controlling forces in their lives will no longer be their parents but instead whatever knowledge, strength, values, standards, and capacity for giving and receiving joy they have developed with the aid of their parents. Inevitably, there must come the time when their only guardian is their own character.

Family Communication About Sex

How can parents and children learn to communicate with each other as the children work out standards for themselves regarding their sexuality? We have already said that much communication among members of the family takes place without words and even unconsciously, and that there is quite commonly little or no open, spoken communication on sexual matters. This is not a conspiracy of silence but an unspoken agreement to be silent, probably because some or all members of the family have gotten the message from each other that sex is a subject to be silent about. Members of a family need not feel guilty or inadequate or angry if silence is the pattern, but opportunities should not be missed to find ways to relieve the silence and let the words flow.

A good time to let down the silence barrier is any occasion of crisis—for example, when a parent is angry or worried about a sex-related occurrence in a child (genital play, too-early dating, use of the car for "parking," inviting a friend into a bedroom alone), or when a child is angry for being forbidden to participate in what seems like innocent activity. If the discussion can center on what actually happened, how each person feels about it, and what the motives and conse-

quences (both good and bad) were or are likely to be, it may be helpful talk. If the talk centers on the person or persons involved—their "goodness" or "badness" as people—rather than on the *actions* themselves, it is likely to be harmful. To express how you feel and how certain behaviors make you feel is fine, but it can be harmful if you get carried away in a spirit of accusation against the person.

If there is a heated exchange of words, it is best that parents not lay down the law while feelings are still hot. Instead, come back to the issues when things are calmer, and then work out some rules or standards or agreements together. A crisis can be the occasion for authentic, valuable communication, and exchange of true feelings, and we can be thankful when crises, openly dealt with, result in keeping the doors open between people who love and care about each other and want to remain a family.

ANSWERING QUESTIONS ABOUT SEXUALITY

When a child, especially an adolescent, asks a question, it is sometimes most fruitful to use the question as an opener for what may become a long and serious exchange of knowledge, ideas, and attitudes. At other times, it may be better to try to answer a factual question plainly, briefly, and factually, not going beyond the question but not hedging either. When you tell children what they want to know, you open the way to further questions and conversation. Be careful not to use a simple question as a springboard for a complete lecture on, say, human biology; if you do, you may turn off further questions. For example, four-year-old Sally points between the legs of her undressed little brother and says, "What's that?" A good answer would be, "That's his penis and testicles; they make him a boy, not a girl. You have a vulva and a clitoris; they make you a girl, not a boy." Later on, unless Sally asks more right then, you can find time to explain, "All boys and men have penises and all girls and women have vulvas outside and vaginas inside, and that's the way it's supposed to be. Little boys use their penises when they go to the bathroom"—you might say "urinate" if it doesn't seem too fancy a word—"and when they grow up they also use them to help make babies. You don't have a penis, but you do have a uterus (or womb) inside you where a baby can grow. You see, it takes both a man and a woman to start a baby."

When questions and comments from the children do come, be very careful not to overadvise or jump in too quickly. Parents should *listen* first to be sure they have correctly heard the question or comment before they answer. And of course, a sure way to shut off further questions is to respond, "Why do you want to know that?"—which may be heard by the child as "You shouldn't be interested in that" or "Have you been fooling around with something you shouldn't?" If you simply answer the question, the reason for the question may well come out sooner or later.

GIVING ADVICE

If you feel you should give advice, and advice is often necessary (for example, if an early adolescent seems to be experimenting with sexual intercourse), let it come as information, not as negative or positive commandments. But when it comes to your own convictions and beliefs about sexual behavior, it is usually best to state these frankly. It is important, however, to label them as *your* beliefs and convictions, not as something you are trying to impose on your children.

By information, examples, and sharing of experiences, you may be able to convince a child to adopt your point of view, but you'll never succeed by insisting that the child think and behave your way only.

One advantage adults have over children and adolescents is that adults have lived longer and can probably see things more in perspective. A mature person doesn't tend to think the world is coming to an end quite so often as a young person does. Even if they haven't been explicitly told some things—about sex, for instance—children know a lot and have imagined or guessed even more. But much of what they think and believe is secret, incorrect, or out of proportion, and this is not their fault but ours for not providing factual information long before.

Parents can therefore be very helpful to their children by using conversation (at the dining table, in the living room, while preparing the children for bed, while driving in the car, while on a walk, during a TV commercial) to put things into context and to ask and answer questions or provide more information. Television shows, news items, school lessons, neighborhood gossip or events, remarks made by peers—all these are good opportunities for communication, sharing, and education. Such sharing is best done naturally and bit by bit, not in large doses of what seem to be prepared lectures.

We mustn't forget that some things that seem important or shocking to an adult are taken in a more matter-of-fact manner by most young persons (for example, news of a rape or an out-of-wedlock pregnancy). It is important to try to react so as to educate rather than frighten young people. Overreaction can easily distort and get things out of perspective.

ENCOURAGING YOUNG PEOPLE TO TALK

Sometimes it is obvious that a youngster doesn't have the courage to express an interest, to make a comment, or to ask a question. He or she may feel the subject is too personal or too embarrassing to talk about in front of the entire family. In this case it can work well to take the youngster aside later and begin a conversation or provide information or make it clear that you are ready to listen. If you let your child know you're ready whenever he or she wants to talk, eventually the child will get up the nerve to ask the question, sometimes of the father, sometimes of the mother. Make it clear you are always available—be "askable."

Books can be helpful in encouraging youngsters to open up. There are a number of books that can be given or left lying around (but better given, with some explanation like, "This is a good book about sex, or at least I thought so. If you read it, then maybe we can talk about it.") The book you are now reading can be left around for any member of the family to pick up. (See pages 267–72 for some other suggestions.)

Other aids can be school or church programs. Learn whether they have a sex education program, what it is like, and how it is taught. Whatever you discover you will be able to use to advantage at home. (See Chapter 11, Planned Sex Education Programs.)

HOW YOUNG PEOPLE CAN IMPROVE FAMILY COMMUNICATION

Many adults would love to feel that young people are trying to keep open the flow of communication and would respond to this. Sometimes it is necessary for young people to take the initiative with parents who are shy. Here, then, young people, are some ways to do this:

• Whenever possible, open up and share feelings.

• Let your parents know how things are and what is going on in your lives.

• Ask questions of fact or opinion.

• When you think your parents (or other adults) are right, tell them so gladly. This makes it unnecessary for parents to keep insisting they are right or to say "I told you so." It also puts you in a much stronger position when you are sure *you* are right; and you will be more likely to be listened to with respect.

Whether you are a parent or a child, if you are hesitant and embarrassed to talk about sexual matters, try to admit it. Don't pretend you know everything or have every issue about sexuality totally decided. If parents acknowledge their questions, children are likely to acknowledge theirs, and good discussion and sharing of information can result in mutual respect and growth.

Developing an Awareness of Differences

In some families all members feel reasonably free to talk together about sexual matters, and the children have learned to talk about body parts and sexual functions naturally and factually. This is a healthy state of affairs, but it can lead to problems when the youngsters go out into the neighborhood or visit other families where there is no such openness. Thus it is good for children to be taught, when they are old enough to understand, that not all families feel the same about what is proper to talk about and what is not, and that many people feel that matters having to do with the body and with sex are not good subjects to talk about. The children should realize that it doesn't mean their family is better than other families, just that it is a matter of differences in feelings and upbringing, and people's feelings should always be respected.

Privacy for Family Members

In most families, both parents and children value their privacy at certain times. If a parent is in the bathroom and really doesn't feel comfortable sharing it with a child, he or she can simply say so. There is no need to do this in a scolding tone. Simply explain, "I like my privacy, so please knock and I'll tell you if it's OK to come in. I'll do the same for you." Or, "I'll feel more comfortable if you knock first and wait for me to tell you to come in." Children can understand that; they often feel the same way.

If parents are in the bedroom together, even if they're simply reading or napping or talking, they may want privacy. Again, a "Please knock when the door's closed and wait to be invited in" is natural and clear and nonthreatening. It's just as important for parents to give the same consideration to their children—once they've reached an age where it matters, perhaps four or five—and to knock if the door is closed and wait to be invited in. A child will be grateful for the respect and understanding shown, and will learn to do the same.

Dealing with Sex Play and Experimentation

Infants quite naturally and quickly learn that it feels good when they touch and play with their genitals, and such play should not be discouraged or punished. Punishment will not stop the activity but will cause the baby to learn to be secretive and to feel guilty about it. Feelings of guilt about such activity may be quite heavy and long-lasting, affecting even the ability to enjoy sexual pleasure later in marriage.

Children in our culture must learn that sex and sexual touching are considered private matters. For example, if a very young child is engaging in genital play in the living room while other people are around, he or she can be picked up in an affectionate way, without the least hint of disapproval, and carried elsewhere. An older child can be told, "I'm glad you've found your body feels good, but when you want to touch your body that way, it's more private to be in your room by yourself." Some parents may ask, "But isn't this simply telling my child that it's OK to go to his (or her) room to masturbate?" The answer is yes, and we believe this is a good thing to reassure a child about. As we have said, masturbation is harmless, except when we make it otherwise by causing a child to feel guilty about it.

An even more difficult situation for parents to deal with is when young children engage in sex play with each other, either with another member of the family or with a friend. It is a fact that children are curious about each other's bodies and that they quite naturally want to satisfy their curiosity. Therefore, unless they are strongly inhibited from doing so, or explicitly forbidden, it is to be expected that they will want to see what another child's body looks like.

Some children will simply and harmlessly look at each other's genitals and perhaps touch them. Usually they will do these things in secret, which shows that they have already learned that any activity connected with the sexual parts of their bodies is taboo—wrong and unacceptable. Others will do their exploring through some sort of game, like playing doctor, to make it seem more acceptable. Such activity is rarely erotic (seeking physical genital pleasure); rather, it is research, learning, trying to find answers to questions, harmful only when adults happen upon it, become vastly upset, and express anger, fear, and the intent to punish. Then the children receive the impression that they are onto something really big and bad and fearful.

If they are observed by a parent, children will usually stop their sex play or genital exploration, and it is an appropriate response for them to do so. If parents feel comfortable enough about it all to say something like "It *is* interesting to find out how other people's bodies look, isn't it?" that's a suitable response. If they can go on to let the children talk about it with them and answer questions, or even to get a book with some diagrams and look at them together, so much the better.

Probably, though, most parents will not feel sure or comfortable enough to do more than put a gentle stop to the incident and then, we hope, find an occasion soon afterward to explain to the child or children what it is they want to know, by conversing or by looking at and reading a book together.

The main reason why parents are apt to make the mistake of becoming alarmed by childish sex exploration and sex play is that they project their own adult attitudes and feelings into the acts of the children. When adults, or late adolescents, engage in sex play, especially when it involves seeing and touching genitals, the activity is highly arousing and closely connected with the urge to have sexual intercourse. But with younger children this is not so. And it certainly does not signify the beginning of sexual promiscuity or "looseness." To them it's just a very interesting kind of looking and finding out. It is usually also part of "You be the Daddy and I'll be the Mommy" play. None of this kind of play upsets parents or other grownups except when it verges on the sexual. Then the children get frightened at the uproar, for they don't understand why something that was cute one minute is bad the next. And the fright and misery can stay hidden within them for years—until they marry or enter an intimate relationship, when it can rise up and cause problems.

When boys and girls who have reached puberty and can impregnate and conceive engage in sex play, it is much more than the relatively simple matter of small-child explorations. The urges are stronger, and the physical, emotional, and social consequences can be major.

By this age, adolescents should have been provided with the straight facts about sexual activity and its consequences so that they will be aware of what they can be getting into. They should also have had previous opportunities to discuss the whole matter at home or at school, preferably both. Those who were unable or unwilling to discuss the subject of sex with their parents, and who had no opportunity to talk about it in a planned way at school or with anyone, will probably have talked about it in bits and pieces with their friends. They may have put together enough information to feel their needs are served, but their knowledge is probably only partial, and apt to be laced with errors or composed of elements quite out of perspective. If their information is not adequate, if they are "innocent" and yet exposed to the pressures leading to intercourse—or perhaps even unaware of what they are being led into—then they are at great risk and in need of help, and quickly, and parents ought to be the ones who can provide that help.

Parents should make clear where they stand on adolescent sexual activity. They should also make clear that they consider that they have the right to set the standards of behavior and limits for conduct within their home. If parents feel it's all right for a young couple to have the privacy of the living room or den for talking only, or for necking and petting, or even for engaging in genital sexual activity or intercourse, that's one thing, and some parents do feel that way. If they feel that it's entirely against their beliefs and standards to have direct sexual activity between their child and someone else's going on in their home, that's another thing, and they should set limits and explain their position as clearly as they can, allowing ample opportunity for questioning and discussion. It may be that their children will agree with them or can be convinced. Simply laying down the law is certainly not going to be as effective in modifying behavior as a conviction developed through information, discussion, and a firm position honestly and lovingly taken.

If parents are convinced that their adolescent children are going to be sexually active no matter what the parents think, then it is certainly better to have a nonpregnant or nonimpregnating sexually active adolescent than a pregnant or impregnating one. In other words, sexually active young people should be provided with contraceptive information, counseling, and methods (see Chapter 4, Family Planning).

If parents react to their children's experiments in sexual activity by anger, threats, or punishment, there are several possible consequences. Most likely, the sex behavior will simply shift to outside the home. Older children often react to strong disapproval that is unaccompanied by explanation and discussion not by conforming to the disapproval, but by ignoring it, while at the same time continuing the behavior elsewhere. In fact, the most common response of young people to overrestrictive parents is to rebel, to do the opposite of what they are commanded to do. The "black sheep" of some families, young people who are heavy drinkers, users of drugs, or sexually promiscuous, may be examples of this kind of rebellion. Still another likely consequence of restrictions tinged with punishment is that the child will come to associate sex with disapproval, fear, and anger and will let sex be driven underground and buried in guilt. Later, this may make happy, pleasurable expression of sex more difficult, but not impossible. After some suffering and struggling to adjust, most people can overcome earlier disadvantages, especially if helped by a loving partner. But one other almost certain consequence of anger and punishment is that the whole area of sexuality will become a subject to be avoided with parents, a sad but quite common loss of opportunity to share caring and learning.

The alternative to anger and punishment is to try to reveal feelings and together to explore consequences. "I'm worried about the way you are experimenting, and I'd like to give you some information that you may not have. Can we talk about it?" is one way to bring up the topic that invites open responsiveness.

Language and Sex

We teach our children something about sex when they are first learning to name the parts of their bodies. Naming their ears, nose, knees, and feet is all right, but in many families it's not so with penis, vagina, testicles, and vulva, and it's a fortunate family in which all parts of the body can be named correctly without discomfort, thus facilitating communication. However, children need to know that the names of the sexual parts of the body are considered special and private by most people, just as are the actual parts themselves.

Children will learn that there are also "dirty" words for sexual parts and acts, words that have shock value. They may hear these words around the neighborhood and come home saying "fuck" or "prick" or "boob" or "pussy." They need to know that these words are not acceptable in most situations. It is important to convey that, although a word is merely a word—a set of sounds and letters that stand for a thing or idea, with nothing inherently bad or good about it—many words carry emotional overtones that arouse feelings as real as the words themselves. Just as people should be considerate in their use of any power—sexual, muscular, intellectual—so they should be considerate in their use of word power.

The same things are true of sex jokes. Human sexuality, like any serious, interesting human activity, is a rich source of humor, but of a kind that should be used with special care. A family may be one in which all kinds of jokes, including sexual ones, are enjoyed. There can be little objection to that as enriching and helpful in sharing laughter privately and keeping communication open. But everyone must understand that sex-related jokes are considered "dirty" by many people and that jokes appropriate in a locker room or in the family car are probably inappropriate with grandparents, another family, or in a classroom. Jokes should never be used to shock or hurt people or to put them down.

Many growing children, especially boys, collect magazines with nude pictures in them which are shared in secret with friends or simply pored over alone and then hidden away for future delectation. When parents come across this kind of thing, what should they do? Nothing. What harm can the pictures do if they are looked at in private?

Sometimes a boy, knowing that his father also has such magazines in the house, will offer to share his own trove with his father. A father should feel flattered at such evidence of openness, even though his enthusiasm for sharing the pictures may be mild at best. But the offer to share may accompany a willingness to talk and an opportunity to help the curious youngster not only satisfy his curiosity but also get things into better perspective.

If parents find a hoard of magazines and quietly remove them, saying nothing, the child may conclude that he has done something pretty terrible, so bad it can't even be talked about (which helps to tie sex and mysterious evil together), or he may resignedly understand that sex is just one more area where he can't talk with his parents. For parents to scold or punish the child for having such magazines is just as bad. A child might rightly protest that the magazines are his and ask what right his parents had to take them, but at least this could begin a dialogue and provide opportunity for each person to give his or her point of view. If curiosity seems to be the child's motive, why not satisfy it by some good factual talk and looking at some accurate drawings or pictures together? Or why not share the beauty of nude art by looking at reproductions of paintings and sculptures by great artists?

We want to reemphasize that it is good for parents to let their children know they do not need to feel guilty about any feelings they may have, because feelings or thoughts or fantasies cannot be completely controlled and guilt about such feelings can be destructive. Children should also know that they need not feel guilty about actions that do no harm to anyone—provided they also understand that harm can be emotional and intellectual, not just physical. Guilty feelings are, however, a good and appropriate response to an action that is harmful, especially if the feelings of guilt lead to an attempt to undo the harm and a resolve not to act in the same manner again.

8

The Different Ones,
the Lonely Ones

"Something there is that does not love a wall," wrote the poet Robert Frost. The people for whom this sentence will surely have meaning are those who are walled in by circumstances, or who have been walled in or out by others because they are different, or who have walled themselves in so they won't be hurt by the fact that they are different. These are the lonely ones.

We have talked about how from birth human beings have a great need and desire for continuing intimacy with at least one person. How is it, then, that some of us find ourselves alone, feeling empty, hungry, just plain lonely, aching for just one person really to need us and us alone because no one else will do?

Who are the lonely ones? They are those with disabilities of one kind or another: those who are mentally slow, who don't understand why they aren't like everyone else but who keep trying to be; those who are deaf, who have to put forth huge efforts day after day just to learn how to communicate; those who have physical disabilities, who have grown up feeling different and ugly, like the teenager with cerebral palsy who wept as he asked, "How can I even invite a girl to date when I'm always drooling?"; those who are disfigured, like the adolescent girl who was born with a cleft lip and wonders if any boy will ever want to kiss her; those born blind, who have no visual way to build good self-images as attractive girls or boys or to exchange the meaningful glances that are so often the beginnings of a human relationship.

Other lonely ones, too, are those older people who may never have married or had a love experience, or who may have had and lost a beloved partner by incapacity, death, separation, or divorce, and now feel isolated by what some parts of our society look upon as the ugliness of age.

And the lonely ones are those children who, through accident or death or abandonment, are deprived of the very people they most need to grow up to become adequate parents themselves. And they are those who, beaten, bruised, burned, and otherwise abused by one or both parents or caretakers, often nevertheless are terrified at any hint of separation from the only people they know well enough to feel they belong to them. Many of these children, even when seen again and again by hospitals and doctors because of their injuries, refuse to accuse or testify and so return "home," knowing that more of the same is in store for them. Their disabilities are not only the bodily scars but also the inner scars of emotions and spirit that can never be totally erased and can make it very difficult for them in adult life to achieve the very relationships they crave so much.

Among the many things the lonely ones have in common with the rest of the world is their sexuality, at the same ages and stages. This means that they have the same sex-related needs as all of us: they need a loving, caring person to be close to; they need the various forms of expression that relate to being sexual, such as tenderness, touching, kissing, stroking, and caressing; and they need the soft words and the pleasure-giving expressions of sexuality, lovemaking, and sexual inter-course.

There is nothing in any book or medical teaching that says any of these lonely ones should be deprived of the possibility of a loving sexual life, including the kind of family experience that is the best preparation for it. For a fortunate few, there may be adoption in childhood, but for the groups we are talking about, adoption is rare. So here are these people of all ages, waiting for someone to care for them and love them, and waiting to give to someone else the caring and loving that waits inside them.

What can we do for these people? We need primarily to change our attitudes by increasing our awareness of the most up-to-date facts about sexuality. Professionals have already changed their views about the emotional and sexual needs of people with disabilities, both those who live in institutions and those capable of living independently. Re-habilitative services for people with disabilities are now doing many things to enrich their lives. Nonprofessionals who are responsible for or close to someone in one of these groups can follow the lead of the professionals in dealing more wisely and caringly with that person.

Sex and People with Disabilities

All too often we assume that people with disabilities somehow do not have the same needs for physical affection, intimate relationships, and sexual expression that people without disabilities do. In almost every case, however, they do have these needs, even though the way they have been treated may make them hesitant to express them for fear they may be rejected.

People with disabilities, given encouragement and training or sometimes even without these, quite commonly are able to accomplish things that non-disabled people would consider impossible under the circumstances. The capacity of the human mind and body to adjust to difficult situations is astonishing.

Of course, it is not helpful to lump all people with disabilities together, for each individual has his or her own special needs. As far as sex and sexuality are concerned, everyone who has a relationship with a disabled person or is in a position to be of help should remember that sexual feelings are there and that the need to give and receive love and affection, both physical and emotional, is also there. We should be sure that neither we nor others regard someone with a disability as someone who is nonsexual.

Youngsters who have disabilities need sexual information and opportunities to talk about their sexual feelings and desires, just as adults do. They may need help and encouragement to reach out to others; they may need special instruction on ways to overcome or compensate for the physical disabilities that might stand in the way of expressing their sexual natures in appropriate, responsible, and fulfilling ways. They need the same sort of sex education as everyone else, but it should be tailored to their special needs. Medical institutions concerned with rehabilitation are now moving toward considering and meeting the sexual needs of people with disabilities under their care.

In our society, so much importance is attached to education that any serious impairment of the capacity to reach a certain minimum educational level constitutes a true disability. Those with intact mental faculties who are physically disabled can go to college or prepare themselves for a vocation or job, but the chances for people with learning disabilities are not so good.

But people with mental disabilities should have the same rights to the happiness of an independent home and family life as the rest of us. Over the past fifteen years, sex education in institutions and schools for

those who are learning-disabled has increased, with emphasis on competence and responsibility. Competence in dealing with oneself and others as sexual beings requires certain information and skills, and so does responsibility. Learning how to care for oneself during menstruation or how to use contraceptives during sexual activity combines knowledge and skills, just as does learning how to get, perform, and hold a job. All add greatly to the possibility of independent, happy living, and many who are learning-disabled can learn these things, many more such people than we thought a few years ago.

Abused and Neglected Children

Children who are abused and neglected tend to become abusing and neglectful parents. Some observers say that it is almost impossible for many such deprived people to know how to form attachments later on or to move into caring relationships with others. One way to break this vicious cycle is to help young abusing or potentially abusing parents become aware of and deal with their feelings, in order to facilitate their capacity to nurture and rear their children. Good sex education can help to create good self-images; and people who have good self-images are better able to care for others. We discuss this increasingly important social problem more fully on pages 161–64, under Child Molestation.

The Single Person

In the United States, until the first twenty-five years of this century, a large family group could almost always find a niche for an extra single person. There is a tradition that these people turned into beloved "aunts" or "uncles," but the truth is that for every one who did, there was another who was barely tolerated or who was turned into a household drudge. The stories we like to believe about the "good old days" too often gloss over or hide the realities of situations that were cruel, heedless, or exploitive.

    Social structures are different today. Families are smaller, and their members may be scattered all over the country or even the globe. And attitudes about what is or is not acceptable behavior are changing. We may be evolving into an age in which the individual will more and more replace the family as the basic unit of society.

    One example of the change in the basic family unit is the increasing acceptance of arrangements in which older, retired single persons, often people who have lost their spouses, form a household but do not marry each other because doing so might jeopardize their total Social Security benefits or their children's inheritances. But living together without marriage is not confined to older age groups. Most of us know of many such arrangements, and people are not as shocked by them any more. Instead, the attitude is becoming more one of satisfaction and acceptance by many on behalf of two people who have eliminated loneliness from their lives by living together to care for and about each other, with the sexual part of it no one's business but their own.

One specific group must be specially identified: it consists of those unmarried persons who live together and who have made a decision not to have children. Generally they are young persons who are concerned about overpopulation in the world or who find the world a difficult one in which to bring up children safely and with benefit to everyone concerned, or who have honestly admitted to themselves that they would make inadequate parents. Both partners in such an arrangement are usually working, and neither perceives a necessity for formalizing the relationship by marriage. This kind of open relationship is called *cohabitation*, which simply means living together. Because cohabitation openly practiced is fairly new, studies of such relationships are far from complete. But the positive attitudes that society has today toward cohabitation, as compared to those of even twenty years ago, are striking. We must remember that the United States is one of the foremost countries in the world to place the welfare of the individual ahead of the welfare of the state. This has been recognized by our Constitution and Bill of Rights, and we can expect that rugged American individualism will continue to assert that "my business is my own and not that of my neighbor"—provided no one else is harmed.

The Elderly

We hesitated to include "the elderly" as a group among "the different ones, the lonely ones" because they are not nearly as different or lonely as most people think. According to a recent survey by the National Council on the Aging of a cross-section of Americans aged sixty-five and over, old people feel quite good about themselves and their lives. Consider the figures in the table on the next page.

Even older people themselves think that *other* elderly people have pretty bad lives—that the individual being asked is an exception.

The problem that a person might have	Percentage of the general public which thinks that elders suffer from the problem	Percentage of elders who say they actually do suffer from the problem
Loneliness	65%	13%
Not feeling needed	54%	7%
Poor health	47%	21%
Not enough jobs	51%	6%
Not enough medical care	45%	9%
Not enough to do	37%	6%
Poor housing	43%	5%
Not enough friends	28%	5%
Average percentage	45%	9%

Adapted from Eric W. Johnson, *Older and Wiser: Wit, Wisdom, and Spirited Advice from the Older Generation* (New York: Walker Publishing Company, Inc., 1986), p. 10.

However, and this is a big "however," there is a large group of elderly people who do live alone and in misery—whether in their own homes or in their children's—or in institutions. We can understand that older people living alone would be lonely, and we can even understand that living in an institution might be lonely. But most people find it hard to understand how living with one's own children could be lonely. Yet it can be. Why?

Because these older people have reached a time in life when they have more to look back on than to look ahead to; when they feel lost without their own possessions around them; when getting up in the morning means that everyone else bustles off to job or school and the day alone in a silent house looms frighteningly ahead; when they have no one to share their private concerns and anxieties with, no one really close and intimate; when day after day goes by without a touch, a kiss, or a hug from someone to whom they mean a great deal; and when the nights are long as they lie wakeful, remembering the comfort of a dear and loving person to reach for in bed—and then they begin to wonder where they are going and if it's worth sticking around for. That's a pretty desperate state to be in at any time of life, but toward life's end it is worst of all.

We should do everything we can to make things better for such

lonely people, and we can begin by recognizing that older men and women are exactly that: men and women. They have the same needs and wishes they always had, but they are no longer in a position to fulfill them alone. For instance, if they have lost a devoted life partner, what social life can they develop? How can they meet new people? How can they learn all over again how to meet, date, and get to know someone well enough to develop a special relationship, when they may have no privacy for dating and no car (or driver's license either) to make dating easier? They need help for all these things.

In our society, too many of us think that an old man who is interested in sex is "a dirty old man," and that once a woman has passed menopause she is no longer sexy or interested in sex, or shouldn't be, since she's past the age when she can become pregnant. When older people become romantically or sexually interested in each other, their children and friends may treat it as a joke, or even with scorn, alarm, or distaste. What right have old people to be starting again, when they're supposed to be decently fading away?

Most homes for the aged, nursing homes, and medical centers, and also some, but not all, retirement communities, have been organized on the assumption that the residents have no need for or interest in intimacy and privacy and sex. Even many doctors and other health care professionals, when asked by older people about sexual problems or their declining ability to have sexual relations, respond with a friendly, amused comment, perhaps supposed to be reassuring and calming, like, "Well, at your age what can you expect?" instead of showing willingness to talk about the problem and to see what can be done—and often a lot can be done.

On the other side, there are those who so closely equate a high degree of sexual activity with the possibility of living a full, vigorous, and rewarding life that they sometimes make older people who have less interest in sexual activity feel inadequate and old in every way. And there are many people, old and young, who may be relatively inactive sexually but are very active and creative in many other ways.

Researchers today almost all agree that the sexuality of the elderly is not very different from that of people of younger ages; that the need for sexual activity in some form and the capacity to enjoy it continues with many people well into old age. But perhaps even more important and universal than the continuation of genital sexual activity in older people is the need of the elderly for physical closeness, touching, stroking, intimacy, affection, and the actions and words of endearment. This is the same need that all of us have when we are born and most of us continue to have throughout life.

Some families may feel threatened if a new relationship for a parent or grandparent might result in a marriage that could mean loss of inheritance. While this is understandable, we believe that the children who feel responsible for an older person should be helped to understand that a new relationship could bring back laughter and sparkle and a sense of independence to two people who had thought these had been lost forever. If a marriage is planned, a premarital agreement can be formalized that will safeguard inheritance rights for both sides. And a surprising number of families are recognizing that what is most important is the happiness and well-being of two human beings and that in the interests of safeguarding Social Security payments and property rights, the marriage ceremony can take second place.

In any case, whether at home with family or in an institution, the early stages of a new courtship deserve the support of everyone and should never be subjected to the jokes that institution attendants or even families too often allow themselves in order to belittle the relationship. When a person is nearing the end of life, he or she seeks out experiences that can make the remaining years real and good. Love and work and playing a meaningful role in the lives of others or in a community—all or any one of these can give an older person a sense that life is still worth living. More and more institutions for the elderly are recognizing this and are making strong efforts to educate their personnel to accept the reality of sexual interest among older people. It costs little or nothing to give the elderly every possible opportunity to enrich their lives.

9

Sex and Sexual Problems

Ways We Make Sex a Problem

Sex and human sexuality are not—or should not be—problems unless we human beings make them so. When and how does sex become a problem? In general terms, when it is used or expressed in ways that are harmful to any person or persons; when people are unable to express their sexuality in ways that they find satisfying and creative; and when sex becomes associated with such negative feelings as anger, jealousy, fear, and guilt. Here is a summary, in no particular order, of some of the kinds of problems sex can cause and the ways sex can be made a problem:

• The basic lack of information among too many people, young and old, about what is known today about sex and sexuality, which can lead to various kinds of trouble. Often that ignorance is deliberately maintained.

• The obsession with the idea that the whole of sexuality is comprised of genital activity; that is, sexual intercourse and the steps leading to it.

• Strong social stimuli, especially in the media, toward sexual activity but few socially approved ways for responding to those stimuli.

• The conflicting messages we get from society, to which our young are especially vulnerable: that sex is the best and most ecstatic, ennobling, status-giving, joy-creating activity; but that it's dirty and bad, so save it for the one you love or stay away from it entirely.

• The way this sexual stimulation acts upon boys and girls, especially during the many years between physical readiness for sex (puberty) and the capacity to form long-term, caring peer relationships that would warrant the full sexual act.

• Adolescent pregnancies—over 20,000 every week in the United States.

• The effects of unrealistic sex fantasies in films, TV, magazines, and advertising upon people whose real sexual lives are so different from those fantasies.

• The unrealistic expectations and requirements for "perfection" and "performance" that people impose on themselves and on others with respect to their sexual lives.

• The overreaction of families and society to sexual events, especially those in the lives of children.

• The tension and unhappiness within marriages in which people feel hopelessly bound yet unable or unwilling to seek help to change and possibly improve.

• The anguish of couples and their children involved in separation and divorce.

• The promotion of the idea, often through advertising or TV or films, that the measure of a man is the number of dollars and women he can make or, of a woman, the number of men she can seduce.

• Our delusion that there can be sexual activity without consequences for human relationships—that sex can be lifted from its human context.

• Grouping sex with alcohol, drugs, tobacco, and violence as problems we should learn to avoid.

• The inability of many to respond sexually when they urgently wish they could.

• The inability of humankind to limit its numbers so that human beings can be decently supported on this planet without eventually destroying it.

USING SEX SELFISHLY

One of the main ways we make sex into a problem is by using our sexuality for our own purposes without thinking of or caring about the consequences for others. Here are some ways people do this:

• A more aggressive partner forces sex when the other doesn't really want it, either because of fatigue or illness or preoccupation with some stressful matter, or a need to talk or simply be stroked and held and comforted, without direct sex play or intercourse.

• One partner is chronically unwilling to take the initiative in sex play that might lead to mutual pleasure. Instead, that person always waits to be wooed, not realizing that the other person may have a deep need to feel loved and lovable by *being* wooed occasionally instead of always having to do the wooing. This is an especially common complaint of husbands about wives; women often feel that it's the man's "job" to take the initiative, to woo, to make her feel "loved" in the physical sense. But men, too, often long to feel "loved" and wooed.

• Some people hurry to get their own sexual satisfaction without thinking of the need for time and loving that the other person feels or needs. (This is an especially common complaint that women have about men: that the man gets his ejaculation and leaves the woman unsatisfied.)

• Some people use their sexual attractiveness to lead another person to expect a genuine short- or long-term relationship, but actually seek only to exercise power or prove themselves attractive.

• Some people use sex to put another person down, to make the other feel inferior or at fault, unattractive, insufficiently sexy, too sexy, or not loving or lovable.

• Some people use "lines" (often really lies) to get sex: "Don't worry, I'm taking care of the contraception"; "Nobody will ever know that we're doing this"; "I love you"; "I don't have VD"; "I don't have AIDS and haven't been exposed to it"; "You're the most attractive person I've ever been with"; "You're not a real man (or woman) if you won't have sex"; "I'm going to marry you"; "I'm not having sex with anyone but you"; "If you loved me you would."

• Some people allow themselves to be overcome by their sexual urges and do not exercise control over themselves.

• Some sexually experienced people use their sophistication and skill in lovemaking to overwhelm a less experienced person, without taking into account the other's feelings or the effects of the experience on the other.

• Some young people use their attractiveness to get attention, money, gifts, and commitments from older people.

• Some people are unaware of how the other person might feel or see things. They assume that their gestures and the words they say mean the same thing to the partner as to themselves.

• Some people treat others as objects to be used and manipulated rather than as complex, feeling beings who are to be respected and considered at all times.

• Some young people use sex to prove to themselves or to their parents that they are adults, whereas it proves no such thing.

• Some older people can be so preoccupied by their own ideas of what is right or wrong about sex that they selfishly block off attempts at communication by young people.

• Some people tell tales about their sexual exploits in order to make their hearers feel inferior and inadequate. (Or, on the contrary, they may proclaim their own righteousness and invoke community standards to make others feel that their sexual patterns are bad.)

NEGATIVE FEELINGS ABOUT SEX; SEX AND RELIGION

Some irreverent wag suggested that it would have been better for the sexual health of Americans if Plymouth Rock had landed on the Pilgrims instead of the other way around. By this he meant that we have inherited from the strongly and narrowly religious people who were important first settlers of our country (and who actually were known as Puritans before they left England and became Pilgrims to America) a rigorous and narrow set of values that set up piety and hard work as the supreme virtues and decried pleasure, especially bodily and sexual pleasure, as evil and animal-like. It is clear that in American society today there is still a strong current of thought that sex, except when used for procreation, is an evil and sinful thing, that it puts us on the level of the animals, and that we should feel guilty about enjoying sexual pleasure.

Dr. William H. Masters and Virginia E. Johnson wrote two very influential books, *Human Sexual Response* (1966) and *Human Sexual Inadequacy* (1970), that reported their pioneering scientific observation and studies of human sexual activity. Their goal was to discover why some married couples are unable to function well sexually, and to develop ways to help them. Masters and Johnson found that in the lives of couples who suffered from sexual dysfunction, a rigid religious upbringing often played an important part in the development of the guilt feelings that ultimately led to their difficulties. It did not seem to matter whether the couple in trouble was Jewish, Catholic, or Protestant. The trouble was caused by the way people interpreted the strongly orthodox "thou shalt nots" of their religion.

Some very religious people have no trouble at all with their sexuality; others, even those brought up in the same families, have great trouble and interpret sex as dirty, evil, sinful. If this interpretation becomes deeply ingrained when they are young, it is difficult later for them to overcome their negative feelings, even after marriage, when their religion would then probably allow full sexual expression. Fortunate are the many who are able without too great difficulty to make the transition from premarital virginity to full enjoyment of sex after marriage in spite of such a rigid background. Fortunate too are those who find that having stuck by their conventional religious standards before getting married has not only strengthened their marriage but also increased their pleasure in it.

For those who find that the strictness of their religious background has tended to interfere with the healthy, responsible expression of their sexuality even in marriage, it may be helpful to know that some of the rules, the orthodoxy, of the Jewish and Christian religions were historically, and to a degree still are, based on a number of mistaken concepts about the biology of reproduction as well as on the need for human survival that no longer exists today. For example, at the time of the birth of Jesus, Jews and most other people believed that it was the man and his semen who provided the actual life, the "seed," and that the woman was merely the soil, so to speak, in which the seed grew to maturity to be born. It was considered almost like murder to allow the "seed" to be "wasted" through masturbation, homosexuality, or sexual intercourse without intent to procreate. It was also erroneously believed (and still is by many people) that semen, "the precious fluid," was limited in quantity so that if it was "wasted" the energy and strength of the man would thereby be reduced.

Furthermore, up until perhaps fifty years ago, human beings were convinced that anything likely to reduce the numbers of children born was evil because it would lead to a smaller tribe or nation and therefore a greater likelihood that the group might be defeated in war or killed off by disease. Many societies still feel this way. Of course today, from a world point of view, the real problem is not too few people in the human race but too many, in most places. It is our rapidly rising numbers that may destroy us.

Mindful of the facts now known to science that were not known several centuries ago, Rabbi Roland Gittelsohn wrote in *Love, Sex and Marriage: A Jewish View* (published in 1976 by the Union of American Hebrew Congregations) that Jews "must respect our tradition without necessarily following it. Most of the ethical concepts of Judaism are at least as valid today as when they were first conceived by our ancestors. In some areas, however, because we have knowledge that was unavailable to them, it becomes necessary to revise or even discard their judgment."

In other words, where religious laws or rules about sex were made on the basis of ignorance of facts now known, laws and rules need to be reexamined and recast to be consonant with these facts. Religious leaders in many denominations have been and are working carefully and intelligently on this reexamination. After all, when Moses and Jesus lived, they (and those among whom they lived) believed that the world was shaped something like our Frisbee, that the sun traveled over it, and that if you went too far you could fall off the edge. Religions have been able to adjust to the new facts here, and they are adjusting also to the new facts about reproduction, sex, and sexuality.

In the Christian religions, there has been an especially deep-rooted belief that the sexual urges of the body are somehow evil and should be put down and denied in favor of spiritual things. As Dr. Walter Harrelson, Dean of the Divinity School of Vanderbilt University at Nashville, commented in a letter to one of the authors:

> The Christian tradition, influenced by Hellenistic religious understandings of the Graeco-Roman world, lost sight of its Jewish roots and tended to spiritualize the Christian faith. One baneful result was the identification of the body as transient and belonging to a material world of less consequence than the spiritual. The solidly biblical understanding of all things as created by God and created good was compromised. The result has been a denigration of the sexual and a loss of that healthy regard for body and for bodily pleasure that ancient Israel understood as a gift of God.

Obviously religion cannot be blamed for all the deep and destructive antisex feelings and emotions that trouble so many people. But what should be blamed is the insistence on negative rules and regulations that can no longer stand in the face of present world conditions and known facts. As we said in the Preface, both of us are religious people. We agree with the thousands of religious leaders of all faiths who are convinced that religious values and insights, in the deepest sense, should not be looked upon as inconsistent with the emerging and expanding scientific knowledge about human sexuality. Instead, with recognition of those scientific facts, our religious values can help us not only to manage but also to express our sexuality in healthy, responsible, satisfying ways, and support our productive living together. We are thinking of such values as respect of the infinite worth of each individual, unselfishness, thoughtfulness of others, and use of our powers for the welfare and happiness of all people. Today many religious and church people are taking the lead in promoting and providing sound education and counseling in the field of human sexuality and working to enlighten a dark antisex dogma based on factual errors and conditions of life that no longer exist. They are also taking the lead in celebrating the fact that God did create us as male and female with the power of sexuality manifest in us from our earliest days of existence.

TALKING ABOUT SEX

Sometimes sex becomes a problem because of our inability to talk openly and objectively about it. People who can't talk about a subject have more difficulty in sharing or getting the information and ideas they may need than do people who are more verbal. Yet the deep-rooted feeling of many people that sex is somehow dirty or evil, or that it should be kept totally mysterious and secret, makes calm discussion difficult. As the father in a cartoon said to his wife, "It's not that I'm opposed to sex education, but six is too young to start calling things by their right names."

Some people, perhaps especially the young, tend to use language about sex, both slang words and standard words, to shock, frighten, and anger other people. The generation gap in sex language helps make sex a problem, both for adults and for children.

It is interesting to note that in the vocabulary of some cultures there is a rich supply of entirely acceptable words to describe the varieties of sexual love and parts of the body especially involved in it. In our culture, however, the language is quite impoverished in this respect. Many of the words we do have are forbidden, so that with children we use terms like "your little thing," "your dicky," or "your bunny" instead of simply saying "penis"; or we go to the other extreme and use threatening words like "prick," "cock," "rod," or "pecker." There appears to be nothing between stilted medical terms or offensive slang terms. How much better if instead we had an ample, pleasant array of language with which to talk to each other about sex! Just as the Eskimos use over twenty words to talk about the varieties of that cold white stuff we know only as "snow," so we might be able to use as many words to describe the variety of activities which, now, we may politely call only "coitus," "sexual intercourse," "making love," or "sleeping together."

"VICTIMLESS" CRIMES

Sex can also become a problem when the law treats as crimes sexual acts that are engaged in willingly and performed in privacy by the adults involved. In such situations there is no victim unless a complaint is made by one of the participants. Complaints usually come from observing outsiders whose moral sense may be offended. Crime that does have victims—whether burglary, environmental pollution, reckless driving, or abuse or exploitation of children—certainly requires the attention of law-enforcement authorities. But treating as "crimes" activities that have no true victims—for example, the sale of pornographic materials to adults, adult homosexual activities mutually consented to, fetishism, prostitution, and sado-masochism—seem to many people examples of misuse of law-enforcement facilities. Such misuse is at best a waste of a scarce service and at worst an abuse of authority for the purpose of imposing the moral opinions of one specific person or group upon other adult persons or groups.

Personal Sexual Problems with Legal Implications

CHILD MOLESTATION

Often confused with rape, but usually quite different from it, is child molestation, a sexual encounter between an adult (a molester, one who molests) and a child. It is estimated that 27 percent of women and 16 percent of men are sexually abused as children, and 75 percent of the abusers are male caretakers or relatives. Molestation is different from rape, because the happening is usually brief and it rarely involves violence or even sexual intercourse.

As we said, most convicted molesters are men (though some women molest children). They usually are men who have little sexual experience and who are generally inept in their relationships with other people. Their average age is about thirty-five, though a few are old and senile and some are mentally retarded. Often the molester has been drinking before his offense. In general, molesters are not otherwise criminal types. For many, molestation is a compulsive, long-term tendency, though the event may happen only once or only a few times. About 85 percent of molesters are known to the children they molest as neighbors, friends of the family, or relatives. About 80 percent of the contacts occur either in the home of the child or in the home of the molester. (The stereotype of the stranger who uses candy to attract a child into his car and then molests the child sexually is largely false, but since such relatively rare events get wide publicity the public thinks of them as common.)

What is the nature of the offense? Sometimes the offense is exhibitionism (see next section), and does not involve any physical contact. Actual physical molestation, as we have said, usually is a brief contact, in which the offender may stroke the child and handle the child's genitals, and that is all. In only 2 percent of the reported cases of molestation is any physical harm done to the child. If there is any possibility that the molestation of the child has involved vaginal or anal intercourse, or oral-genital sex, it is essential, without making a big deal of it, for the child to have a blood test for the AIDS virus after a few weeks, and again after six months. (See Chapter 10 on STDs and AIDS.)

What effect will molestation be likely to have on the child? According to the best evidence available (interviews with people who as children were molested), the molested children are hardly ever sexually excited by the experience. Their reaction is more likely to be quite slight and to involve puzzlement and a vague fear. The major effects of such incidents are caused not by the event itself but by the outraged, angry, fearful, and shocked reactions of the adults who learn of it, whether they be parents, relatives, or police. It is these immoderate reactions that may cause whatever psychological damage occurs. The problem seems to come from the fact that adults tend to react to such an invasion of the child's sexual innocence and privacy by projecting their own adult feelings onto the child. They may forget that children before puberty do not see or feel the event as a big, threatening sexual happening, for their experience and feelings are childlike, not adult. This is an example of how we often make sex a problem by assuming that others are feeling just the way we ourselves would feel in the same situation, instead of making a calm effort to put ourselves into the position, experience, and circumstances of the other person.

There is a widespread impression that, in the case of a homosexual molestation, a child's sexual orientation may be shifted from heterosexual to homosexual. As we explained in Chapter 5, a person's sexual orientation toward heterosexuality or homosexuality is established relatively early in life—although no one knows how—and certainly not by a single, brief, genital sexual experience. (And in fact, a considerably smaller percentage of homosexuals than heterosexuals molest children.)

It is difficult to make a single recommendation for the best way to deal with a child who reports having been sexually molested. Certainly, if the child is disturbed and fearful, he or she needs comforting. And children should always be assured that the event was not their "fault." It can and does happen that such children's needs as those for physical affection, for approval, for good grades, for having a feeling of control over adults, even for the good taste of candy or for an attractive gift, may cause them to act in ways that the children themselves see as merely attractive but that the adult may read as seductive and sexual. (That's why we enclosed the word *fault* in quotes.)

We should remember that children are even less likely than adults to report events accurately or completely. Therefore parents should probably, in a calm, objective, nonfrightening way, try to elicit information: What happened? Where did it happen? Who did it? Did you know him? What did he actually do? The parents should try not to appear greatly upset when suggesting to the child how to avoid such situations in the future: "It is always wise to stay away from men who approach you in an overfriendly manner or who try to touch you or persuade you in a secret way to be alone with them. This is true even if they are people you know quite well. Never accept gifts from strangers and certainly don't accept a lift in a stranger's car." But parents must be careful not to warn so strongly that the child grows fearful about meeting and being friendly with new people or about responding with physical affection to relatives and friends.

If the child is old enough, he or she will certainly benefit from being given some facts about the sexual side of life, but immediately after an experience of molestation is not the best moment to do this. Better wait until things have calmed down and an opportunity arises at another time.

If the event seems serious to you, that is, if rape or attempts at penetration occurred or if bleeding resulted, then we strongly recommend reporting the incident to the police. Here parents must balance the advantages of having the molester apprehended and prevented from molesting other children (although the extreme punitive treatment that most molesters receive does little to remedy their condition and is more likely to make it worse), and the disadvantages arising from the likelihood that the child will have to give evidence to officials, perhaps even in court, which may increase his or her fears and reinforce the harmful emotional effects of the experience. The balance of the decision is more delicate if there was only simple touching.

Let us repeat that the harm most likely to come from a case of molestation is not from the event itself so much as from the reaction of adults who may, by the example of their own emotions and even with the best of intentions, help to tinge all the child's subsequent feelings about sex with negative feelings and fear. Instead, calm and quiet good judgment should be called into play.

EXHIBITIONISM

Exhibitionism involves the compulsion a man has to exhibit his penis, usually erect, to a woman or girl. There is no physical contact. In fact, the exhibition usually takes place from a distance, and as soon as he is seen by his "victim" (who is usually a stranger to him), the exhibitionist almost always flees.

Although the most common reactions to exhibitionists are surprise, puzzlement, scorn, disgust, fear, or panic, many females simply laugh off the whole thing as something done by "some sort of nut." Others are afraid that the exhibition may be a preliminary to attack and rape. Such fear is unnecessary, for exhibitionists are usually timid, harmless people who are very much afraid of actual sexual contact. They get their kicks in some unexplained way from the reactions evoked in females by the exhibition.

Exhibitionism is a truly compulsive act, for the man cannot help himself and often repeats it until he is arrested. When he is released, he is in many cases unable to resist the urge to repeat the offense. Many exhibitionists have been arrested and convicted a number of times.

Most girls are likely to encounter an exhibitionist at some time in their lives. Parents should not overreact but simply explain that the man is a disturbed person and that all the child need do is keep her cool and walk away toward other people. Women can leave the scene and should avoid showing the shock or surprise that is so important to the exhibitionist. They might decide to report the matter to the police in order to protect others from being so annoyed.

INCEST

Incest is sexual activity of any kind between members of the same family. It is not as rare in our society as most people believe, and it is more frequent between brothers and sisters, and fathers and daughters, than between mothers and sons. The term *incest* includes sexual intercourse between a person and any close relative: brothers, sisters, uncles, aunts, grandparents, adopted children, stepparents, and in-laws. In some societal groups, first cousins are included; in others they are not. In every culture that has been studied, there is a strong taboo against incest, and it is deemed a crime in every state in the United States.

The taboo is so deeply ingrained that we rarely stop to ask why it exists. A reason often given, but rarely true, is that children born as a result of an incestuous relationship are likely to suffer from hereditary diseases. Other reasons given are: If sexual intercourse were permitted between members of the same family, the inevitably resulting competition, jealousy, deception, hatred, and confusion might well destroy the family. Or, children would be subject to exploitation by older, stronger members and have no way to escape. Or, if a young person experienced sexual ties within the family, it could be more difficult for him or her to establish good sexual attachments outside the family in adult life. Whatever the reasons, the taboo exists.

It is important not to confuse incest with the usual, pleasant physical expressions of affection between members of a family. We have talked about the importance of body contact between young children and their parents, and especially between mothers and infants. The distinction between incest and healthy contact is found in the motivation for it. If the motivation is simply to express love and fondness and to give a feeling of comfort and support, it is healthful and good; if the specific motivation of the adult is sexual arousal and gratification, it is not. If young people find themselves in a situation where they are being pressured or seduced into sexual contacts within the family, they should seek counsel from someone in the family or outside, and seek it as soon as possible.

According to the psychoanalytic theory of psychosexual development as put forth by Sigmund Freud, as children develop they normally go through a stage of strong attraction, boys for their mothers, girls for their fathers. Most of us probably do not remember going through this stage, because we were very young and felt so guilty about it that we suppressed the memory. The attraction of son to mother is called the "Oedipus complex," after the Oedipus of Greek mythology who, as a result of many confusing events, married Jocasta, his own mother, neither one knowing who the other was; when they discovered their relationship, Jocasta killed herself and Oedipus put out his own eyes. The attraction of daughter to father is called the "Electra complex," after another mythological figure, Electra, who avenged the death of her father, Agamemnon, by helping to kill her own mother, Clytemnestra. These historic myths serve to illustrate the concern of the ancient Greeks about people who broke the age-old incest taboo.

An interesting modern-day extension of the anti-incest feeling is reported among college students who live together in the proximity of coeducational dormitories, where the style of life and sharing somewhat resembles that of a very large family. In such situations, dating and sexual attachments are known most often to occur with people outside the dormitory. It may be that sexual attachments developing within the dorm are seen unconsciously as in some way violating the incest taboo, although dorm-mates would probably not think of it that way. Similar dating patterns have been seen among young people raised together from infancy in the same kibbutz in Israel.

One thing is certain: in any cases of sexual contact between a child and an adult, where there has been no force or violence, the greater the fuss and uproar, the greater the possible damage to the minor.

PEDOPHILIA

Closely related to the problem of child molestation is a condition called pedophilia. The word comes from the Greek *paedo-* (child) and *-philos* (loving) and means sexual desire in an adult for children. A pedophile, then, is a child-lover, one who gets sexual gratification from contacts with children. Almost all known pedophiliacs are men. Only people whose strongest sexual feelings are aroused by children rather than by adults are pedophiles. Since sexual activity by adults with children is so strongly condemned by our society, it is quite possible that most people who have pedophilic feelings either suppress them or recognize them but never act them out. Pedophilic activity is considered a serious criminal offense.

There is both heterosexual and homosexual pedophilia. The common impression, doubtless conveyed by occasional cases highly publicized in the press, is that homosexuals are likely to try to seduce young boys. But the highest rate of seduction is of young girls by adolescent or adult males. The vast majority of homosexuals are active with adults only and scorn those who have, or attempt to have, sexual relations with young boys.

PORNOGRAPHY

What is "pornography"? No one is certain. The word is a combination of the Greek words *pornē* (prostitute) and *graphein* (to write) and meant, in ancient Greece, "the writing of prostitutes." Today it is often paired with the word *obscenity* to refer to writing and/or pictures designed solely to arouse the reader or viewer sexually. In a famous case in 1957, the U.S. Supreme Court defined as pornographic or obscene material (1) whose dominant theme is designed to appeal to morbid or shameful interests, (2) which goes beyond contemporary community standards, and (3) which lacks any redeeming social value. This isn't a very helpful definition, because words like "morbid and shameful" and "social value" and "contemporary community standards" are so subject to individual interpretation. One Justice said, "I can't define pornography, but I know it when I see it," a common-sense statement with which most people might agree but which did nothing to enhance understanding of the decision and led someone to remark that pornography is "anything that turns the Supreme Court on." A term that is more precise and descriptive than pornography or obscenity is *explicit sexual material*—material that portrays sexual behavior in words or pictures with specific intent to arouse. Whether or not it does so depends on individual reaction to it.

No one knows for certain whether pornography is a problem of sex or not. Many people make the confident statement that it is, and many say just as confidently that it is not.

Let's summarize the arguments for and against explicit sexual material and the right to publish it:

For: With the possible exception of children, people have the right to read or look at any kind of material they wish—a right protected by the First Amendment to the Constitution. If we take away this right, what rights will we take away next? Forbidding is a dangerous business and not democratic. No one forces pornography on anyone; people can choose whether they wish to look at it or not. Pornography meets needs, it doesn't create them. For some, it provides entertainment and harmless and pleasurable sexual arousal and release; for others it can even be educational, showing or describing human sexual organs and activities that otherwise are kept unhealthily forbidden and mysterious. There is no reliable evidence that pornography causes people to commit sex crimes; on the contrary, research shows that people guilty of such crimes report having seen significantly less pornography than those guilty of other kinds of crimes. Pornography is a harmless human phenomenon, desirable and rewarding to some even though repulsive and shocking to others.

Against: It is only common sense that one who wallows in filth is going to get dirty, and pornography is filthy, a tasteless yet arousing depiction of promiscuous and disgusting genital sexual activity, produced for money and exemplifying sex glorified for its own sake, without love, caring, or commitment. Furthermore, pornography arouses sexual desires which are

SEX AND SEXUAL PROBLEMS   169

likely to overstimulate those exposed to it so that they go out and try the things they have seen; thus, it leads to rape, to sex outside of marriage, to the breakdown of families, to young people going astray, and to unnatural and repulsive sex acts. The authors of the First Amendment did not have in mind the legal protection of a kind of material they never could have imagined anyone publishing. People who commit sex crimes admit to having been stimulated by pornography, and many police officers, who are as close as anyone to crime, report that pornography leads to crime and that some criminals are found to possess pornographic material. Common sense and moral sense dictate that pornography, and the activities of those who profit from it, should be outlawed.

It is very difficult to define what is and what is not pornographic or obscene. One person's pornography may be another person's art. There are many Americans, both men and women, who desire and are willing to pay for explicit sexual materials of various kinds. About 85 percent of adult men and 70 percent of adult women have at some time in their lives been exposed to explicit sexual material, most of them voluntarily and with enjoyment, and many of them by the time they are eighteen years old. There are also many Americans who find any kind of explicit sexual material absolutely distasteful and immoral—even including the simple diagrams and explanatory text found in serious teaching manuals or books like this one.

Viewing explicit sexual materials does sexually arouse many people and, contrary to common belief, probably arouses women almost as much as men, although up to now most pornography has been pro- duced to appeal to men. The arousal simply tends to cause people to be more active in their habitual patterns of sexual activity, whatever these are, whether within marriage, outside marriage, heterosexual, homo- sexual, variant (other than penile-vaginal intercourse), masturbatory, or other. But this response lasts for only a short time and does not change basic sexual attitudes or patterns of behavior.

Correlation does not mean causation. Indeed, one should be very surprised if those people of any age who had constitutionally stronger- than-average sex drives would not be more highly motivated than the average person, both to seek out pornography and to seek out sexual activity. The point is that there is no reliable evidence that the pornog- raphy *causes* the sexual activity.

Explicit sexual material can be educational in that it plainly shows what human bodies, and especially genitals, look like, how they react, and how they are used in sexual activity. But pornography can seriously mislead the viewer if he or she takes it seriously, for it can give the impression that life is just a series of excuses or opportunities for genital

acts. It can also give the erroneous impression that most people most of the time are panting for sex, and that they are endowed with very large sexual organs and extremely sexy-looking bodies. It also promotes the false idea that sexual activity is almost always orgiastically passionate and that it can be engaged in without human consequences and quite independently of human feeling and relationships.

We have heard practically no one argue in favor of exposing children to pornography, nor do we favor it. However, there is no solid evidence, except the urgings of common sense, that such exposure is harmful. There is no reason to go out of our way to introduce children to it, but neither is there any reason to get hysterically upset over it when they do seek it out—as many always have and still do today—or to deny even young children access to sound sex information when they want it, including simple pictures and diagrams to make it understandable.

PROSTITUTION

Prostitution is the exchange of sex for money. Although some prostitutes are men and some are boys or girls, the vast majority are women who sell their bodies as a commodity. Prostitution is sometimes called "the oldest profession," for throughout recorded history there have always been prostitutes. (Two other words for a prostitute are *whore*, which today has become a put-down term, and *harlot*, now seldom used.)

In most parts of the world, prostitution is not considered a crime. In all of the United States, however, except in certain municipalities in Nevada, prostitution is outlawed in one way or another. Despite this, prostitution is widespread, the best estimates being that there are between a third to half a million full-time prostitutes and many more part-time ones.

What kinds of people become prostitutes? We must be careful not to make sweeping generalizations, but scientific studies of prostitutes make possible some careful statements. Many prostitutes are poor and go into the work for economic reasons: to support their children, to get off welfare, to avoid the job discrimination that many women experience. Some prostitutes are drug users and need the earnings to pay for their addiction. Many prostitutes come from broken homes; a few are mentally deficient; many, when they are not on the job, show an active dislike of men. Prostitutes may stay in the business for only a few years, after which time they often marry and enter the mainstream of society.

Many people see prostitutes as emotionally ill people, unable to adjust to life in a normal way. The American Psychiatric Association, however, classifies prostitution not as a disease but as a "social maladjustment, without manifest psychiatric disorder." Although most prostitutes are not by ability and training very good at defending their profession in public (and, since almost everywhere in the United States it is illegal, it would be dangerous for them to do so), there are increasing numbers of prostitutes who refuse to accept for themselves the shameful role in which most of society has cast them. They reject the psychiatrists' classification of them as socially maladjusted, and they resent it when well-meaning people investigate their lives in the conviction that they are objects of pity leading a debased life and needing rehabilitation. What they need, they themselves say, is not rehabilitation but money and good jobs. Also, they maintain that they fill a genuine need (otherwise why would people be willing to pay them?) and help make rejected and lonely men feel satisfied and understood, and that they have a perfect right to do with their bodies what they choose. No one is forced to go to a prostitute, they say.

Prostitution is carried on in many different ways. There is the independently operating "streetwalker," who solicits her own customers. Other prostitutes work in houses of prostitution, also called brothels (or, in informal language, whorehouses), where facilities are provided for the customers. The woman who runs a brothel is called a madam, and people, usually men, who go out and solicit customers and control the earnings are called pimps. People who attract women to prostitution or help find a place to work for those who decide to become prostitutes are procurers or panderers. There is a common notion that prostitution is closely linked with the world of organized crime, but because the business is difficult to organize, it is not particularly attractive to organized crime. Therefore, some women operate independently. Also, since prostitution is an underground activity almost everywhere in this country, prostitutes are seldom willing or able to defend themselves against assault or robbery by customers, because this would open them to arrest for the crime of practicing their profession. The prostitute is much more often a victim of criminal action than are her customers.

Some women, *call girls,* engage in a more sophisticated form of prostitution than that of streetwalkers and those who work in brothels. They have their own apartments, which are in many cases very attractive and comfortable, for providing entertainment and services, or they will go to the apartments of their customers. Call girls provide sexual services only by appointment, commonly arranged through a telephone "call" by a middleman, who shares the earnings.

Another, rather different group of women who provide sexual services are mistresses, sometimes simply called "girl friends," women who are supported on a long-term basis by one man, for whom they provide sexual services and perhaps meet other needs that society would expect usually to be met in marriage. Between men and their mistresses there may indeed be genuine affection, considerate sharing, and even love. (It is interesting that many prostitutes have somewhat similar relationships with their pimps; they love the man who obtains their customers for them, provides them with protection, manages their finances, and provides bail for them when they are arrested.)

Not all prostitutes are females. There are male prostitutes, more of them homosexual than heterosexual. Many male prostitutes are capable of erection and often ejaculation between three to six times in twenty-four hours. There are also men who are paid by women to provide companionship and sexual services. A term for such a man is *gigolo*.

Prostitution involving children is today being identified as especially objectionable. Runaway teenage boys and girls are all too often enticed into prostitution. Since they usually are desperate for money and some sort of love and security, and are unaware of the possible long-term consequences of the activity they are entering, they are easy to victimize. In large cities there are numbers of boy prostitutes, nicknamed "chickens," who are patronized by older adolescents and men, nicknamed "chicken hawks."

During the past 20 to 30 years the prostitution "business" has declined. A number of trends explain this. Many more women now feel free to engage in sexual relations with men to whom they are not married, for their own satisfaction as well as for that of the men, and without pay. Also, there is probably a wider acceptance of masturbation as a normal, harmless activity to achieve sexual release. Perhaps an even more important factor is that married women—indeed, women in general—have become more ready to see sex as something to be enjoyed by both sexes and are therefore better prepared to be satisfying sexual partners for their husbands, who thus have no need to seek sexual gratification outside their marriage. Also, fear of the disease AIDS has made people much more cautious about having multiple sex partners.

Why do men go to prostitutes? Many men know of no other way to satisfy their sexual urges. Some have a deep feeling that masturbation is sinful, harmful, or somehow unmasculine, or they do not find it satisfying. Other men find a fascination in trying something new, something forbidden. Still others prefer, at least from time to time, a sexual encounter where there is no complicating human relationship and where they can get whatever kind of sexual service they want, without hangups. Some are just plain curious and turn to a prostitute for sexual experiences different from those they have with their wives.

Prostitutes are most commonly arrested and prosecuted for *solicitation* of customers (or "hustling"). But in many states a woman need not be caught in the act of soliciting or engaging in sexual relations to be arrested. If because of previous acts she can be proved guilty of *being* a prostitute, she can be convicted and punished. The usual punishment is a fine and then release—usually to go right back to prostitution.

It is interesting that the law considers the activity of the prostitute to be criminal, and in most states that of her customer as well. One could ask why it is that *both* the partners in the act are not always considered equally guilty, or equally innocent. The American Civil Liberties Union states: "laws against prostitution represent one of the most direct forms of discrimination against women in this country today. The woman who sells her body is punished criminally and stigmatized socially while her male customer . . . is left unscathed." However, in recent years there has been a trend toward equal prosecution.

A common notion is that prostitutes are a principal cause for the spread of sexually transmitted diseases (STDs)—often still called venereal disease (VD) in our country. In fact, the STD rate among prostitutes is somewhat higher than in the general population, but not nearly as high as that in the group of the general population aged fifteen to thirty. It is not possible to eradicate STDs among prostitutes, because even if they are examined and treated frequently, one customer who has gonorrhea, a very common major sexually transmitted disease, can reinfect the prostitute immediately, and she can then infect the next customer even though she has no symptoms. Most prostitutes, however, are quite aware of the danger of sexually transmitted disease and take every precaution to avoid it, to be examined, and, if necessary, to be treated. (See Chapter 10 on Sexually Transmitted Diseases.)

An important question to consider is whether or not prostitution should be decriminalized in this country, as it has been in most other Western countries. Here are the main arguments:

In favor of decriminalizing prostitution: Prostitution should not be considered a crime. A prostitute has the right to do with her body what she wishes, and the state should not interfere with her privacy or the privacy of her customers. The purpose of the law is to protect people and property, not to legislate individual moral conduct. Outlawing prostitution does not prevent it; it only drives prostitution underground. The history of the prohibition of alcoholic beverages demonstrates the impossibility and vast expense of trying to enforce laws against any activity for which many people feel a need and to which they are convinced they have a right. Furthermore, prostitution cannot be a crime since there are no victims (except in the case of associated violence or robbery); all parties enter into it voluntarily to meet what they consider to be their own needs.

Against decriminalizing prostitution: Prostitution is an immoral and debasing human activity, both for the prostitute and for her clients. It separates sex from love and tends to break up marriages by providing sexual satisfaction outside the marriage bond. It commercializes and trivializes in the most crass way what should be a meaningful, deep, unifying experience within the context of love. If the state says yes to prostitution, it is saying yes to sexual license and permissiveness, yes to the breakup of the family, yes to those who go against all accepted moral standards. If prostitution is decriminalized it will increase, because it will be available to people who now, restrained by the law, stay away from it. It is a responsibility of the state to use its laws to strengthen and uphold the commonly accepted standards of morality and to protect the structure of the family. To decriminalize prostitution would do just the opposite.

RAPE

Any human activity can become a problem when it is mixed with violence, and sex is no exception. Rape is an act of violence, in which sexual activity is forced on one person by another. Usually the victim is a woman, although boys and men are raped, most frequently in prison and by heterosexuals. On rare occasions even babies and very old women are raped, and it is not unknown for grown women to force sex upon adolescent boys, which could be considered a kind of rape.

Here are some figures about rape in a typical large metropolitan area: *Age of victim:* 11 and under, 18%; 12 to 17, 28%; 18 to 35, 45%; 35 to 54, 8%; 55 and over, 1%. *Sex of victim:* female, 94%; male, 6%. *Relationship of offender to victim:* stranger, 33%; caretakers or relatives, 24%; superficial acquaintance, 31%; knew each other well, 12%. *Location of rape:* indoors, 79% (30% of these in the victim's home; thus, about one-quarter of all reported rapes take place at home); on the street, 21% (this includes the 11% that happen in cars).

Note that these figures represent only *reported* rape cases. Government authorities estimate that less than 10% of rapes are reported, probably because of the victims' fear and emotional turmoil.

There is no simple, single explanation of why some men (and even a few women) become rapists. Many are people whose behavior is generally oriented toward crime and violence. They often lack a moral sense and are prone to aggression. Not a few are true psychotics, deeply troubled people who need psychiatric help and from whom society needs to be protected. Many male rapists feel an overwhelming need to find a victim to dominate and terrorize; otherwise they cannot perform sexually. Many have histories of relationships with women, often starting right within their own families, which have left them fearful and resentful of females generally. Still others believe, in a distorted way probably accentuated when they see a woman whom they find sexually provocative, that the woman they select as a victim really desires to have sexual intercourse with them, that she is "asking for it," even when she struggles and protests. Also, there is a good deal of evidence that acts of sexual violence like rape originate in emotional deprivations suffered by the rapist in early childhood.

Obviously, a woman should try not to allow herself to get into situations where she might be raped. That means avoiding dark, lonely streets or city parks, whenever possible; it means not acting or dressing in a sexually provocative manner in situations where a rapist might see her; it means staying aware of her surroundings and noticing whether she is being followed; it means not showing herself to be alone in a house or apartment, and keeping doors and windows locked; it means having her keys ready when she gets to her door or, if she's inside, always finding out for certain who's at the door before opening it; and it means, in the longer run, working with community organizations to try to make a safer environment.

Rape crisis workers generally agree that it is most important for a woman to look confident, strong, and purposeful and, even in the most tense, threatening, and emotional situation, to stay cool if she can. It will also be well for her to try to think out in advance what she would do if she were threatened with rape.

An experienced counselor who has worked for several years in a rape crisis center wrote us some wise words about the question of what a woman should do when faced with a rapist. She said:

> Please be very careful about giving specific advice on what to do. There is great disagreement on the subject. Some rapists say that if a woman had screamed or resisted loudly, they'd have run; others report they'd have

killed her. Self-defense training is valuable in that it helps a woman feel and act more assertively, but it is risky in that none of us really knows how we would use it when scared to death—and badly or ineffectively used active self-defense could get us killed. Some say it is best to seem to give in quietly so as to avoid being injured or killed, and to try to calm the rapist, to win time, so that escape is more likely should the opportunity arise. The trouble with telling a woman she *should* resist and yell is that she adds to her already large burden of guilt if she does not do so, and it plays into the hands of prosecutors and those who insist (against the law) that a woman isn't really raped unless she is beaten up or shows signs of struggle. I think it is best to give various options and then say that each woman and each rapist and each situation are unique, and the woman should respond in whatever way she thinks best.

If a woman when threatened by a rapist does decide to fight back, here is what Women Organized Against Rape (WOAR) recommends:

- USE YOUR VOICE! Yell and keep yelling. (This may sound obvious but you would be surprised how few people have ever really yelled. It takes practice and you should do it today.) Yelling will clear your head and start your adrenalin going. It may scare your attacker and also bring help.
- If you just throw your hands out for striking, they can be grabbed by an attacker and used to get you down.
- If an attacker grabs you from behind, use your elbows for striking the neck or his sides, or even his stomach to take him by surprise.
- Don't forget that a rapist also feels pain and is also afraid of pain, plus he is afraid of getting caught. Try to use this weakness to get away.
- Your legs are the strongest part of your body—they have been carrying you around all of your life. Your kick is longer than his reach and a series of hard, fast kicks should keep him away from you. Always kick with your rear foot and with the toe of your shoe. Aim low to avoid losing your balance.
- His most vulnerable spot is his *knee;* it's low, difficult to protect, and easily knocked out of place. The most effective kick is a glancing one across his kneecap.
- Don't try to kick a rapist in the groin. He has been protecting this area all of his life. In addition, he may grab your foot, knocking you off balance.
- Trust your gut feelings. If you feel you are in danger, don't hesitate to run and scream. It is better to feel foolish than to be raped. In any situation, screaming and a general uproar are strongly recommended.
- When you do decide to fight, always accompany it with a strong bellowing war cry.
- Don't ever expect a single blow to end the fight. Don't give up, keep fighting. Your objective is to get away, and to get away as soon as you can.
- If a rapist is carrying a weapon, you shouldn't fight unless absolutely necessary.

Cruel and psychologically devastating as rape is, it does not mean the end of the world for the woman, who knows it is not her fault. Although she feels the shock and will never forget the experience, she is alive and probably not seriously injured physically. It is important that she be helped to get over the experience by talking with someone, preferably a skilled counselor, so that she may receive the support she needs. There are a number of organizations across the country that deal with rape. Most are locally organized, and they have various names, such as Women Against Rape or Women Organized Against Rape (WOAR). To find the one nearest you, look in the telephone directory under "Rape" or "Rape Crisis Center." Usually there will be a hotline number to call and women on duty twenty-four hours a day to give confidential advice and help.

If a woman has been raped, what should she do? The Philadelphia WOAR gives the following advice:

If you are raped:
1. Tell what happened to the first friendly person you meet.
2. Call the police. Use the emergency number. Give your location and tell them you were raped.
3. Try to remember as many facts as you can about your attacker: clothes, height, weight, age, skin color, etc. Try to remember his car, license number, the direction in which he went, etc. Write all this down right away.
4. *Don't* wash or douche before the medical exam, or you destroy important evidence. *Don't* change your clothes, but bring a new set with you if you can.
5. At the hospital you will have a complete exam, including a pelvic exam. Show the doctor any bruises, scratches, etc.
6. Tell the police simply but exactly what happened. Try not to get flustered. Have a friend or relative accompany you if possible. Be honest and stick to your story.
7. If you do not want to report the rape to the police, see a doctor as soon as possible. Make sure you are checked for pregnancy and venereal disease.
8. If you need help or have questions, call WOAR. We're here 24 hours a day.

An important thing to remember is that reporting the rape to the police is not the same thing as pressing charges against an accused rapist who has been caught and identified. A woman has to decide whether she wishes to press charges; that is, to attempt to have the rapist convicted of a crime. If she does, there must be an investigation and hearings, for it is not unknown for women to engage willingly in sexual relations with a man and then claim to have been raped, and every person, under our system of justice, is presumed to be innocent until or unless he or she has been proven guilty. The accused rapist has civil rights, too.

Also, a woman who has been raped should be tested for sexually transmitted diseases (STDs). Rape crisis centers generally do this testing and also prescribe and administer an antibiotic. Further, if the victim consents, a "morning-after" pill is given to prevent pregnancy. (See the Concise A–to–Z Encyclopedia.) As for AIDS, the woman is given full information (orally and in writing) about the disease and offered the possibility for blood tests later. Since raped women are generally in a serious state of stress, crisis centers follow up later to see whether the victim wishes to be tested for AIDS.

Statutory Rape

"Statutory rape" is the term for sexual intercourse with a girl who is below the legal age of consent, which varies from state to state between the ages of fourteen and twenty-one, most commonly between sixteen and eighteen. The girl may have been an entirely willing partner in the intercourse, but because of her age the law does not consider her responsible and considers the man as having raped her—that is, if she, her family, or someone else brings a complaint. Obviously, millions of girls under the age of eighteen are willingly having sexual intercourse. Their male partners, if it is clear that they are physically mature enough to achieve penile penetration, could be found guilty of statutory rape. Complaints are rarely brought, however.

SADO-MASOCHISM

Sadism, in the sexual sense, is the condition in which sexual gratification depends largely upon inflicting physical pain on others. (The term derives from the name of the Marquis de Sade, a Frenchman who practiced and wrote about such activities.) *Masochism,* the condition complementary to sadism, is the condition in which sexual pleasure depends upon undergoing physical pain or humiliation.

Sadists and masochists, whether heterosexual or homosexual, thus match each other as partners, and as long as each satisfies the needs of the other, there seems to be no great problem. Usually the masochist more or less controls the relationship, not allowing the infliction of pain to go further than he or she wishes, since if it did, the sadist would lose a desired partner. Sadists use, and masochists consent to, whipping and gagging, chaining, and other restraints such as leather wrist and leg straps, sometimes called "bondage."

Obviously, if a person with sadistic tendencies gets involved with or marries a person who is not a masochist, serious problems can develop, for in the eyes of the law, sadistic activity is criminal, whereas masochism is not. There are more sadist and masochist heterosexual males than there are females to match.

TRANSVESTISM

A transvestite is a person who dresses in clothes designed for members of the opposite sex in order to be able to perform sexually and achieve orgasm. Transvestites are almost always males. Like voyeurism (see below) and exhibitionism, transvestism can be considered merely a "public nuisance offense" in that it may be annoying or repulsive but is otherwise harmless.

Many transvestites confine their "cross-dressing" to their homes. Often they are married men; others are homosexuals. But whether heterosexual or homosexual, the transvestite can get into trouble with the law if he publicly flaunts his behavior in female clothing. Transvestites are quite clear that they are not transsexual (see pages 181–82).

VOYEURISM

A voyeur (a French word meaning "one who sees") is a person, almost always a man, who gets sexual satisfaction from looking at a sexual act or at a person undressed or undressing. Being sexually aroused by seeing people doing sexual things or dressed (perhaps undressed) in a sexual manner is certainly nearly universal among men and increasingly common among women. Often the voyeur masturbates while he is looking, or soon afterward.

Voyeurism is considered a deviation only when the seeing is preferred to sexual intercourse, when it is done at considerable legal risk to the voyeur (and thus contains an element of the forbidden), and when the person or people being seen are unaware they are being observed. Usually voyeurs watch strangers, and they are for the most part entirely passive and harmless, except as they are considered nuisances or offensive. Voyeurs are in most cases reported to the police by neighbors rather than by the person being observed.

A common term for voyeur is "Peeping Tom," the name coming from Tom the tailor, who according to an eleventh-century legend was the only villager who failed to close his shutters but "peeped" out when Lady Godiva rode nude down the main street of Coventry, England, as a gesture to persuade her husband to stop oppressively taxing the poor.

Personal Sexual Problems Without Legal Implications

FETISHISM

Fetishism means experiencing sexual stimulation and gratification from touching, fondling, or just looking at an inanimate object that is not in itself sexual, as for example pieces of clothing, leather garments, chains, or shoes. In some ways it can truly be considered that, in our society, women's breasts, although not inanimate, obsess men to such an extent that they are treated almost as fetishes. Fetishism is a condition of men, very rarely of women. How a fetishist becomes fixed upon a certain object is not always clear, but it does have to do with some kind of conditioning, association, or deeply affecting experience during the very early years—sometimes before memory.

It is usual for the fetishist to masturbate into or onto the inanimate object that is the fetish. However, a fetish should not be confused with what might be called a "masturbation aid"; say, a picture or recording that stimulates the fantasies that often accompany masturbating.

TRANSSEXUALISM

Transsexuals are people who wish they were, or are convinced that they are, of the sex that is opposite from that shown by their anatomy and chromosomes. They are genetically of one sex but psychologically of the other. No one knows the origins of transsexualism.

There are three to four male transsexuals to every female transsexual. A male transsexual is convinced that he is "a woman imprisoned in a male body" and has a compelling and never-ending desire to have his body reconstructed to conform with what he considers to be his true sex. His condition is to him serious and is not to be confused with the wish of some men and women that they had been born as members of the other sex. The medical profession is learning how to study, appraise, and test the transsexual's compelling drive for a sex-change operation.

Many transsexuals, usually after long periods of suffering followed by much counseling, achieve the surgery. In male-to-female sex-change surgery the penis and testes are removed entirely, and an artificial vagina, which usually functions very well sexually, is constructed. The patient is required to live for a full year as a female before surgery is granted. Prior to the surgery, the patient undergoes female hormone treatment to modify as far as possible his secondary sex characteristics toward femaleness, and this results in growth of the breasts and change in body-fat distribution. Hormone treatment must continue for the rest of male-to-female life. Finally, as a woman, a male-to-female transsexual can legally marry, can enjoy penile-vaginal intercourse, usually with orgasm, but, of course, cannot become pregnant.

People often confuse transsexualism with homosexuality, but the two are entirely different. Homosexuals like their own maleness and enjoy sexual love with people who have the same sex organs as themselves. Transsexuals are also interested in members of the sex they were born into, but this interest is actually heterosexual. They wish to be transformed into the other sex they truly believe they are. They want their bodies to be reassigned as far as possible to the other sex to conform with what they are convinced is their true gender identity so that thereafter their sexual relationships can, in fact, be heterosexual.

As we mentioned above, female-to-male transsexuals also exist; they too request surgery, and where appropriate receive it. Female-to-male sex-change surgery includes removal of uterus, tubes, ovaries, and vagina, inclusion of plastic testicles in a scrotal sac constructed out of the labia, and construction of a penis from skin. Even though the surgically constructed penis cannot function as successfully as the surgically constructed vagina, many female-to-male transsexuals legally marry women, and many such couples are able to lead contented lives.

DRUGS, ALCOHOL, AND SEX

When sexual activity becomes associated over a period of time with the use of drugs or alcohol, problems arise. Drugs used for nonmedicinal purposes, and alcohol (which medically is considered a drug, even though it has wide social acceptance), tend to lower people's capacity to reason straight, to make responsible decisions, or to have the will-power to carry out those decisions. When this effect is injected into a sexual situation, tragedy may well be the result, especially if the sexual activity that may be affected is carried on outside the context of a stable relationship like marriage.

Insofar as sex is concerned (and many other human activities too), it is not possible to separate the actual physical effects of drugs and alcohol from the psychological effects. If a person thinks that a drink or a drug will make sex better for him or her, then quite possibly it will seem to do so, in spite of the fact that for others the capacity to perform sexually may actually be lowered.

One of the main effects of drugs and alcohol is to reduce people's inhibitions, to make them feel more relaxed. Since inhibition, worry, and tension about sex, conscious or unconscious, make it difficult for some people to enjoy their sexuality, anything that reduces these may temporarily increase pleasure. But if inhibition is so reduced that a person loses his or her sense of judgment and responsibility, trouble can result. Also, if there is dependency on drugs or alcohol for the enjoy-ment of sex, that can be a serious problem requiring professional help.

Here are some facts about specific substances that affect, or are believed to affect, sexual behavior. Keep in mind that different people are affected in different ways by different substances and that for some people there is a greater factor of risk than for others.

Alcohol

Alcohol lowers the capacity to reason and to make sound decisions, increases vulnerability to sexual or other impulses, reduces inhibitions, and may temporarily increase a person's sense of pleasure. However, even small amounts lower the capacity—from a purely physical point of view—to perform sexually, especially in males. Large amounts of alcohol produce temporary impotence in males and have a negative effect on sexual desire.

Marijuana

Marijuana is believed by many of its users to enhance their sexual pleasure and reduce inhibitions. Long-term use, if excessive, impairs mental faculties and sexual judgment.

Heroin

Heroin temporarily appears to increase desire and potency. But as a person becomes addicted, his or her capacity to enjoy sex is greatly impaired. This impairment may continue even after the habit is kicked.

Amphetamines and Cocaine

At first, amphetamines and cocaine seem to increase sexual desire and activity. With their continued use, however, the ability to perform and to enjoy is reduced, as exhaustion, nervousness, and even serious irrationality set in. In the female these substances can cause vaginal dryness and irritation.

10
Sexually Transmitted Diseases — STDs

Another major set of problems connected with human sexuality is sexually transmitted diseases, STDs. A term still commonly used for STDs is *venereal disease,* VD. (The word *venereal* means "having to do with sexual intercourse" and comes from the name of Venus, the Roman goddess of love.) We shall use STD, the now correct and accepted term.

What evidence is there that sexually transmitted diseases are a problem? According to the best evidence, and no one knows for sure, from 6 to 10 million Americans, the majority of them under age twenty-five, are infected by one or more STDs each year. The U.S. Public Health Service estimates that STDs cost the nation over 3 billion dollars annually. The amount of suffering, both physical and psychological, is impossible to estimate. It involves not only the infected people, but also their partners and families. And the terrible, lethal disease AIDS (acquired immune deficiency syndrome) is spreading rapidly in the United States, although until now the number of people infected has been small compared to the number infected with chlamydia (inflamation of the urethra in men and women), trichomoniasis (infection of the vagina), gonorrhea, and herpes. However, for AIDS there is as yet no known cure, and almost all of those who get a full case of the disease die of it. (See the special section on AIDS, beginning on page 189, toward the end of this chapter.)

One problem in dealing with sexually transmitted diseases, both in writing and medically, is that they are so closely related to sexual behavior. Most people, many doctors included, find it hard to be objective about sex and sexual behavior, so often it is difficult for the average person to get accurate information about the diseases; for example, how they are spread and how widespread they are. Thus, although doctors and public health workers are legally required to report all cases of most major STDs to the public health authorities, the U.S. Public Health Service estimates that only one case in four that is medically treated actually is reported and entered into the statistics.

If it were possible for people's attitudes about sex and sexual information to be more understanding and realistic, health workers and others interested in public and individual health might be more successful in their efforts to control the STDs. There must be sober acceptance that sexuality and sexual behavior are facts of life and that many people of all ages, for better or worse, are and will continue to be sexually active—as they have always been. The job of STD health workers is not to deal with the moral apsects of the situations they are concerned with—important as these are in other kinds of work and teaching—but to deal directly with the problems of prevention, control, and cure of the sex-related diseases.

We speak of sexually transmitted diseases, and yet it is often not accurate to say that certain diseases are sexually transmitted and certain others are not. An unborn baby will contract syphilis from its syphilitic mother; if not protected immediately after birth by drops or ointment applied to its eyes (as almost all babies now are in the United States), a newborn can be infected with gonorrhea in its eyes as it passes through its infected mother's birth canal, with the risk of permanent blindness. An AIDS-infected mother will transmit the disease to her child during pregnancy or birth, and the child will almost certainly die before reaching school age.

In general, the organisms causing most sexually transmitted diseases can live only in the warm, moist conditions found inside the human body. They die almost at once if exposed to air or allowed to become dry or cool. The organisms of STDs are transmitted mainly by contact between the warm, moist *mucous tissues* of an infectious person and those of another person, as in sexual intercourse or heavy petting. The mucous tissues are the soft, moist linings inside almost all the passages of the body that open to the outside: the penis, the vagina, the anus, the mouth, and the throat. The germs can also enter through the eyes or through those parts of the skin that are quite delicate, like the skin on the penis or in and around the genital area or on the face or the nipples. Syphilis germs can enter the body through a cut, a scratch, or an opening in the skin; gonorrhea bacteria (but almost certainly *not* AIDS) can be transmitted through using towels or sheets immediately after an infectious person has used them *and* while they are still damp and warm. The germs of STDs cannot be transmitted by means of toilet seats, doorknobs, swimming pools, or drinking glasses.

The disease AIDS is indeed an STD, but it is also transmitted by any exchange of blood, such as that occurring when people share needles or syringes when they use intravenous drugs. It is *not* spread by casual contact, living together in a family, or by going to school together, but only by the exchange of semen or blood.

Everyone who is sexually active should have some knowledge about the symptoms of the main sexually transmitted diseases. In the Concise A–to–Z Encyclopedia at the back of this book, we give a summary of the information about the most common of the STDs, each in its alphabetical position: the causes of each disease, its symptoms, the time from contact to first symptoms, the method of diagnosis, and the complications of each disease. We do not, however, describe the treatment, since people with symptoms should go to a doctor or STD (VD) clinic to be examined and to have treatment prescribed. The diseases explained are: AIDS, chancroid, chlamydia, crab lice, gonorrhea, herpes progenitalis, lymphogranuloma venereum, nongonoccocal (or nonspecific) urethritis, pelvic inflammatory disease (PID), syphilis, trichonomiasis, venereal warts, and yeast infections.

Self-treatment of any sexually transmitted disease should never be undertaken. To find a clinic, look for the telephone number and address in the telephone directory under "Health," or under the name of your city or town and then "Health Department." If you or any people you know have questions about symptoms, diagnosis, or treatment and where to go to get help, you may call, toll-free, the STD National Hotline seven days a week. The number is 1-800-227-8922 (outside California), 11:30 A.M. to 1:30 A.M., Eastern Time, 8 A.M. to 8 P.M., Pacific Time. In California, call 1-800-982-5883. The calls are confidential. No names are asked, no records are kept. But the VD National Hotline has available in its office the names, addresses, and hours of service of STD clinics throughout the United States. There is also a national AIDS hotline. The number is 1-800-342-AIDS.

Most of the sexually transmitted diseases, except AIDS, can be cured by one or more injections of penicillin or another antibiotic. The cure is usually quick and inexpensive, and free of charge at a public clinic. Examination, testing, and treatment are done confidentially.

Even if they are minors, young people may be diagnosed and treated entirely legally without their parents' knowledge, although young people would be well advised to share their problem with their parents.

The Prevention of Sexually Transmitted Diseases

While, with the exception of AIDS, STDs are not the worldwide disaster they were before the discovery and application of antibiotics, they are still a terribly serious health problem. For instance, although antibiotics can cure syphilis, they cannot repair the serious damage it may already have done. Also, there is every possibility of reinfection after a cure. As far as prevention of STDs goes, there are two parts: individual protection and public protection.

INDIVIDUAL PROTECTION

There are a number of ways by which you as an individual can help to protect yourself and your partner from sexually transmitted diseases:

1. *Don't have sexual intercourse or engage in heavy petting with just anybody.*

2. *Be sure you and your sexual partner are free of STDs.* The only way to be certain is to be tested at a clinic or by a doctor and then have intimate sexual contact only with your partner, and your partner only with you.

3. *Use a condom if you have sexual intercourse with a person you are not certain is free of STDs.* And even condoms are not 100 percent "safe sex." (See page 78 for instructions on this.)

4. *Know the symptoms of the sexually transmitted diseases.* These symptoms are described in the Concise A–to–Z Encyclopedia in the back of this book. In general, if you have soreness or pain in your genital area, severe itching, inflammation, unusual discharges, ulcers, warts, or any other unusual conditions, especially if you are sexually active, assume that you may have one of the STDs.

5. *Get diagnosed and, if necessary, treated.* If you have symptoms, go at once to a clinic or doctor and follow the instructions you receive. If you don't know where to go, call the STD National Hotline (see page 187). Do not try to treat yourself. It can be dangerous.

PUBLIC PROTECTION

The U.S. Public Health Service's Center for Disease Control, in Atlanta, Georgia, and various state and city public health services attempt to keep track of the spread of sexually transmitted diseases in the United States. They publish the latest information about the extent and location of the diseases and the ways of diagnosing and treating them. One of the most important aspects of this work is locating all people who have STDs and confidentially treating them. You can assist in this work by being sure that if you become infected this is reported by you or your doctor to the public health authorities. You should also report, again confidentially, the names of all your sexual contacts, so that if infected they can be diagnosed and treated. The chain of infection cannot be broken without this contact tracing.

AIDS

We have already spoken of AIDS, a disease caused by the human immunodeficiency virus (HIV), which is a major threat to the health of people in the United States and the rest of the world. Although the number of people who actually have AIDS is as yet small compared to the number of those infected by other STDs, the disease is rapidly expanding, and all of those who have it will almost certainly die within a few years.

AIDS stands for
- *acquired*—something you can catch
- *immune deficiency*—not enough protection against disease
- *syndrome*—a group of signs and symptoms characteristic of a given disease

AIDS was first recognized in the United States only in 1981. By late 1988, about 40,000 people in the U.S. had developed AIDS and, of those, over 35,000 had died. The number of cases is doubling about every 18 months, and by 1992, Public Health officials estimate that there will be at least 450,000 AIDS victims, of whom 265,000 will have died. (According to the U.S. Public Health Service, another 1,500,000 Americans carry the HIV virus in their blood and can infect others, even though they themselves, for reasons not fully understood, do not have AIDS or display its symptoms.) According to the World Health Organization, a United Nations Agency, by 1991 over 100 million people in the world will have AIDS, although this figure is difficult to check accurately.

Until a cure for AIDS is discovered, or a vaccine against the AIDS virus is developed, these figures will escalate. AIDS deaths are long, emotional, and frightening, for the victim, for the victim's family and friends, and for the health care providers. The deaths often are caused by a kind of pneumonia caused by a parasite *(pneumocystitis carinii)* or a rare kind of cancer of the blood vessels *(Kaposi's sarcoma),* both of which the body's normal immune system resists, but not the weakened immune system of AIDS victims.

The situation is so alarming that in October 1986, Surgeon General C. Everett Koop urged an all-out effort to educate everyone in the country about the dangers of AIDS. He then advocated that "safe" sex education begin as early as third grade so that children can "grow up knowing the behaviors to avoid [in order to] protect themselves against the AIDS virus."

Here are some facts about AIDS:

• The symptoms of AIDS virus infection are: unexplained fevers, sweats, dry coughing, swollen glands, swollen lymph nodes, continuous weight loss, diarrhea, tiredness, fleshy purplish skin lesions, and a heavy whitish coating on the tongue and in the mouth, called thrush. However, note well that a person may have any or all of these symptoms and still *not* have AIDS.

• AIDS is spread by the exchange of semen or blood.

• AIDS, thus, is spread by sexual intercourse, especially by anal intercourse (in which the penis of one partner enters the anus of another), but also by vaginal intercourse. Anal intercourse is particularly dangerous because the anal blood vessels and membranes are delicate and breakable so that semen containing the HIV virus can enter the bloodstream. Much less dangerous is oral sex, although there is some risk.

• The AIDS virus is spread also by intravenous (IV) drug users who share needles or syringes. This is deep blood-to-blood contact.

• The groups of people who are at greatest risk of getting AIDS are homosexual or bisexual men; women who have sexual intercourse with infected men and men who have had sexual intercourse with infected women; IV drug users who share needles or syringes; and infants born to HIV-infected mothers. About 50 percent of such infants get the virus while in the womb or during birth. They almost all die before they reach school age.

• For people who are sexually active, condoms, if very carefully used from start to finish of intercourse, provide some protection against the spread of the AIDS virus, but they are not foolproof. (See page 78.)

• When a person's blood contains the HIV virus, a blood test will reveal it, by means of the antibodies the body produces. However, many who show positive in HIV blood tests do not themselves suffer from AIDS.

• AIDS, unlike colds, the flu, or measles, is not a contagious disease in the usual sense of the word. It requires a definite action on a person's part to "catch" it. Thus, *anyone can avoid catching it,* except for infants and people who had blood transfusions prior to 1985. AIDS is different from the great plagues of the past, which killed people no matter what they did.

• Until 1985, people who received transfusions of blood were at some risk because some donated blood carried the HIV virus, but since 1985, a simple, inexpensive and highly reliable blood test has become available, and now all blood and blood products are routinely screened, and there is virtually no danger from transfusion. (The only exception to this statement is that a person who has just been infected by the HIV virus and then donates blood within a period of two weeks to three months, before the antibodies to the virus have developed in his blood, may test negative but actually have AIDS-infected blood.)

• You do not get AIDS from tears or saliva, from people coughing or sneezing, from sharing food or eating and drinking utensils, from toilets and basins; nor do you get it from hugging, kissing, or fondling. You don't get it from insect bites. If a person has a bleeding cut and it touches another person's bleeding cut, no AIDS virus has been shown to be passed, probably because the fluid from cuts oozes outward, not into the bloodstream.

• As far as we know, there are fewer than 100 AIDS-infected children in all the schools in the United States. The widely reported fear that young AIDS victims who attend school are a threat to the health of other children is a mere bugaboo. There is no known case of AIDS having been passed from child to child in school (unless they have had sexual intercourse or shared IV drug needles or syringes on school premises). However, the American Academy of Pediatrics, which affirms that children with AIDS should be allowed to go to school, recommends that if a child is incontinent, has open sores, or, for some reason, frequently bites other children, he or she should have his or her contacts with classmates closely monitored.

One of the great dangers about the fear of AIDS is that it is, in some areas, creating a great fear of homosexuality and homosexuals. The term for such irrational fear of homosexuality is *homophobia*. In the light of the facts you have just read about AIDS, this fear is unjustified. Examples of hysteria based on ignorance are a proposal that a house that an AIDS victim has lived in may not be sold without informing the buyer, and the suggestion that all bodies of AIDS victims should be cremated.

One last point: We can all reassure ourselves by remembering that, thus far, humankind has found ways to end these vast threats to human life—the Black Death, cholera, yellow fever, smallpox, and others. Now that we are mobilizing our knowledge and facilities to attack the AIDS threat, it is likely that a cure, or at least a preventative, will be found, tested, and approved. Already, scientists can reproduce the AIDS virus in the laboratory so that they can study ways to kill it, although it remains an elusive and complex virus, difficult to isolate and define, and there may be several forms of it. According to the American Foundation for AIDS research, about twenty drugs show promise and some 10,000 drugs a year are being screened. Some of these may provide a cure, or at least an effective treatment, for AIDS—but a solution to the problem is probably still several years away, perhaps longer, and at this writing most scientists are feeling discouraged, as nothing really seems to work.

Fortunately, recent public polls are showing that many Americans are becoming less outraged about AIDS and its dangers, and increasingly compassionate toward AIDS victims and their terrible suffering. A well-known physician in New York who specializes in AIDS research and treatment reports that, typically, people go through three stages of response to the AIDS situation: first disbelief, then denial, then compassion.

Remember that information about AIDS is developing and changing rapidly. To get up-to-date answers to any questions you may have, call the National AIDS Hotline: 1-800-342-AIDS.

The Biggest Sex Problem of All

In the previous chapter and in this one, we have said a good deal about ways that sex can get turned into a problem by human beings. The length of these chapters is an indication of how often this happens. But undoubtedly the biggest problems are the fear and guilt that our society attaches to the expression of human sexuality, as the result of the ignorance—today—about the simple and complex physical and emotional facts about sexuality. All too often this ignorance is willfully and stubbornly maintained by individuals who refuse to read, listen, and learn, and who thus deprive themselves—and usually their children—of the calm, informed attitudes and understanding about sex that might give them sexual peace and happiness in their lives.

And that brings us to the subject of our next chapter.

11
Planned Sex Education Programs

The following exchange of letters recently appeared in the "Dear Abby" column:

Dear Abby: I may be old-fashioned, but I can't see teaching sixth and seventh graders sex in the schoolroom. They are a long way from needing that kind of information. Why rush them? If you start putting ideas about sex into their heads, first thing you know, they'll start experimenting.

No wonder we have so many unmarried mothers among teenagers. I read in your column that venereal disease is now an epidemic in this country.

What can be done to stop all this sex education, Abby?

Concerned in Illinois

Dear Concerned: If there really were all the sex education you claim there is, we'd have less teenage pregnancy and VD—not more.

No one has to put "ideas" about sex into the heads of children. It's there already. Sexual feelings and curiosity about sex are natural and normal in all children. And so is experimenting.

Ideally, parents should provide their children with a proper sex education, but surveys show that most of them do not, so some schools provide it. . . .

The old saying, "What you don't know can't hurt you" is not true. On the contrary—it can hurt you. And it's hurting all of us.

Although Abby makes her point strongly and clearly, we doubt that "Concerned in Illinois" was, or could ever be, convinced. The fear that "Concerned" expresses—that information leads to ideas which in turn lead to experimentation which in turn leads to illegitimate babies and sexually transmitted disease—is widespread, deep-rooted, and based on error.

Why Sex Education Outside the Family?

We have already explained how parents are their children's primary sex educators, whether or not they know it or want to be, even though about two thirds of eighth- and ninth-graders say that they have never talked with their parents about sex. Most of the education is done unconsciously, by example and attitudes, rather than directly in words. There are, however, a number of reasons why today a sex information program outside the home is considered beneficial, not to replace but to supplement home teachings:

• Some parents—or their children—are so embarrassed when a sexual subject or action comes up in family or community life that they are simply unable to discuss the matter. ("My mother says, 'Go talk to your father,' and my father says, 'I'm busy.' ")

• Some parents keep waiting for their children to ask the questions, but the children never do, or else the parents fail to recognize implied questions.

• Some parents simply do not have the information—beyond the simple facts of where the babies come from—to answer their children's questions. (This book is one resource for all family members to use when information is needed. Sometimes a book is a good "third party" to get families talking together. You can start off talking about the book.)

• Information and opinions can often be shared more easily in a clear, friendly, and objective way by people trained as teachers than by parents, who are quite naturally and properly very emotionally involved with their children.

• Once children reach puberty and begin to struggle with the four tasks of adolescence (see Chapter 7), sex and sexuality become an area in which they feel they must try especially hard to achieve independence. They resist the idea that their parents might be worried about their sex lives. They very much want and need physical and psychological privacy with respect to sex, yet they need to be able to talk about it with each other and with respected authority figures.

• In most families there is little chance for the children to talk about sex and sexuality with people their own age, but this is an important skill for people of any age to learn. Such talk helps to prepare boys and girls for communicating with their future mates and for the responsible, intelligent choices they must learn how to make.

• A classroom can provide a "safe," somewhat structured situation in which young people can speak out more easily than in the more intimate environment of the home. It also provides the opportunity to be silent and learn from listening to the exchange of ideas by others.

Many parents worry that a sex and family-life education program will promote or suggest ideas they would not approve of. But we must remember that, as the Dear Abby column pointed out, ideas and feelings about sex and sexuality are already in the heads of normal children. However, it would certainly be wrong for a public school to promote any given point of view or set of morals, other than the basic one of responsibility for one's own actions *and* their consequences. Generally, the fear in this connection is that teachers, in their enthusiasm, will promote a pro-sex, go-out-and-try-it point of view. In actual practice, this has not proved to be the case; in the rare instances where it did happen, the community outcry was so immediate and vigorous that it soon stopped. A far greater danger is that the subject of sex and sexuality will be grouped with "problems"—like drugs, alcohol, and smoking—or that it will be taught by teachers who are not trained to deal with the subject. Parents are quite right to be concerned about this.

In this connection, see the statement of widely acceptable values on which a sex education program can be based (pages 197 and 200–201).

Essential Elements for Planned Sex Education

It would be a mistake for anyone to prescribe a sex education program, since the content should be developed by a school's educational staff in cooperation with a broadly based committee from the community, as far as the basic approaches and areas are concerned. Community needs and degrees of readiness do differ from place to place. However, here are the elements we consider to be essential to any sex education program:

1. The complete biological facts of sex and reproduction.

2. The basic facts of birth control and family planning. Even people who are for religious reasons opposed to the medical birth control methods need to know these facts, for if they don't they will accept rumor and half-truths.

3. The differences in sexual behavior between other animals and

human beings. The sexual behavior of animals is largely programmed by instinct and innate physiology, so they have no choices to make, whereas the sexual behavior of human beings is mostly learned. Humans can make choices about how they will behave sexually, and they are therefore directly responsible for the results of their choices. Too many youngsters, aware of the copulation of animals, conclude that the sexuality of men and women is the same as the reproductivity of animals.

4. The differences between men and women, not just the biological differences but the differences in sexual roles, in sexual response, in personality, and in what society expects.

5. The facts about masturbation. Because of students' embarrassment, this subject is unlikely to come up spontaneously in class and therefore needs to be introduced, if only to make sure that misconceptions about its role throughout the life cycle are cleared up.

6. The facts about homosexuality, and a discussion of the rights and special social problems of people with homosexual preferences.

7. The facts about sexually transmitted diseases—not to scare young people, but to help them protect themselves against a real and widespread health danger.

8. The possible results, both good and bad, of sexual intercourse, and the steps that lead up to it.

9. The place of sex in family life.

10. The place of sex in the social life of teenagers.

11. Through discussion and through literature, the recognition that the feelings experienced by one individual are often not the same as those experienced by another individual. Students need help in putting themselves in the places of other people.

Sometimes it is helpful to give students a worksheet on which they can indicate what they would like to talk about. We have reproduced one on the next two pages, for use with modifications appropriate to the specific situation.

Sex Education in the Public Schools

We have suggested that teachers should stick to facts and preside over the discussion, making sure that the major issues get discussed. But mere facts and discussion are not enough. They need to be undergirded by a set of values. (We use the word *values,* not beliefs or dogmas. A church or church school has the right to teach a specific set of religious

Girl_____   Boy_____   Section_____   Date_____

I. Sex education unit: eighth or seventh grades

In order to make sure that the days we spend on sex education are as helpful as possible to you and the rest of the class, please write out in the spaces below any questions you'd like answered or subjects or issues you'd like to discuss.

FACTS AND INFORMATION

Questions of fact or information you'd like answered. Be as specific or as general as you want. No question is too large or too small.

(Use other side if you need more space)

ISSUES AND MATTERS OF OPINION

Controversial issues; questions of behavior, what to do or how to do, morals, standards—what's right or wrong, wise or unwise, when—that you'd like the class to discuss.

(Use other side if you need more space)

Girl_____ Boy_____   Section_____ Date_____

II. Please put a check beside any of the subjects below that you'd like to be sure the class deals with.

_____ abortion, how does it work?

_____ abortion, right or wrong?

_____ adoption

_____ AIDS

_____ bases for a good marriage

_____ birth control

_____ childbirth

_____ contraception (birth control)

_____ dating

_____ divorce

_____ drugs and sex

_____ extramarital sex

_____ feminism

_____ going steady

_____ guilt and sex

_____ homosexuality

_____ how talk about sex with members of the other sex?

_____ how talk about sex with parents

_____ incest

_____ "living together": without marriage or before marriage

_____ love—what is it?

_____ masturbation—and men

_____ masturbation—and women

_____ molesters

_____ necking, petting, making out

_____ natural family planning

_____ nonmarital sex

_____ orgasm

_____ population problems

_____ pornography

_____ pregnancy

_____ premarital sex

_____ prostitution

_____ rape

_____ religion and sex

_____ selfishness and sex

_____ sex in other animals

_____ sex roles, male & female

_____ sex, words, and language

_____ sexual intercourse

_____ sexually transmitted diseases (STDs)

_____ sterilization

_____ unwanted babies

_____ venereal disease (VD)

_____ when is it "safe" to have sex?

_____ OTHER:

_____

_____

_____

_____

_____

_____

beliefs, dogmas, or rules about human sexual behavior, but a public school does not have that right.) The following eight values should be acceptable to any community in our American democracy.

• *The value of each individual person.* The infinite value of others is worthy of our most caring and loving consideration.

• *The value of consideration.* The welfare and needs, both short-term and long-term, of oneself, of others involved, and of society, must be considered in whatever one does.

• *The value of communication.* It is good to have opportunities to talk over our questions and ideas, to test them out against the ideas of others, to make our feelings known and to learn the feelings of others through discussion and conversation.

• *The value of marriage and the family.* Sexual activity, or refraining from it, should be decided upon partly on the basis of one's thoughtful judgment of what will strengthen marriage and the family.

• *The value of responsibility.* An action, sexual or otherwise, taken in the light of all its possible consequences, good and bad, present and future, can be called responsible. An action taken without regard for the consequences is irresponsible.

• *The value of pleasure and good feelings.* We all know, and have known since we were infants, that our bodies can give us good feelings. For many people—though not all—feelings of bodily pleasure, called sensual feelings, are an important part of a good life, right through old age.

• *The value of control.* Sex is a power, and, like any other power, it can be used for good or for bad. Therefore it must be controlled by the individual for good purposes. (Automobiles and fire are two other examples of power where responsible and knowledgeable control can mean the difference between benefit and tragedy.)

• *The value of information.* Correct information is better than ignorance or wrong information; it makes responsible action possible, while ignorance can lead only to irresponsibility. There is no evidence that sound knowledge leads to experimentation and trouble, for those who get into what we call "trouble" are usually those who are not truly and fully informed. There are people in every community who will argue for ignorance in matters that concern human sexuality, but we believe that the great majority favor information. Imparting information, and teaching people how to get it and use it, is a main function of the schools.

We suggest that these eight values make an excellent basis for class discussion, or discussion by the school community.*

Teaching According to Age Level

In general, we have found that in kindergarten through about fourth grade it is best to proceed in sex education somewhat as an enlightened family would proceed at home; that is, to (1) deal with questions as they come up, (2) answer them briefly and factually (either before the entire group or simply to the individual who asks them, whichever seems most natural), and (3) ask if there are any other questions. This is the method of using opportunities as they arise, taking advantage of the moments of teachability. If classrooms have animals (hamsters, mice, guinea pigs, rabbits, and the like) that from time to time mate and have young, this is a good extra resource for teaching, as much for teaching how animals and human beings differ as for teaching reproduction. (But the birth of baby rabbits, for example, should *never* be explained by saying that "the mommy and daddy rabbits got married.")

For children in kindergarten or first grade, it is also useful to read aloud, look at together, and discuss a carefully chosen book written especially for this age so that these children will know at least basic, simplest facts about "where babies come from." (See list of books beginning on page 267.)

By fourth or fifth grade, children are ready for a planned unit on the facts of human reproduction. Children of this age are in that wonderful period of life when they are enthusiastic about all sorts of facts, can learn them without discomfort or silliness, and are likely to have lots of serious questions, all of which should be answered. Very few will have reached puberty, so their interest will still tend toward the facts rather than toward their own emotional involvement. A number of books are available for this age group.

Beginning at grades 7 or 8, the planned portion of the sex education program really should have two parts: (1) use of the entire school curriculum to deal with questions and information about human sexuality as they come up, and (2) scheduled units of instruction and discussions.

*Permission is hereby given to copy this statement of values for use in classes or at meetings. Please acknowledge the source, *The Family Book About Sexuality*, © 1989 by Mary S. Calderone, M.D., and Eric W. Johnson; Harper & Row, Publishers, New York.

THE CURRICULUM-CENTERED PART

The curriculum-centered part can make valuable use of such subjects as social studies (history, current events, anthropology, sociology, and the like), English (especially literature, which is rich in the materials of human behavior), and science (especially biology), as well as opportunities that arise in counseling situations. To make intelligent but not excessive use of the curriculum, it is important for faculty members from time to time to discuss together what information and understandings they wish to be ready to convey or develop, so that they can have in their minds an informal agenda of items relating to sexuality. In such faculty discussions it is useful, too, for the staff to share and talk about classroom experiences that have been especially successful or unsuccessful.

SCHEDULED UNITS

From grade 4 or 5 on through the teenage years, there should be scheduled units of sex education, perhaps once every two years—say grades 5 or 6, 7 or 8, 10, and 12. Grades 7 and 8 are crucial years, in which more children reach puberty than in any other, when interest in the social as well as the physical aspects of sexuality becomes high, and yet before many students are deeply involved personally (most are still only thinking about getting involved). A month- or six-week-long unit, planned on the basis of the content suggested on pages 196–97, with reading, discussion, and writing and with the students being tested on facts, is a valuable focal point.

By grade 10, students have grown in maturity and experience and are ready to discuss again, at new levels, the factual and behavioral aspects of sexuality. A shorter planned unit is probably sufficient here—say, ten days. Then in grade 12, as students are about to experience the greater freedom of the world outside of school, on the job or in college, they should be helped by another planned unit to prepare for being independent and for meeting with value systems other than their own. In all of the *factual* material presented in grades 5 through 12, students should be tested for mastery of the information, and marked, just as they are in any other subject. They should *not* be tested or marked on non-factual questions that have been discussed and for which there are no clear right-or-wrong answers.

Learning by the Discussion Method

As we have said, schools and other public institutions serve best if they do not promote a certain point of view or set of morals, other than the set of acceptable values that we presented earlier in this chapter. Teachers should stick to established facts. Where the facts are not known, or where they do not know them, the teachers should be frank and say so. For example, no one can or should say that it is a fact that premarital intercourse does or does not improve a person's chances of having a happy, satisfying, and long-lasting marriage. Research on this question has come up with no consistent evidence one way or the other.

If a student asks, "Is it OK for a boy and a girl to have sex if they're in love and know what they are doing? Will it hurt them later when they get married?" some teachers, afraid of parental reaction, might be inclined to answer, "Well, if you have sex with somebody you're not married to *before* you are married, you are likely to go on having sex with people you're not married to *after* marriage, and that's bad for marriage, isn't it? Also, it's immoral." Other teachers, not wanting to cause hang-ups in the children, might say, "Well, I don't know, but you certainly don't want to get so turned off about sex that when you get married you will have difficulty enjoying the sexual part of your marriage." The best way to handle a question like this is to say only that it's a very good question and then turn it back to the class for discussion, making sure that all aspects of the question get talked about. Such an approach emphasizes that questions like these have to be answered by each individual for himself or herself, and also that there are some things the teacher—or science itself—just can't answer.

When discussed fully, freely, and openly by the class, this question about premarital sex provides almost enough material for an entire unit of sex education! Look at the questions in it:

- What do you mean, "having sex"?
- What does "OK" mean? OK with whom?
- What does "in love" mean?
- What do you mean, "know what they're doing"? Know physically? Know emotionally? Know intellectually?
- What do they need to know? How do they know that they know it? What were their sources for finding out?
- What do you mean by "hurt" them? In what ways could it hurt them?

• In what ways could it be good for them? How could it hurt, or be good for, their eventual marriage?

• What makes a good marriage?

In our experience, a discussion of subjects like these, if there is free expression of all points of view, is likely to result in a balance of opinions and the gradual emergence of a clear wisdom of the group. There are two main benefits: the chance to hear the views of others, especially those of the other sex, and the chance to think through, with others, various issues of behavior and feeling—what to do and what not to do, and what the consequences are likely to be. This process requires teachers skillful in facilitating group discussions. The main role of the teacher is to be the moderator for the discussion (only one person talking at a time), to correct any misstatements of fact or to inject any factual knowledge that may enlighten the discussion, and to make sure that questions raised keep being turned back to the class for further exchange. Thus, without preaching and without forcing, a maturity of thought, opinion, and choice-making develops in the group and in each individual, even among those who prefer listening to talking.

Studies of the effects of sex education show that a course or unit based on facts and discussion raises the age at which young people first have sexual intercourse. Thus, far from just "putting ideas in students' heads," the courses help them to understand that full sexual experience is a serious thing and that there's a lot more to sexuality than just "doing it"—that it's a matter to be carefully and thoughtfully considered.

Teachers of Sex Education

Who should teach about human sexuality? Not necessarily the persons with the most factual knowledge. Facts can be mastered rather quickly by people chosen and trained to teach. Nor should teaching about human sexuality be the monopoly of any traditional field. It can become integral to courses in English, history, social studies, biology, general science, physical education, health, or family life.

People who teach sex education should:

• be able to communicate simply, openly, and truthfully with boys and girls.

• feel unembarrassed by any aspect of the topic and comfortable in a dialogue-centered classroom.

• be secure in their own sexual feelings and have developed for themselves a set of values that they feel confident about but do not preach or try to impose.

• be skilled in facilitating discussion and especially be able to resist talking too much, giving all the answers, or providing advice.

• be ready to acknowledge that there are things they don't know (which makes it easier for the students to admit that there are things *they* don't know).

• be able to maintain a nonjudgmental attitude, especially about things they feel strongly about, for criticism of student ideas about sexual behavior will destroy rapport and communication. Rather let the students criticize themselves.

• absolutely respect each student's right to silence and to privacy. (Also, certainly any faculty member who does not feel comfortable in discussing matters of sexuality and sexual behavior with a class should not be asked to do so.)

TRAINING IN TEACHING ABOUT HUMAN SEXUALITY

When courses in human sexuality are provided in schools, churches, and other institutions, parents are right and prudent to inquire who will be teaching these courses and what their training and qualifications are. In recent years more and more courses in human sexuality and sex education have been offered by universities, special institutions, school districts, and other professional organizations. These courses train school and university teachers, doctors, nurses, clergy, and social workers. It is important that teachers and schools be wary of courses that are taught from a biased or propagandistic point of view.

Rather than attempt to list here some of the hundreds of courses now available, we suggest that readers write to SIECUS (Sex Information and Education Council of the U.S.), New York University, 32 Washington Place, New York, NY 10003, or telephone them at 1-212-673-3850. SIECUS will send, at modest cost, a list of available courses.

The Relationship Between Sex Education Programs and the Home

Some parents fear that teaching outside the home about human sexuality will somehow take from them their right and duty to bring up their children to believe and behave as they, the parents, want them to. Parents who feel this way can be assured that a school's provision for sex education does not mean it is attempting to take over the parents' role as the primary sex educators of their children. As far as sex education is concerned, educators see it as their job to supplement and complement the education that has been going on at home since the birth of each child. When schools follow guidelines like those suggested earlier in this chapter, there is no danger. The real dangers lie in the unplanned, distorted, sensationalized messages of society, whose onslaught on children is continuous, and in the gossip, rumors, and assorted revelations of fact and fancy that circulate among young people of school age. Many children need help from the school as well as from their families in the task of separating fact from distortion and in making judgments in the light of full scientific information and in the perspective of open discussion.

THE SCHOOL'S OBLIGATIONS TOWARD THE PARENTS

To deserve and win the confidence of parents, schools should provide full information in advance about any sex education program, so that parents may know what its objectives are and what to expect. Parents should have an opportunity to see and comment on all materials to be used, to hear an explanation of the teaching methods, to know how the teachers have been trained, and to be told exactly when their children will be studying a given unit on sex education. (The *when* is important because it enables parents to take advantage of the school's program to open up discussion at home. Otherwise children sometimes will say nothing about it, and good chances for communication will be lost.)

If some parents do not want their children to participate in the program, the school should respect this wish and furnish an alternative, even if it is only a supervised study period. Sex education is a sensitive area for some parents, and thus it should remain optional. Experience across the nation has shown that, given this option, 1 to 2 percent of parents ask that their children not participate.

The school should be open to parents' suggestions and objections, and to acting upon those that give promise of improvement.

HOW PARENTS CAN ENCOURAGE SOUND PROGRAMS

Many teachers and especially school administrators hesitate to start a sex education program for fear that parents will object. So if parents want to have a sex education program in their school, we suggest that they first discuss the matter with other parents who are likely to feel the same way. Then, very early in the process, they should talk with the principal or superintendent to find out what his or her thoughts are, to explain their views, and to ask for advice on how to proceed. The administrator will appreciate being brought in at the earliest stages. Next, the parents may want to assemble an informal committee of lay and professional people—some teachers, perhaps a doctor or two, some clergy, maybe a couple of lawyers and other professional people, some school administrators, a cross section of parents, and perhaps one or two thoughtful eleventh- or twelfth-graders.

It would be unwise to prescribe a course of action from this point on. What parents do will depend on the community and on people's attitudes and convictions. They may find that once the administrators know that a responsible group of parents is ready to back them, they will go ahead and take the necessary steps themselves, keeping parents informed. Or they may want to continue to have parents involved up until the program is established. Of course, no such program is ever finally established, for it will need modification over the years, as those involved gain experience, as conditions in the community change, and as new research knowledge becomes available.

Furthermore, we must remember that no sex education program can succeed if it goes beyond what the community is ready or can be educated to accept. This does not mean giving in to the objections of a small group of determined objectors (whose children, as we suggested, need not participate); it means letting the program grow, with guidance and organization, out of the values of the community itself and its sense of what it needs. Many a program has been wrecked because it was launched without the necessary preliminary discussions or because those teaching it allowed themselves to get out of touch with the community.

If some parents have been influential in getting a program started, it is important for them to remember that it is the school people who will be carrying out the program. Once the climate of acceptance is created and communicated to the school, the detailed development of the program and its teaching are the professional responsibility of the school, not of the parents. It is, however, the responsibility of the school and the parents to keep their communication going, so that parents never feel things are happening behind their backs.

WHAT TO DO IF YOU AS A PARENT HAVE OBJECTIONS

If you have objections to the school program, what is the best way to get heard and to get constructive results? First, be sure you have the facts straight. The first place to go for information is your own child. Find out as calmly as possible exactly what took place. (But remember what one teacher reportedly said to parents at a first PTA meeting: "If you will promise not to believe everything your children tell you happens at school, I'll promise not to believe everything they tell me happens at home.")

If your objection is to something said by another student in class, think twice before doing anything. The school is not responsible for what children say in class, only for how this is dealt with by the teacher. In a healthy school discussion of human sexuality, many points of view will be expressed by different children. This is good because young people must develop discrimination and skills in dealing with opinions and assertions they come in contact with and, putting them into proper perspective, in deciding whether they agree or disagree and why.

If you wish, you might check with another parent to see if you are the only one who is disturbed, but be sure that the other parent is responsible and unexcitable. It is never a good idea to call ten parents and ask, for example, "Did you hear that Mrs. X is having those sixth-graders look at illustrated, dirty sex books and discuss them, and what are we going to do about it?"

If you are sure of your facts and still firm in your objection, the best policy is first to make an appointment with the teacher concerned. After talking together, both you and the teacher may be better educated about the feelings and purposes of the other, and the matter may be settled right there. If the teacher does not want to talk with you, or if you do not feel satisfied after you talk, then it would be well to ask to see the principal, not as a threat but as a way of getting the objection dealt with sensibly. There's no doubt that teachers do from time to time make errors in judgment—they're as human as anyone else.

Only rarely are there situations that cannot be resolved by frank, calm discussion. If you feel you must organize support for your view, do it with the full knowledge of the school authorities and the officers of the PTA, so that the discussions can be well-informed and constructive action will be likely to result.

If you are a parent who feels that a small group of people is making a large fuss over a minor event, and if you basically agree with the school and disagree with the objectors, let the school know and offer your help if it is needed. Too often the strident protests of a small group of parents, or even of outside people, have weakened or wrecked a good sex education program because those who were in favor of it did not make themselves known.

Sex Education Programs Outside the School

According to the best estimates, about half of American students are offered planned sex education in school, and that half includes those whose courses deal only with the facts of human reproduction, plus some information on the dangers and treatment of diseases, with very little opportunity for the kinds of discussion of human sexuality that we have been talking about. Since some teachers, administrators, and school boards are afraid or unwilling to provide adequate sex education in the schools—often because they feel they have enough troubles without facing the objections of the minority of parents who oppose it—we can be thankful that there are other ways to provide opportunities for boys and girls to learn about and discuss human sexuality under expert leadership and outside the home. Many churches and other religious organizations offer excellent, carefully planned programs, as do the YWCA and the YMCA, the Big Brother Association, the educational outreach departments of some hospitals, and many Planned Parenthood affiliates.

If you find that no schools in your community provide sex education acceptable to you, we suggest that you investigate other community organizations to see what they can offer. You may find it possible to join forces with other parents and families to encourage organizations with which you have connections to provide what is needed. And there is always SIECUS as a source of information (see page 205).

Planned programs of sex education to complement the education at home are not panaceas. They can inform, enhance communication, and put matters in perspective, but they are not likely, by themselves, to transform a selfish, exploitative person into a responsible and altruistic one or to free a fearful person from crippling inhibition and guilt, although they might provide nudges in these directions. We think, though, that the results can be more than merely modest. Stated briefly, good sex education can develop in boys and girls knowledge and attitudes that will enable them to make sound choices about the use of their sexual powers—choices that are intelligent, because they are based on solid information; responsible, because they are made in light of all possible consequences; and moral, because they are not harmful to the decision-makers themselves or to any others involved, now or in the future. In this way, young people will begin to learn not to fear the sexual part of their natures, but to understand and accept it, and to be prepared to manage it and use it as a part of life and for the good of life.

12
Making Sexual Decisions

This chapter is addressed to young people especially. What kind of sexual person would you like to be, and how can you become that kind of person?

In his play *Hamlet*, Shakespeare wrote:

> This above all: to thine own self be true,
> And it must follow, as the night the day,
> Thou canst not then be false to any man.

What does it mean to be true to your own self in all that concerns sexuality? Does it mean telling the truth to yourself? That certainly is part of it—actually the very first step in decision-making. Lying or fabricating to oneself about sexuality makes it impossible to get a clear and true picture of it, especially if you need to make clear-cut and well-grounded decisions about your sexual life. Insisting on remaining ignorant of the known facts about human sexuality also leads to difficulties in decision-making. That is why in this book our aim has been to present only the facts about sex and sexuality now known through responsible research. So the first question is: How best are you going to use the facts that you read in this book and elsewhere or that you experience? The answer lies largely with you, for no one else can answer your questions as well for you as yourself.

Next comes a second question: How well do you know yourself? Well enough to predict how you will make decisions about sexual situations in the light of all the facts? And are you strong enough to carry out what you decide? What kind of sexual person would you like to turn out to be—or turn into from what you already are?

Of course, it is possible to get away with making very few decisions at all in life about anything, to slide along and live from day to day, taking what comes and doing things on impulse. Most people can get away with this when it comes to unimportant things, but should such an important thing as your sexual life be left to chance and luck?

Or maybe you could choose to drift along about sexual decisions as long as you are the only person involved. But sooner or later, sex almost always involves at least one other person, and as soon as that happens things change. Involving someone else in your life, especially sexually, means that you are affecting the life of that person as well as your own. Are you ready and able to accept responsibility for that?

Feeling comfortable about yourself as a sexual person is important. But how do you decide what's right and what's wrong about sex? How do any of us decide what we'll think or imagine or wish or feel or do about our sexuality? As with most of our actions—past, present, and future—there are only two ways of answering these questions: One is, when a moment for sexual decision descends on us, to rely on inspiration, intuition, or impulse, and hope for a good answer, one we can feel comfortable with for the rest of our lives. The second is to develop a set of moral values that we would choose for governing all our life's actions and relationships, including the sexual ones. Once we are aware of what these values are, and have accepted them for ourselves, nothing should be able to catch us off base; that extraordinary computer, our brain, can sort out the elements in any decision we face, including a sexual one, test these elements against the values we have set for ourselves, and give us an answer. That answer may not be the one we would like it to be at a given moment, and so we may try to put it through the computer again. But we must face the results of our reasoning process honestly, and this is where knowing ourselves is so important. How good are you at accepting responsibility for your actions, at being aware of how what you do or think can affect others?

To be involved with others every day in your activities is inevitable, and the involvement is tinged with sexuality, for you relate to each other never as a non-woman or a non-girl or a non-man or a non-boy but always, in part, as the sexual person you are, female or male. How you relate, though, depends on the kind of person you are—dependable or not dependable, honest or cheating, willing or unwilling to take advantage of others, caring or not caring, open to learning or closed to it. And the kind of person you are is always reflected in the way you go about making your decisions, especially those that affect other people's lives.

There are certain ethical principles that are basic to all the great religions: respect for human life and dignity; putting yourself in the other's place; and modifying your actions and demands to fit the rights and needs of others, even though this may interfere with or postpone your own immediate wants. The Hebrew Scriptures—the Old Testament—put it this way: "Thou shalt love they neighbor as thyself" (Leviticus 19:18). In the New Testament, Jesus of Nazareth put it this way: "All things whatsoever ye would that men should do to you, do ye even so to them" (Matthew 7:12).

Treating others as you would like them to treat you is easier said than done, whether we're talking about little things or big things. Sex is a big thing for almost everyone, and when another person is involved, it becomes much bigger. When you knowingly risk involving not one but two persons in your sexual life, the need to make moral decisions rather than purely selfish ones is imperative. For example, sexual activity risks pregnancy. Each year in the United States, an estimated 1 million young women under the age of nineteen, or 1 out of 10, become pregnant, and 600,000 of these young women deliver babies. This is still happening, at the rate of almost 20,000 pregnancies every week in girls under nineteen—20,000 babies conceived, usually unwanted, most of whom, if they are carried full-term and are born, will have to be cared for by persons other than the unmarried teenage boy and girl who begot them.

Mature thinking would have meant avoiding intercourse, or protecting against pregnancy by taking the trouble to use contraceptives, because a baby really needs two people to bring it up—a mother and a father who can take care of it until it has reached the age of eighteen at least. Using this reasoning, the couple would have shown awareness that their actions did not involve just themselves, but might also harm a third person—a baby brought into the world when they were not ready to be a real mother and father to it.

Learning how to reason in arriving at decisions can help you develop a system of moral values to rely on in making sexual decisions, not only to analyze your own reasoning processes, but also to see how other people reason. Research has found that most people seem to prefer to accept a set of rules someone else has made, although they may not always be able to live up to those rules. Mere rule-minding spares such people from having to think out carefully *why* they are or are not going to do a certain thing. However, if the rules are good and the circumstances favorable, reasoning by rules may work.

But in a very real sense, moral decision-making, whether about your sexual actions or about anything else, must eventually involve growing beyond unthinking obedience to rules. It requires accepting responsibility for thinking through your own wishes, needs, decisions, and actions in the light of the needs of all the other persons involved, and it requires using the rules you have made and tested and live by. That is your responsibility to yourself—and to the world you live in.

Concise A–to–Z Encyclopedia

In the main chapters of this book we tell in as readable and connected a way as possible everything that members of a family might be interested in finding out about human sexuality. But people often want to know about a specific matter, and quickly. Arranged alphabetically, the items in this Encyclopedia will help you find out immediately what you need to know. Many of the subjects are also discussed in the main part of this book more completely or in a different context. Refer to the General Index to find where else in the book a subject is discussed.

Words set in SMALL CAPITAL LETTERS the first time they appear in an entry are also separate entries in the Encyclopedia. Look them up for more information as you need to.

A

ABDOMEN. The area of the human body, both the external part and and the internal cavity, that lies between the diaphragm and the PELVIS; the belly.

ABNORMAL. Not average, typical, or usual. The word is carelessly and often harmfully used to label unfavorably certain sexual behaviors or conditions of which the person doing the labeling may not approve. Two other words carelessly used as put-downs are *deviant* and *perverted.* The best word to use scientifically is *variant,* which is a neutral descriptive term meaning "different." *See also* NORMAL; UNNATURAL

ABORTION. The premature expulsion or removal from the UTERUS of the products of CONCEPTION, that is, of a FERTILIZED EGG, an EMBRYO, or a FETUS. A *spontaneous abortion,* often called a MISCARRIAGE, is an abortion that occurs without intention on the part of the PREGNANT woman and without the use of any artificial method. An *induced abortion* is one intentionally brought about by medical or surgical means. A *self-induced abortion* is one deliberately brought about by the pregnant woman herself, usually by methods that are dangerous and can result in her illness or death. *Therapeutic abortion* is a medical term used for an abortion induced to protect the life or health of the prospective mother or to prevent the birth of a baby likely to be deformed or incurably diseased. *See also* DILATATION AND CURETTAGE; SALINE ABORTION; VACUUM ASPIRATION.

ABSTINENCE. Abstaining from any action. With respect to sex, it generally refers to not having SEXUAL INTERCOURSE. Abstinence is one of the principal methods of CONTRACEPTION, especially by people before they are married. *Periodic abstinence* during that part of a woman's MENSTRUAL CYCLE when she is FERTILE—that is, may become PREGNANT—is the basis for the method of CONTRACEPTION called NATURAL FAMILY PLANNING. Note that abstaining from sexual activity does not necessarily mean abstaining from sexual urges. *Permanent abstinence* is held by some religious groups to be the only holy way to deal with one's SEXUALITY, as with nuns and priests, for example. *See also* CELIBACY; CHASTITY.

ACNE. A condition of the skin, especially of the face, that causes pimples, often rather deep ones. It seems to be the result of the chemical changes in the body during PUBERTY, when the oil glands in the skin begin secreting increased amounts of an oily substance that clogs the pores. The condition is more common in boys than in girls and, fortunately, is usually temporary. Although it is generally more noticeable to the sufferer than to his or her friends, it can be very embarrassing while it lasts. The severity of acne can be lessened by frequent washing of the skin with soap and water, which helps to unclog the pores. If acne becomes severe (with many painful, deep swellings), infections and scars may result. Therefore, if acne persists, the young person should seek a doctor's advice about treatment. A simple, well-balanced diet with ample fruits and vegetables and a minimum of sweets and fats can help reduce or avoid acne. There is no connection between acne and sexual activity, except that acne and the beginnings of desire for sexual satisfaction both happen to come at about the same time in the lives of most persons.

ACQUIRED IMMUNE DEFICIENCY SYNDROME. *See* AIDS.

ADOLESCENCE. From the Latin *adolescere* (to grow up). The period of time between PUBERTY and adulthood, when a person is neither a child nor an adult but at various times behaves in ways characteristic of either or both.

ADOPTION. The process by which a person, usually a child, is legally made a part of a family into which he or she was not born. The person can be of any age from newborn up and can be a blood relative, relative by marriage, relative by out-of-wedlock birth, or someone unrelated to the adoptive parents. Adoption meets the needs of an unwed mother who does not want to or is unable to raise her own child and does not wish to have an ABORTION. When children are adopted, they have full legal rights as members of their adoptive family. Most adoptions in the United States are arranged through licensed social agencies, although quite a few are arranged by physicians or lawyers. Before a social agency approves an adoption, it makes a thorough investigation to be sure that the family will be a good one for a child to grow up in; in most states the child spends a trial period of from six to twelve months in the adoptive family before the adoption is made final. Adoption agencies generally agree that parents should tell their child that he or she has been adopted, although there is no agreement as to what age is best for this. Children should be told as soon as they are old enough to understand, certainly before they go to school, and they should be told as simply and naturally as possible.

ADULTERY. The historic and legal term for SEXUAL INTERCOURSE between a married person and someone who is not his or her wife or husband. Another term for it is extramarital sexual intercourse. Adultery was formerly one of the few grounds for DIVORCE; today, however, irreversible breakdown of the MARRIAGE, rather than adultery, is generally accepted as more realistic and humane grounds for divorce. *See also* EXTRAMARITAL SEX.

AFFAIR. A romantic relationship, usually but not always of brief duration, between two people who are not married to each other.

AFTERBIRTH. The product of the third stage of labor, when the UTERUS expels the PLACENTA and with it the sacs or coverings that contained the amniotic fluid in which the baby floated during GESTATION. In most mammals, the afterbirth is usually eaten, for it provides the mother with HORMONES that stimulate the milk flow to nourish the baby animal. In humans, the afterbirth is disposed of.

AIDS (ACQUIRED IMMUNE DEFICIENCY SYNDROME). A SEXUALLY TRANSMITTED DISEASE first recognized in the United States in 1981. It causes the body to lose its immunity to disease. By 1993 there will have been about 450,000 AIDS victims in the United States, of whom about 300,000 will have died. The fatal disease is spreading rapidly throughout the world, especially among HOMOSEXUAL men and people who share intravenous drug needles. *Causes:* exchange of SEMEN or blood with a person infected with HIV (human immunodeficiency virus). AIDS is not caught by ordinary family living together, sharing utensils or bathrooms, coughing, sneezing, etc. *Symptoms:* fevers, sweats, extreme tiredness, dry coughs, swollen GLANDS, weight loss, white coating on tongue and in mouth. *Time from contact to first symptoms:* from a few days to many years. *Method of diagnosis:* since 1985, a highly reliable blood test for the HIV virus. (Many people, however, test positive but do not come down with full-blown AIDS; nevertheless, they might infect others.) *Complications:* a long, anguished period of decline and inevitable death. No vaccine against or cure for AIDS has been discovered, nor is expected for a number of years. Death in AIDS patients often is caused from a kind of pneumonia or a cancer of the blood vessels. AIDS is one of the world's worst health problems, although it is incorrect to call it a "plague" in the ordinary sense, since, except for babies of AIDS-infected mothers, individuals must perform a definite action to catch it.

ALCOHOL AND SEX. Many people believe that alcohol increases SEXUAL DESIRE and the ability to perform sexually. Actually, alcohol is a depressant, and its initial effect is to depress feelings of shyness, inhibition, and control. Thus people whose tensions, worries, and emotional conflicts about sex prevent them from relaxing and enjoying it may be helped by a modest intake of alcoholic beverage. But taking more than a moderate amount of alcohol in a sexual situation may also seriously impair judgment and good sense and cause a person to do things that he or she will later regret. For young and inexperienced persons, it is certainly foolish to mix alcohol and sex. Far from improving sexual performance, too much alcohol has actually been found to be a major cause of decreasing a man's capacity to have an ERECTION and a woman's ability to have an ORGASM.

AMNIOCENTESIS. A procedure by which a doctor inserts a hollow needle into the ABDOMEN directly through the wall of the PREGNANT UTERUS and into the amniotic fluid surrounding the FETUS to draw out a small sample. Analysis of this fluid can in certain cases provide information important to the coming child's welfare—for instance, whether the child will be a male or female. But unless there is a very high probability of a GENDER-linked genetic disorder, the procedure is very seldom done for this purpose, because any such procedure has some, but slight, risks: possible infection, possible damage to the fetus, and possible induced ABORTION. *See also* GENETIC COUNSELING.

AMNIOTIC SAC. Also called the *amnion.* The thin membrane within the cavity of the UTERUS forming a closed "bag of waters" that surrounds the developing baby during PREGNANCY and cushions it from bumps and shocks. The "waters" are called *amniotic fluid* and, during LABOR, rupture of the sac allows the fluid escaping through the VAGINA to act as a LUBRICANT for the passage of the baby.

ANAL INTERCOURSE. A form of SEXUAL INTERCOURSE in which the PENIS is inserted into the partner's ANUS. It is practiced by HETEROSEXUAL as well as HOMOSEXUAL couples as one of the ways of having sexual pleasure. It is one of three forms of sexual activity to which various states apply the legal term SODOMY. Unless considerable care is taken about soap-and-water cleanliness, anal intercourse preceding intercourse through the VAGINA can result in vaginal or URINARY TRACT infections. Because the blood vessels in the anus are very delicate, inserting an erect penis is likely to break them and cause bleeding. Thus SEMEN and blood become mixed. This explains why anal intercourse is a likely way to spread the disease AIDS. CONDOMS may reduce the risk slightly, but they are likely to break as a result of the strenuous stretching involved in anal intercourse.

ANDROGEN. The HORMONE that produces the male sex characteristics and influences the growth and development of the male body. It is also responsible for the level of SEXUAL DESIRE (LIBIDO) in both male and female. Derives from the Greek word *andros* (man). *See also* ESTROGEN; TESTOSTERONE.

ANDROGYNOUS. Containing or exhibiting the characteristics of both sexes; BISEXUAL, not specific to male or female. The word can refer to physical characteristics, to behavior, to clothing, etc. It is a combination of the Greek words *andros* (man) and *gynē* (woman).

ANUS. The opening in the human body leading from the lower end of the intestines to the outside. Through this opening passes the solid refuse of digestion (bowel movements, or feces) in the process called defecation. See diagrams on pages 34 and 41.

APHRODISIAC. Any substance that is believed to stimulate SEXUAL DESIRE, such as odors (see PHEROMONES) or certain foods or drugs. For centuries, people have searched for substances that would increase sexual excitement, but not one has been found that works consistently or safely. It has been said that the most important sex organ is "between the ears" and that, therefore, if a person really believes a certain substance will increase sexual desire then it probably will, at least temporarily. Some substances that have enjoyed popularity over the years are potatoes, oysters, ground rhinoceros horns, pigs' testes, finely ground beetles, and peanuts. Some drugs are considered by uninformed persons to be aphrodisiacs when in fact they are not. The best advice is not to search for a magic aphrodisiac substance, because disappointment and possibly danger will almost certainly result. The best aphrodisiacs are good health, good diet, positive attitudes toward SEXUALITY, freedom from emotional tension, and a partner who turns you on and is turned on by you. See also ALCOHOL AND SEX.

ARTIFICIAL INSEMINATION. The injection of SEMEN into the VAGINA or UTERUS by means of a syringe. The procedure is used to inseminate a woman who desires a child but who may be unable to conceive one by means of SEXUAL INTERCOURSE, perhaps because her husband's SPERM COUNT is too low or of poor quality. The semen may be collected from several EJACULATIONS by MASTURBATION, quick-frozen, and stored in a glycerine solution until sufficient sperm have been collected. Then the collection is used to inseminate the wife. If the husband produces practically no sperm at all, donor sperm from another man—who is usually anonymous—may be used, with the consent of both husband and wife. It can be taken from a SPERM BANK or directly from a donor who is known only to the physician performing the insemination, never to the woman being inseminated or to her husband.

AXILLARY HAIR. Hair under the arms. Its first appearance is one of the signs of approaching PUBERTY. Axillary hair usually appears somewhat later than the first PUBIC HAIR.

B

BASAL BODY TEMPERATURE (BBT). The usual body temperature. In many but not all cases, a woman's BBT rises just after OVULATION and remains elevated until she next menstruates. Using a special BBT thermometer, if a woman takes her temperature at the same time each day, preferably immediately upon waking up in the morning and before getting out of bed, and keeps a chart of her readings, she may be able to tell when she has ovulated. The BBT method of NATURAL FAMILY PLANNING is more useful for telling when ovulation *has* occurred than for predicting when it *will* occur. Minor illnesses like colds or even emotional stress can throw off the normal BBT pattern. *See also* NATURAL FAMILY PLANNING.

BIRTH CANAL. The passage in the female body through which the baby is pushed during the process of being born, in other words, the VAGINA. It begins at the exit from the UTERUS, that is, the upper end of the cervical canal (*see* CERVIX), and ends at the outer opening of the vagina. In all, it is not more than 3 or 4 inches in length. See the drawings on pages 39 and 64. The walls of the birth canal are capable of expanding greatly to accommodate the baby's head.

BIRTH CONTROL. *See* CONTRACEPTION.

BISEXUAL. Sexual attraction both to people of one's own sex and of the other sex, or a person so attracted. It is likely that most people in their FANTASIES, even though not in their actual sexual behavior, have bisexual potentiality. People who are bisexual may vary in the kind of bisexuality, at times preponderantly active with their own sex, at other times preponderantly active with the other sex.

BLADDER (URINARY). An expandable, muscular sac into which the two kidneys secrete urine through tubes called *ureters.* The urine is accumulated in the bladder until the sensation of pressure leads to emptying by urination through the URETHRA. The opening and closing of the urethra is controlled by two muscles, the internal and the external urinary sphincters. The urinary bladder is not related to the gallbladder. *See also* CYSTITIS.

BREASTFEEDING. The feeding of an infant at the BREAST. Bottles for the artificial feeding of infants are often called nursing bottles. Breastfeeding is being more and more recognized as somewhat better than bottle-feeding for two reasons: (1) physically, breastfed infants tend to develop better; and (2) psychologically, the bond between mother and baby that is so important to both of them tends to be established more strongly and faster than it is with artificial feeding. However, most bottle-fed babies do thrive, and the mother-baby bond can be established if the baby is held closely and cuddled while it nurses from the bottle.

BREASTS. Two milk-producing organs on a woman's chest, known also as *mammary glands.* The breasts contain many lobules (sacs) which, after a woman gives birth and is breastfeeding her baby, manufacture milk. The milk is led by many small ducts to a small reservoir just under the NIPPLE, so the baby has a constant supply to suck. As the time for giving birth approaches, the breasts' glandular tissue increases to supply more milk. Women with small breasts are just as successful at nursing their babies as those with large breasts. The pink or brown area surrounding the nipple is called the *areola.* The breasts of women—and of men—are EROGENOUS ZONES. In our society there is preoccupation with breast size as a symbol of the supposed sexiness of a woman. There is, however, absolutely no relation between the size of a woman's breasts and the degree of her SEXUAL DESIRE. Preoccupation with breast size on the part of both women and men is unfortunate, since it is unconnected with the meaningful aspects of relationships between them, sexual and otherwise.

BROTHEL. A house of PROSTITUTION.

C

CALENDAR METHOD. A method of NATURAL FAMILY PLANNING based on a woman's carefully keeping a record of the date each MENSTRUAL PERIOD begins. Theoretically, this enables her to estimate when OVULATION will occur, so that she and her partner know when to abstain from SEXUAL INTERCOURSE if they do not wish her to become PREGNANT. The method works fairly satisfactorily only for those couples in which the woman has a regular MENSTRUAL CYCLE. However, absolute menstrual regularity can rarely be counted on, since stress, fatigue, or even a cold can unexpectedly lengthen or shorten the cycle. *See also* NATURAL FAMILY PLANNING.

CALL GIRL. A female PROSTITUTE with whom an appointment may be arranged by a telephone call.

CARNAL. A word deriving from the Latin word *carnalis* (fleshly). Generally used in the sense of "having to do with the pleasures of the flesh," principally sexual activity. "Carnal knowledge" means SEXUAL INTERCOURSE, especially in legal or biblical language.

CASTRATE. To remove the SEX GLANDS—the TESTICLES in a male, the OVARIES in a female. Castration of males used to be a method of STERILIZATION, but VASECTOMY has taken its place. Castration has also been used as punishment for sex criminals, and it still is in some of the less developed parts of the world. Castration can be necessary to save the life of a man who develops cancer of the testicles, and this often results in the loss of SEXUAL DESIRE.

CELIBACY. Voluntary ABSTINENCE from SEXUAL INTERCOURSE. Historically there has been a strong current in Christianity and in some other religions to attribute nobility and holiness to the celibate way of life. Catholic priests and nuns take vows of celibacy. (In the case of nuns, it is usually called a vow of chastity.) *See also* ABSTINENCE; CHASTITY.

CERVICAL CAP. A CONTRACEPTIVE device, 1 inch in diameter, made of latex. It fits over the base of the CERVIX. Used with a SPERMICIDE, it prevents the passage of SPERM into the UTERUS.

CERVIX. The lower end or neck of the UTERUS; constitutes the passage between the uterus and the VAGINA. SPERM pass upward through the cervix and into the uterus during and after SEXUAL INTERCOURSE, unless certain methods of CONTRACEPTION block the passage. In the other direction, from uterus to vagina, pass the MENSTRUAL FLOW and, during birth, the baby. The cervix's powerful muscle holds the FETUS in the uterus until birth, when the cervix relaxes to become an extraordinarily flexible passageway.

CESAREAN SECTION. Also called *cesarean birth.* Delivery of a child by means of a surgical incision through the ABDOMINAL wall and the UTERUS. A cesarean is performed when the doctor determines that childbirth via the BIRTH CANAL may be dangerous to the mother or the baby. This might be because the mother's bony PELVIC opening is too small or the baby's head too large to permit a normal birth, or because the baby is positioned in the uterus in such a way that the birth would be very difficult. In the United States, about 6 percent of all births are cesarean, and cesarean babies develop just as well as those born the usual way. A mother may have several children by this means; occasionally, a cesarean birth may be followed at another time by a normal birth. (The name cesarean comes from that of Roman Emperor Julius Caesar, who according to tradition was born by this method.)

CHANCROID (pronounced SHAN-kroid). One of the SEXUALLY TRANSMITTED DISEASES. Occurs most often in men. Also called *soft chancre,* as distinguished from the firm, "hard" chancre of SYPHILIS. *Cause:* bacteria *(Hemophilus ducreyi). Symptoms:* one or more shallow, painful sores on the GENITALS, which bleed easily. Usually causes painful enlargement of lymph nodes in the GROIN, which may break open and drain pus. *Time from contact to first symptoms:* one week or less. *Method of diagnosis:* microscopic examination. *Complications:* can destroy tissues of the genitals.

CHANGE OF LIFE. A now rather old-fashioned term for MENOPAUSE and CLIMACTERIC. Change of life refers mainly to that time when a woman ceases to OVULATE and MENSTRUATE, commonly between forty-five and fifty-five years of age. Many people used to assume that along with a woman's loss of capacity to become PREGNANT went a loss of SEXUAL DESIRE and attractiveness. Now we know that this is not necessarily so. *See also* CLIMACTERIC; MENOPAUSE.

CHANGE OF VOICE. The lowering of the voice in boys during PUBERTY. Increased male HORMONE from the TESTICLES makes the voice box grow larger, resulting in a lower voice. At the same time, the ADOLESCENT boy's whole body usually undergoes a rapid spurt of growth. Most commonly, the change of voice becomes noticeable some time after a boy's first EJACULATION of SEMEN. While a boy is adjusting to his new voice, he has a tendency toward sudden, brief breaks into falsetto. This experience should not be, but too often is, cause for embarrassing jokes and laughter by those who hear it. Girls have a similar deepening and maturing of the voice at puberty, but not in such an obvious way.

CHASTITY. The state of being chaste; abstention from SEXUAL INTERCOURSE. The word comes from the Latin *caste* (pure, clean), and it implies a connection between sex and impurity or uncleanness, as if not having had sex means being pure and clean. The word is most commonly used in reference to women—nuns take vows of chastity, monks and priests vows of CELIBACY. In the Middle Ages some married women wore iron chastity belts, locked on by the husband to prevent his wife from having sexual intercourse during his absence.

CHILD MOLESTER (one who molests). A person, usually a man, HETEROSEXUAL or HOMOSEXUAL, who seeks sexual satisfaction from physical contact with young girls or boys. Often the children are not aware of what is really happening, for the molestation may be only simple touching of the GENITALS. Molesters behave compulsively in this respect and need help, but they are rarely dangerous. Most often they are older relatives or friends rather than strangers. Young people will do well to steer clear of contact or being alone with such people, and to go immediately to someone they can trust, to tell them about the experience. It will probably make them feel better, and it may make it possible for the molester to get help. A young person can be helped to know that the molesting was not his or her fault and that there is no reason to feel guilty about it. Child molestation is a crime against a minor (defined by the American Law Institute as a person under age sixteen), provided the molester is at least four years older than the child. About 38 million Americans have been sexually abused as children, and 10 percent of American males have abused a child. *See also* PEDOPHILIA.

CHLAMYDIA (pronounced kla-MID-ia). A SEXUALLY TRANSMITTED DISEASE that appears in various forms. It began in the tropics but now is the most common STD in the United States, affecting more than three million Americans a year, three times more than gonorrhea. *Cause:* a bacterial microorganism, *Chlamydia trachomatis.* The disease is still called NONGONOCOCCAL URETHRI-TIS (NGU) or nonspecific urethritis (NSU), "nonspecific" meaning that scientists originally really didn't know what caused it. *Symptoms:* in men, discharge from PENIS and burning sensation when urinating; burning and itching around opening of penis; symptoms may be very mild and come and go. In women, VAGINAL itching or discharge; chronic ABDOMINAL pain; bleeding between MENSTRUAL PERIODS; later, low-grade fever. Many women have no symptoms and if they think they have been exposed to chlamydia should be diagnosed by a doctor or at a clinic. *Time from contact to first symptoms:* two to four weeks (if there *are* symptoms). *Method of diagnosis:* special tests, accurate and painless, based on a CULTURE made from fluids taken from the URETHRA or CERVIX. *Complications and effects:* infection of the EPIDIDYMIS in men, the FALLOPIAN TUBES in women, sometimes causing scar tissue and STERILITY; PELVIC INFLAMMATORY DISEASE (PID); complications in pregnancy that may kill the baby and sometimes the mother; ear, eye, and lung infections in babies.

   The chlamydia organism also causes LYMPHOGRANULOMA VENEREUM (LGV).

CHROMOSOMES. Minute rod-shaped bodies in the nucleus of every living cell. The number and shapes of the chromosomes are characteristic for each plant or animal species of life. Each chromosome carries the thousands of GENES that determine the characteristics a person inherits from his or her parents. One pair of the chromosomes always determines the sex of the child: the mother's OVUM chromosome is always X, but the father's SPERM are of two kinds, X or Y. An X-bearing sperm uniting with the ovum (always X) will produce an XX, or female, baby. A Y-bearing sperm uniting with the X ovum will produce an XY, or male, baby. Thus it is the sperm from the male which determines the sex of the baby. *See also* HEREDITY.

CIRCUMCISION. A minor operation that removes the FORESKIN of a boy's or man's PENIS. In the United States it is usually done on the second day after birth. The operation is performed for reasons of cleanliness, appearance, custom, and, among Jews and Muslims, for religious reasons. The American Academy of Pediatrics now recommends against circumcision unless it is required by a family's religion. Despite that recommendation, many doctors still favor circumcision. In 1985 in the U.S.A., 59 percent of newborn boys were circumcised, down from 68 percent in 1979. Research has shown that circumcision in no way affects later sexual response.

CLIMACTERIC. The group of physical and psychological changes that occur around the time of MENOPAUSE in women, which is the time of reduced production of ESTROGEN, or female sex HORMONE. Climacteric, a very difficult phenomenon to define, both as to time and effects, can show itself in a combination of ills and miseries, both physical and emotional. In women, emotional effects are mostly related to loss of feelings of sexual adequacy. In some men, similar effects can be traced to a feared loss of sexual attractiveness and power. *See also* CHANGE OF LIFE; MENOPAUSE.

CLIMAX. The high point of sexual excitement and pleasure—whether during SEXUAL INTERCOURSE, SEX PLAY, MASTURBATION, FANTASY, or dreaming—when ORGASM is reached.

CLITORIS. The small, very sensitive, erectile organ in the female, located just in front of the opening of the URETHRA and under a hood at the top of the small lips of the VULVA. It becomes ERECT when the female is sexually stimulated. The nerve endings in the clitoris are quite similar to those in the head (GLANS) of the PENIS. Pleasurable stimulation of the clitoris is an important part of the process by which a woman reaches ORGASM. See drawing on page 41.

COHABITATION. Literally, living together. In terms of human sexuality, the term usually refers to a couple (sometimes more people than a couple) who live together, having SEXUAL INTERCOURSE, as a way of discovering whether or not they wish to marry. But many couples these days cohabit simply as a matter of pleasure and convenience, with no commitment to serious consideration of MARRIAGE.

COITUS. *See* SEXUAL INTERCOURSE.

COITUS INTERRUPTUS. *See* WITHDRAWAL METHOD.

COLOSTRUM. The substance ready in the BREAST of a mother immediately after birth, even before the infant has suckled. It is slight in amount, yellowish and watery but rich in protein, and helps the digestive system to begin normal functioning. It also provides the infant with immunity to infectious diseases during its first few months. Within two or three days after birth, the baby's sucking stimulates the breast GLANDS to make true milk that is more nutritious.

CONCEIVE. *See* CONCEPTION.

CONCEPTION. FERTILIZATION, the moment at which the SPERM and OVUM join, at which time the woman is said to have *conceived.*

CONDOM. Also called *rubber, prophylactic.* A sheath, usually made of rubber, which is placed over the ERECT PENIS before SEXUAL INTERCOURSE to prevent the EJACULATED SPERM from entering the VAGINA. If properly used, condoms are a very effective method of CONTRACEPTION and also provide quite good protection against SEXUALLY TRANSMITTED DISEASES.

CONTRACEPTION. The use of any device (CONDOMS, IUDs, DIAPHRAGMS), the PILL, VAGINAL SPERMICIDES, or action (WITHDRAWAL or NATURAL FAMILY PLANNING) designed to prevent CONCEPTION. Another term for contraception is *birth control.*

CONTRACEPTIVE. A device or medication used to prevent CONCEPTION. *See also* CONTRACEPTION.

COPULATION. SEXUAL INTERCOURSE. The term copulation is usually used to refer to the sexual activity of animals, sexual intercourse being used to refer to that of people.

COUNSELING. The formal or informal process by which a professional who has been trained in counseling talks with a person, couple, or family to help them become aware of and solve or manage their problems. Besides sex counseling, there are a number of kinds of counseling that might be related to human sexuality: MARRIAGE counseling, singles counseling, ABORTION counseling, CONTRACEPTIVE counseling, RAPE counseling, and various combinations of these. A distinction is usually made between the skills of counseling and those of therapy and the training necessary for each.

COWPER'S GLANDS. Two GLANDS in the male, one on each side of the URETHRA near the PROSTATE GLAND. Cowper's glands secrete a slippery substance that neutralizes any acid remaining from urine (which might kill sperm), becomes a part of the SEMEN, and sometimes oozes down the urethra after ERECTION of the PENIS and LUBRICATES its tip.

CRAB LICE. A sexually transmitted insect that lives in the warm, wet folds of the body and lays eggs on the PUBIC HAIR. Also called *pediculosis pubis, crabs, cooties, lice. Cause:* tiny lice and eggs (or "nits"); lice barely visible, nits invisible. *Symptoms:* intense itching, especially in pubic hair; pinhead blood spots on underwear. *Time from contact to first symptoms:* four to five weeks. *Method of diagnosis:* examination. *Complications:* none. *See also* SEXUALLY TRANSMITTED DISEASES.

CRUSH. A brief, romantic fixation or ir_atuation, often by a younger person toward an older person. Quite commonly the older person is entirely unaware that the younger "has a crush on" him or her. Crushes can be same-sex or other-sex. The concept of and behavior involved in the crush seems to some people old-fashioned, but it still happens.

CULTURE. In medical terms, a method of putting a sample of possible disease microorganisms onto a special gel surface (called an *agar plate*), where the germs, if any, are allowed to grow. When there are enough germs well enough developed to be examined under a microscope they can be identified, thus making it possible to prescribe treatment of the disease.

CUNNILINGUS. The act of using the tongue or mouth to stimulate the VULVA of a female, one sort of oral sex, a common practice for both HETEROSEXUAL couples and female HOMOSEXUAL couples, LESBIANS. The word derives from two Latin words, *cunnus* (vulva) and *lingere* (to lick). *See also* FELLATIO; ORAL-GENITAL SEX.

CURETTAGE. Emptying the UTERUS by means of a curette, a spoonlike instrument used for scraping. *See also* DILATATION AND CURETTAGE.

CYSTITIS. Infection and inflammation of the BLADDER caused by invasion of the bladder by bacteria, usually through the URETHRA. The symptoms are painful (burning) and frequent urination. It should always be treated by a doctor. Cystitis is more common in women than in men, because a woman's urethra is very short and therefore bacteria can easily and quickly enter the bladder.

D

D & C. *See* DILATATION AND CURETTAGE.

DELIVERY. The act of giving birth to a child, including the assistance given to the woman while she is delivering.

DES. Diethylstilbestrol, a strong ESTROGEN which used to be prescribed as a "MORNING-AFTER" CONTRACEPTIVE. Because of the danger of harm to the female offspring of women who took it while PREGNANT, it is now used only in emergency situations such as RAPE.

DEVIATION. A sexual behavior that is considered by the user of the word to be not "NORMAL." Deviation and sexual deviancy are terms that tend to be used as put-downs. Terms that are more scientific and less judgmental ones are *variance* and *variant. See also* ABNORMAL; VARIANT SEXUAL BEHAVIOR.

DIAPHRAGM. A CONTRACEPTIVE device—a round rubber cap—about 2 to 3 inches in diameter, which a woman places in her VAGINA to cover the CERVIX before having SEXUAL INTERCOURSE. Used with a SPERMICIDE (cream, jelly, or foam), it prevents SPERM from entering the cervix.

DIKE. Also *dyke.* A slang term for a female HOMOSEXUAL or LESBIAN.

DILATATION AND CURETTAGE. Often called *D & C.* Stretching open the CERVIX to permit surgical curettage, which means scraping out the lining of the UTERUS and any contents of the uterus. There are three primary reasons for a D & C: to diagnose possible disease, to correct habitual heavy bleeding during MENSTRUATION, and to perform an ABORTION. For abortion, the method has now been largely replaced by VACUUM ASPIRATION.

DILDO. An artificial ERECT PENIS. Dildoes are used by a man who is unable to achieve an ERECTION so as to give pleasure to his partner; by a woman for self-stimulation during MASTURBATION; or by two women for mutual stimulation.

DIVORCE. In the legal dissolution of a MARRIAGE, divorce releases both the husband and wife from all marital obligations to each other and returns them to the single state.

DNA. Deoxyribonucleic acid, a chemical substance making up the GENES that are carried on the CHROMOSOMES and that determine the inherited characteristics specific for each living organism.

DOUBLE STANDARD. The concept that there is one standard of sexual behavior for men and another for women. In the traditional double standard, society has tended to view PREMARITAL or EXTRAMARITAL SEX as acceptable for men but not for women, and to expect that men may actively seek many sexual contacts, whereas "nice" women will limit sex to marriage. The double standard is much less widely accepted in the United States now than it was a generation ago, but it still persists, often in subtle forms, despite the efforts of believers in equality of sexual rights, pleasures, and obligations to eradicate it. *See also* SEXISM.

DOUCHING. Cleansing or rinsing the VAGINA with a jet of liquid, usually squirted from a douche bag or syringe. A totally ineffective means of CONTRACEPTION, and unnecessary in the healthy vagina.

DYSFUNCTION. When used in connection with sexuality, the term means a problem that interferes with or prevents a satisfying sexual life. (The prefix *dys-* comes from a Greek word or affix meaning "bad" or "ill.") The most common sexual dysfunctions in the male are IMPOTENCE and PREMATURE EJACULATION, and in the female DYSPAREUNIA (painful SEXUAL INTERCOURSE), VAGINISMUS, and inability to reach ORGASM.

DYSMENORRHEA. Literally, painful MENSTRUATION, which may involve cramps, headache, backache, and nausea. The cramps are probably caused by spasms of the muscles of the UTERUS or CERVIX. In most cases, dysmenorrhea disappears after the age of twenty or after the birth of a woman's first child.

DYSPAREUNIA. Painful SEXUAL INTERCOURSE. The most common cause is fear, tension, and anxiety accompanying intercourse. This can make the VAGINAL muscles tighten. There are several medical causes possible that should be diagnosed only by a GYNECOLOGIST.

E

ECTOPIC PREGNANCY. A PREGNANCY in which the FERTILIZED OVUM IMPLANTS somewhere outside the UTERUS in the ABDOMINAL cavity. A pregnancy in a FALLOPIAN TUBE is known as a *tubal pregnancy*. The *ectopic* means "out of place," from the Greek words *ec* (out) and *topos* (place). The most common cause of ectopic pregnancies is scar tissue that is the result of an infection by GONORRHEA or other bacteria, so blocking the fallopian tube that, even if the SPERM can proceed up the tube, the much larger fertilized ovum is unable to pass down it and into the uterus to implant. An ectopic pregnancy is very painful and may cause death of the mother from bleeding, especially if the fallopian tube ruptures. It must be recognized early and terminated by surgery to avoid this.

EGG. *See* OVUM.

EJACULATE. To eject SEMEN from the PENIS at the male CLIMAX resulting from SEXUAL INTERCOURSE, MASTURBATION, NOCTURNAL EMISSION, or other sexual activity. Ejaculation comes in a series of quick spurts caused mainly by contractions of the PROSTATE GLAND and the muscles around it, as well as the muscles at the base of the penis. In a healthy man, one ejaculation contains about a teaspoonful of semen containing from 200 to 400 million SPERM.

EMBRYO. The unborn young from the time of IMPLANTATION in the UTERINE wall until, in human beings, about the end of the second month of PREGNANCY, after which it is known as a FETUS.

ENDOCRINE GLANDS. In contrast to GLANDS such as the salivary glands that deliver their product through ducts, the endocrine glands secrete their products, called HORMONES, directly into the bloodstream. The PITUITARY, adrenal, and thyroid glands are among these, as are the TESTICLES and OVARIES, which secrete the sex hormones TESTOSTERONE and ESTROGEN, respectively.

ENDOMETRIUM. The soft, velvety lining of the UTERUS, richly supplied with small blood vessels. Into this the FERTILIZED EGG implants itself and begins its development. If no egg is implanted, the lining, along with the blood and blood vessels that are a part of it, is discarded monthly through the process called MENSTRUATION.

ENGAGEMENT. A period during which a man and a woman have a formal understanding that they will be married at some time in the future. Engagement is usually marked by the gift of a ring from the man to the woman. It is looked upon as a period during which the betrothed (engaged) couple become better acquainted with each other as preparation for their eventual MARRIAGE.

EPIDIDYMIS (plural, epididymides). In the male, a collection of about a half mile of extraordinarily tiny tubes coiled behind and against each TESTICLE. In these tubes the SPERM that have been manufactured by the testicles are stored, to mature before they pass into the VAS DEFERENS, ready for EJACULATION. See the drawing on page 34. *See also* SEMEN.

EPISIOTOMY. A small surgical incision made in the PERINEUM, usually toward the end of the second stage of LABOR. This is done to enlarge the opening of the VAGINA and thus prevent the tissues from being overstretched and possibly tearing as the child's head emerges. After DELIVERY, while awaiting the AFTER-BIRTH, the OBSTETRICIAN stitches the episiotomy. Such clean incisions heal faster than would an accidental tear in the tissues.

ERECTION. Erection occurs when, during sexual stimulation, a supply of blood becomes temporarily trapped in the spongy tissues of a usually limp SEX ORGAN. Such stiffening and enlargement of the PENIS usually occurs as a result of sexual excitement. The CLITORIS also becomes erect during sexual stimulation, as do the NIPPLES. When the erection is over, the blood supply returns to the body. One interesting fact about male erection is that penises that are varying sizes when they are not erect all tend to approach approximately the same size in erection. Many boys and men, whose unerect penises vary in size, often worry unnecessarily about this, especially if their penises appear small in comparison to those of others. In any case, a large erect penis is a no more effective giver of pleasure, or of SEMEN and PREGNANCY, than a somewhat smaller erect penis.

The area of the VAGINA in which the pleasure-giving nerve endings are located is near its entrance, not far inside and near the CERVIX. Thus, whatever the size of the erect penis, it will stimulate that area.

EROGENOUS ZONES. These are the areas of the body which are especially sensitive to sexual excitement, such as the GENITALS, the BREASTS, the mouth, and the inside of the thighs. People vary in their responses, however, and almost any part of the body if touched or stroked in a sensual manner can prove to be an erogenous zone.

EROS. The ancient Greek god of love. When not capitalized, eros refers to SENSUAL love or SEXUAL DESIRE. The ancient Romans called this god Cupid.

EROTIC. Having to do with arousing SEXUAL DESIRE. Erotic material is anything—prose, poetry, pictures, music, perfume, etc.—that causes, or is designed to cause, sexual arousal. *See* PORNOGRAPHY.

ESTROGEN. One of two HORMONES produced by the OVARIES. It is the hormone that produces the female sex characteristics and affects the way a woman's MENSTRUAL CYCLE functions. Synthetic estrogen is one of the chemicals in the contraceptive PILL, which mimics the state of PREGNANCY and therefore suppresses OVULATION. Synthetic estrogen can be prescribed for older women during MENOPAUSE, when their ovaries cease to produce natural estrogen, to reduce the physical and psychological effects of menopause. Carefully prescribed doses of estrogens after menopause are an important method of preventing osteoporosis, a weakening of the bones due to the body's decreased ability to absorb calcium. This is called estrogen therapy.

EUNUCH. A CASTRATED male, that is, one whose TESTICLES have been removed. The word derives from the Greek words *eun* (bed) and *-ouchos* (keeping) and literally meant "guardian of the bed," when eunuchs were often used as guards of the women in harems.

EXHIBITIONIST. In the sexual sense, a male who feels a compulsion to expose his PENIS publicly and who derives sexual satisfaction from so doing. Such exhibitionists, often called "flashers," are almost always harmless and tend to keep a safe distance from their "victims." However, their activity often is disturbing and frightening to people who do not understand it, and to most people it is upsetting. Exhibitionism is a minor crime and more of a nuisance than a menace.

EXTRAMARITAL SEX. SEXUAL INTERCOURSE by a married person with someone other than his or her SPOUSE. The legal and religious term for it is ADULTERY. It should not be confused with PREMARITAL SEX (strictly speaking, sex before MARRIAGE between two people who expect to marry each other) and NON-MARITAL SEX (sex between two unmarried people who do not expect to marry each other).

F

FALLOPIAN TUBE. The tube or duct that extends from near each OVARY to the UTERUS. After an OVUM has been produced by the ovary, the FIMBRIAE and the tiny cilia of the tube wave it into the entrance and transport it toward the uterus. If on the way the ovum meets a SPERM, FERTILIZATION takes place, and the fertilized ovum (or ZYGOTE) begins its cell division and continues its trip down the tube, dividing into more and more cells as it goes. Each tube is from 4 to 8 inches long. At the uterine end, the passage is between $1/16$ and $1/8$ inch in diameter, about twenty times larger than an unfertilized ovum and large enough to allow the zygote to pass through into the uterus where it can IM-PLANT. See the drawing on page 39.

FAMILY PLANNING. Another term for BIRTH CONTROL or CONTRACEPTION. It consists of planning by a couple for the number of children they wish to have and for how far apart they should be spaced.

FANTASY. In sexual terms, fantasy means imagining scenes and events, usu-ally sexual and romantic, that rarely are actually carried out. Most people's sexual lives involve a lot of fantasy, though many feel needlessly guilty about it, for fantasies or dreams cannot be controlled and therefore we are not re-sponsible for these. Rather it is our *actions* for which we are responsible and which we need to learn to manage. For most people, an active sexual fantasy life is a harmless, indeed often beneficial, way of enriching their sexual satis-faction.

FELLATIO. Taking the PENIS into the mouth to give sexual satisfaction, one sort of oral sex. It is common practice for both HETEROSEXUAL and male HOMOSEX-UAL couples. *See also* CUNNILINGUS; ORAL-GENITAL SEX.

FEMINISM. Advocacy of legal, social, political, economic, and sexual rights of women to be equal to those of men. A *feminist* is a person, male or female, who advocates feminism. Another term for feminism, now seldom used, is "women's liberation."

FERTILE PERIOD. The days during a woman's MENSTRUAL CYCLE when she can become PREGNANT. *See* NATURAL FAMILY PLANNING.

FERTILITY. The state of being fertile, that is, capable of CONCEPTION. The opposite state is INFERTILITY or STERILITY.

FERTILITY AWARENESS. A term used especially by people involved in NATURAL FAMILY PLANNING. It refers to a woman's awareness that she is about to OVU-LATE or has ovulated.

FERTILITY TESTING. Various tests made to determine whether a man is capable of producing sufficient healthy SPERM to IMPREGNATE, or whether a woman is producing an OVUM every month so she can CONCEIVE.

FERTILIZATION. The moment of union of OVUM and SPERM that results in CONCEPTION.

FETISHISM. A type of VARIANT SEXUAL BEHAVIOR that has fixated sexual re-sponse by a male on some object or part of the body as necessary to reach sexual satisfaction or ORGASM. Objects commonly so used are a foot or a shoe or rubber boot, female underwear, or a lock of hair.

FETUS. The unborn young from the beginning of the third month after CONCEP-
TION until birth. Before the third month, it is called an EMBRYO.

FIMBRIAE (singular, fimbria). The fingerlike fringes at the ends of the FAL-
LOPIAN TUBES nearest the OVARIES. After OVULATION the fimbriae wave the
OVUM into the tube for its journey to the UTERUS. See the drawing on page 39.
See also FALLOPIAN TUBE.

FOAM. See SPERMICIDE.

FOLLICLE. See GRAAFIAN FOLLICLE.

FOREPLAY. The beginning stages of SEXUAL INTERCOURSE, during which the
partners kiss, caress, and stimulate each other before the PENIS enters the
VAGINA, in other words, SEX PLAY before INTERCOURSE. One problem with
such sex play may be that one partner interprets it as a preliminary to intercourse, which he or she expects will occur, while the other may think that it
is merely touching and caressing for their own sake and not really foreplay at
all. Another even more serious problem is the failure of one partner, usually the
male, to understand the importance of foreplay before sexual intercourse begins, in order that both partners may be ready—that is, the woman aroused,
with the vagina LUBRICATED, and the male with the penis ERECT. A difficulty
with the term foreplay is that it assumes that sexual play or PLEASURING will
necessarily end in intercourse, whereas often it is a pleasure to be enjoyed
without intercourse or ORGASM. See also SEX PLAY.

FORESKIN. The skin covering the tip of the PENIS, which is drawn back when
the penis undergoes ERECTION. See also CIRCUMCISION.

FORNICATION. SEXUAL INTERCOURSE between two unmarried people. Fornication is still a crime in some states in the United States, although it is rarely
prosecuted. It is not legally the same as ADULTERY.

FRENCH KISS. A KISS involving the use of the tongue within another's mouth
for erotic pleasure. Although it is called "French," it is not now, nor was it ever,
limited to France. See also KISSING.

FREUD, SIGMUND (1856–1939). The Austrian neurologist who developed the
theory and practice of psychoanalysis and was one of the first widely known
professionals to recognize the all-pervading influence of human sexuality on our
lives and behavior, especially the influence of infant and childhood sexuality.
Many people mistakenly equate Freud and sex, as if he had somehow invented
it. What he did was to make us more aware of it and help us to understand its
power, and its pervasiveness of all human life processes, of which we are often
not aware. Later physicians, psychiatrists, psychologists, and scientists have
developed Freud's theories, which are far from being universally accepted at
present.

FRIGIDITY. A term formerly applied to the state of being unresponsive, indif-
ferent, or cold with respect to sexual activity and especially SEXUAL INTER-
COURSE; also, the state of being unable to experience sexual pleasure and OR-
GASM. The term has been applied primarily to women rather than to men,

although there undoubtedly are some "frigid" men. Several different kinds of sexual DYSFUNCTIONS have been lumped under the term *frigidity,* but the term is now not considered scientifically useful.

G

GAY. A widely accepted term meaning HOMOSEXUAL, whether male or female. *Gay* is the term preferred by most homosexuals themselves. Used as a noun, as "He is a gay," or adjective, "She is gay." The term originated in the fourteenth century, and referred, among other meanings, to happy and irresponsible (no possibility of pregnancy) love between people of the same sex. It is not a word "taken over" by homosexuals, although, since 1953, it has been commonly used to refer to homosexuals, especially males. *See also* HOMOSEXUAL; LESBIAN.

GAY LIBERATION MOVEMENT. A movement, participated in by HETEROSEXUALS as well as HOMOSEXUALS, promoting equal rights for homosexuals in all matters, legal, social, political, economic, and sexual. It is made up of a number of organizations such as the Gay Activist Alliance and the Gay Liberation Front. Gay liberation is especially concerned with equal rights in employment, including the teaching and religious professions, and in private sexual expression.

GENDER. The overall term used for whether a person is male or female.

GENDER IDENTITY. The awareness a person has of being either male or female. A person's gender identity is established by how he or she is treated from the moment of birth, usually by three years at the latest. Once established, it can be destructive to the personality structure thereafter to try to alter it. *See also* TRANSSEXUAL.

GENDER ROLE. The types of behavior that a given society expects and tends to assign differently to males and females. Gender role is the public expression of GENDER IDENTITY. Traditionally, boys have been supposed to show their "masculinity" by being aggressive, active, brave, and not crying, while girls were expected to show their "femininity" by being passive, pleasing to others, dainty, and emotional. These behavior stereotypes are rapidly losing their strength in many segments of our society, but they still influence our behavior, for better or worse, according to the very different convictions that people still hold. *See also* SEX ROLE; SEXUAL STEREOTYPES.

GENES. Genes, the basic units of HEREDITY, are made up of DNA and are carried on the CHROMOSOMES. People's genes, which come from both their parents in the moment of FERTILIZATION, determine their inborn characteristics, which are then acted upon by environmental influences after birth. *See also* FERTILIZATION.

GENETIC COUNSELING. Counseling with prospective parents regarding possible hereditary diseases or conditions that may afflict a child they might CONCEIVE or have already conceived. The purpose of such counseling is to give the parents the information to help them determine whether or not to risk CONCEPTION or, if PREGNANCY has already begun, whether the FETUS is abnormal and whether or not to carry it to term if it is. There are some kinds of mental and physical defects which, if carried by one or both parents, may result in a badly defective or deformed child. *See also* ABORTION; AMNIOCENTESIS.

GENITALS. Also *genitalia.* The external SEX ORGANS. See the illustrations on pages 34 and 41.

GESTATION. The period between FERTILIZATION and birth, on the average 266 days, or about eight and one-half to nine months. Since fertilization comes about two weeks after the previous MENSTRUAL FLOW begins, a woman can expect her baby about nine months after her last flow—eight and a half months plus two weeks. *See also* PREGNANCY.

GLAND. An organ that produces a secretion. Glands of internal secretion (ENDO-CRINE GLANDS) have no duct but secrete directly into the bloodstream. The glands that relate to the REPRODUCTIVE SYSTEM and sex and are ductless are the PITUITARY, the OVARIES, and the TESTICLES. Other sex-related glands, like the PROSTATE and COWPER'S GLANDS, have ducts.

GLANS. The smooth, rounded, cone-shaped head of the PENIS. When an unCIR-CUMCISED penis is limp, the glans is covered by the FORESKIN. When the penis enlarges in ERECTION, the glans is always exposed.

GONORRHEA. Also called *clap, strain, dose, drip.* A SEXUALLY TRANSMITTED DISEASE. *Cause: gonococcus* (plural, *gonococci*) bacterium, a microscopic germ. *Symptoms:* in men, painful urination and milky, puslike discharge from the PENIS, but sometimes no symptoms; in women, usually no noticeable symptoms unless the infection spreads to the URETHRA. Therefore, it is extremely important that infected persons inform their sexual partners so that they can be treated and not unknowingly spread the disease to still others. *Time from contact to first symptoms:* two to ten days, sometimes as long as thirty days. *Method of diagnosis:* for men and women, examination, smear, and CULTURE. *Complications:* in women, PELVIC INFLAMMATORY DISEASE (PID) a painful infection of the pelvic organs, often causing fever; STERILITY from scar tissue that closes the FALLOPIAN TUBES (about 50,000 women a year are rendered sterile from gonococcal infection of their tubes); in men, sterility caused by scar tissue blockage of the VAS DEFERENS; in both sexes, arthritis, which may be crippling if the disease is not treated promptly; also, blindness in babies whose mothers have gonorrhea at the time of delivery and whose eyes are not medicated. A present-day problem concerning gonorrhea is that new strains of *gonococci* are appearing which are resistant to penicillin; the infections they cause therefore may be very expensive or even impossible to cure. Gonorrhea can be spread both HETEROSEXUALLY and HOMOSEXUALLY by ANAL and VAGINAL INTERCOURSE and by FELLATIO, but rarely by KISSING or CUNNILINGUS.

GRAAFIAN FOLLICLE. A small sac at or near the surface of the OVARY which forms around (usually) one maturing OVUM during each MENSTRUAL CYCLE and then slowly swells and bursts open to discharge the ovum in the process called OVULATION. After ovulation, the follicle develops special cells that secrete the

HORMONE PROGESTERONE, which is necessary to maintain the PREGNANCY if one occurs. *See also* OVULATION.

GROIN. The frontal area of the body where the ABDOMEN joins the thighs. Contains LYMPH NODES and important blood vessels.

G-SPOT (*Gräfenberg spot*). A pea-sized spot in the VAGINA that is very sensitive to stimulation. When a woman is lying down, the G-spot is on the upper side of the vagina, next to the URETHRA. It can be found by exploring with a finger (hers or her partner's) until a strong pleasurable sensation is felt.

GYNECOLOGIST. A physician especially qualified to treat the female REPRODUC-TIVE organs. Derives in part from the Greek word *gynē* (female, woman). *See also* OBSTETRICIAN.

GYNECOMASTIA. Temporary enlargement of the BREASTS in about 80 percent of boys during PUBERTY. Harmless and soon disappears.

H

HEART TROUBLE AND SEX. Many people, knowing that breathing and heart rates show a marked increase during SEXUAL INTERCOURSE, believe that a heart attack should be followed by extreme caution in resuming sexual activity. A person should consult with the doctor as he or she resumes regular activities after a heart attack, but most physicians today are aware of the great psychologi-cal importance, for most people, of sexual activity and feel confident in saying that, if the patient can walk up a flight of stairs without stress, then it is safe to resume his or her sex life. At first the partner of the heart attack victim may assume a more active role in SEX PLAY and intercourse until the patient feels secure and comfortable about his or her accustomed sexual preferences.

HEAT. The periodic and well-defined times during the life of a female animal when she is OVULATING and when COPULATION will almost certainly result in PREGNANCY. When the female is "in heat," she gives forth certain scents (*see* PHEROMONES) and signs, which stimulate the male and cause him to become sexually aroused and desirous of mating—that is, he "ruts" or becomes "rutty." In most mammals, only when she is in heat will the female be willing to copulate, and only then is the male responsive. In human females, there is no such thing as heat and little obvious connection between their desire for SEX-UAL INTERCOURSE and the time they may become pregnant. In the human male, there is no season for being "rutty." Thus, in sex, animals, except for some primates, are governed by their seasons and driven by their instincts, whereas human beings have the capacity to make choices and decisions about their sexual lives.

HEREDITY. The parental characteristics that are passed on to an individual, via the CHROMOSOMES of the father's SPERM and the mother's OVUM. Two factors determine the life of an individual: HEREDITY (inborn characteristics) and envi-ronment (what happens to him or her after CONCEPTION). In studying the life of an individual or a group, it is usually impossible to identify completely the comparative influences of heredity and environment (often called nature and nurture). *See also* CHROMOSOMES; GENES; GENETIC COUNSELING.

HERMAPHRODITE. An individual born with incomplete SEX ORGANS, partly male and partly female. Most plants and some lower animals are true hermaphrodites—that is, can reproduce by themselves—but there are no true hermaphrodites among human beings. Much more common, but still appearing in only about one in every thousand infants born, are babies born with TESTICLES in the ABDOMEN but whose external GENITALS appear somewhat female, or whose sex glands are OVARIES but whose external genitals look somewhat like a PENIS and testicles. People with such a disorder are called *pseudohermaphrodites,* and since their genetic GENDER is difficult to determine, they may be assigned at birth and brought up as members of the wrong sex. HORMONAL therapy and/or surgery can sometimes be helpful. Hermaphrodites should not be confused with TRANSSEXUALS.

HERPES PROGENITALIS. Also called *herpes, herpes 2, genital herpes.* A SEXUALLY TRANSMITTED DISEASE, often mistaken for SYPHILIS. At first, it appeared in the tropics but now affects about 20 million U.S. citizens. There is no cure for the disease. *Cause:* herpes 2 virus. *Symptoms:* swollen, tender, very painful sores on GENITALS; sores somewhat like fever blisters or cold sores on the lips, but caused by a different virus. *Time from contact to first symptoms:* about one week, but often there are no symptoms. *Method of diagnosis:* examination, smear, CULTURE. *Complications:* in some cases destroys genital tissue, causing damage and scarring; some research suggests that it is an important factor in the development of cancer of the CERVIX; very dangerous to newborn babies, in whom it can cause damage to the central nervous system (encephalitis) and sometimes death.

HETEROSEXUAL. Sexually attracted to the other sex, or a person so attracted. The opposite of HOMOSEXUAL. The prefix *hetero-* is from the Greek meaning "different" or "the other of two."

HIV (HUMAN IMMUNODEFICIENCY VIRUS). *See* AIDS.

HOMOPHOBIA. A recently coined word to describe the condition of being afraid of or despising HOMOSEXUALITY and homosexuals. A person suffering from this condition is *homophobic.* Comes from the Greek word *phob* (fearing).

HOMOSEXUAL. Sexually attracted to people of the same sex, or a person so attracted. The opposite of HETEROSEXUAL. The prefix *homo-* comes from the Greek *homos* (the same), *not* from the Latin *homo* (man). *See also* GAY; LESBIAN.

HORMONE. One of a number of chemical substances produced by the ENDOCRINE GLANDS, which have specific effects on various organs of the body. Three hormones especially important in relation to sex and reproduction are ESTROGEN and PROGESTERONE in the female, and TESTOSTERONE in the male.

HORMONE THERAPY. The treatment of any condition by use of synthetic or natural HORMONES. Perhaps the most common type is insulin therapy for diabetes. Sex hormone therapy is not as specific or well-developed, but it can be useful at times, especially in reducing the symptoms of MENOPAUSE and occasionally some symptoms of aging in women. *See also* ESTROGEN.

HOT FLASHES. The best-known (and most disliked) symptom of MENOPAUSE. Consists of feelings of sudden, intense heat accompanied by more or less heavy perspiration. Caused by a quick change in the diameter of the surface blood vessels, resulting in a more rapid and larger flow of blood through the skin. The change in the blood vessels is the result of the drop in ESTROGEN production that comes with menopause. These flashes last from a few seconds to a few minutes.

HOTLINE. A telephone service available, usually toll-free, to people in need of emergency help, especially when they may wish their request to be kept confidential. In many communities, and often nationwide, there are hotlines for SEXUALLY TRANSMITTED DISEASES (STDs; VD), AIDS, RAPE, child abuse, MARRIAGE COUNSELING, and SEX THERAPY.

HYMEN. The membrane (a very thin layer of tissue) that partially closes the entrance to the VAGINA in most females who have not had SEXUAL INTERCOURSE or used TAMPONS. It is also called the *maidenhead,* since its absence was traditionally considered by many—often wrongly—to be the sign that a female was not a "maiden," that is, an unmarried VIRGIN. When a woman has sexual intercourse for the first time, the hymen seldom "tears" but is stretched or forced open farther by the entrance of the PENIS. In the flush of sexual excitement, this opening up is hardly felt, and the amount of bleeding is slight or none. See the drawings on pages 41 and 42. *See also* SEXUAL INTERCOURSE.

HYSTERECTOMY. The surgical removal of the UTERUS for medical reasons such as fibroid tumors, cancer of the CERVIX, or uncontrollable bleeding. The OVARIES are generally not removed unless they too are diseased, and thus the secretion of female sex HORMONES remains unchanged. Hysterectomy was once a principal method of female STERILIZATION, but today, if the uterus is healthy, TUBAL LIGATION is considered preferable. Nevertheless, about one half of all women in the United States will have had a hysterectomy by age sixty-five.

I

ILLEGITIMATE CHILD. A child born to an unwed mother. Traditionally in our society such children have been looked down on, even though the children had nothing whatever to do with the conditions of their CONCEPTION and birth. In recent years, with the increasing amount of NONMARITAL SEX, the number of babies born out of wedlock has greatly increased, and social attitudes and actions both toward the children and toward their mothers have become much less punitive.

IMPLANTATION. The settling into the UTERINE ENDOMETRIUM of the FERTILIZED OVUM. If all goes normally, the implanted fertilized ovum will grow to a full-term baby.

IMPOTENCE. A sexual DYSFUNCTION among men, characterized by the inability to achieve and maintain an ERECTION sufficiently or long enough to have SEXUAL INTERCOURSE or to EJACULATE. Most men have occasional episodes or periods of impotence (secondary impotence), while some others are impotent all their lives (primary impotence). The various causes of impotence, far more often psychological than physical, are often treatable, and the condition can often be cured—or it may cure itself with a change of conditions or attitudes. As a man grows older, if he expects to become impotent he probably will, but some men remain potent well into their seventies and eighties.

IMPREGNATE. To make a female PREGNANT. The ability to impregnate is unique to males; to be impregnated, or CONCEIVE, is unique to females.

INCEST. Sexual relations (usually but not always HETEROSEXUAL) between close relatives, for example, between father and daughter, mother and son, brother and sister, uncle/aunt and niece/nephew, or cousin and cousin. The TABOO against incest is found in almost all societies. Yet in the United States recent research is revealing that incest is very much more common than most people realize.

INCUBATOR. A small heated, enclosed, boxlike bed in which a PREMATURE baby is kept warm, protected, and fed until he or she is ready for life outside.

INFANTILE SEXUALITY. A universal characteristic of infants and very young children, demonstrated by their SENSUAL pleasure in being touched, caressed, and held and their pleasure in touching and caressing themselves, especially their GENITALS. Although many people deny or attempt to suppress the sexuality of children, and of course have no memory of their own sexuality as infants, we can say that the period of infancy is one of the most sensual of our whole lives, even though it does not involve SEXUAL INTERCOURSE.

INFERTILITY. The inability of a female to become PREGNANT or of a male to IMPREGNATE. More than 10 percent of U.S. couples have difficulties in achieving pregnancy. The causes of infertility (also called STERILITY) are often multiple and complex, but in many cases can be dealt with successfully. *See also* STERILITY.

INTERCOURSE. *See* SEXUAL INTERCOURSE. (Note that the simple term *intercourse* can be applied to any social interchange between persons, including conversation.)

IUD. The initials stand for intrauterine device, a plastic or metal object to be placed in the UTERUS by a doctor or specially trained clinician to prevent PREGNANCY, probably by interfering with IMPLANTATION of the FERTILIZED OVUM in the ENDOMETRIUM. IUDs are one of the most widely used and effective means of CONTRACEPTION in the world, but they must be used exactly according to instructions. Recently, because of the enormous costs of litigation, most IUDs have been withdrawn from the American market, but consultation with PLANNED PARENTHOOD will enable most women to obtain one if they wish. Two IUDs now approved and on the market in the U.S.A. are Progestasert-T and Copper T 380-A.

J

JEALOUSY. A state of resentment, uneasiness, suspicion, and discomfort felt toward another person who may be seen as a rival for the attention and affections of the person feeling jealous. For example, a husband may (quite against his will) feel jealous of the new baby in the house because of the love and attention it receives from his wife, or a wife might feel jealous of her husband's business friends and acquaintances who seem to be taking his attention away from her. We have observed that in the sexual and affectional aspects of most people's lives, jealousies are likely to rise from time to time. Probably the best way to deal with it is for the jealous person to express his or her feelings rather than to stifle them, and thus give the partner a chance to understand, to explain, to put things into perspective, and, if necessary, to change his or her behavior in order to ease the harmful feelings. The jealous person should also be helped to become aware that feelings of possessing the other person are what underlie jealousy.

K

KINSEY, ALFRED C. (1894–1956). The American entomologist and biologist who became aware of how little was known about human sexual behavior and, with a team of researchers, succeeded in collecting sex histories from more than 18,000 volunteer men and women across the United States. The results were published in two major volumes, *Sexual Behavior in the Human Male* (1948) and *Sexual Behavior in the Human Female* (1953). These studies proved revolutionary, for it was the first time such complete information on human sexual behavior had been collected from so many varied individuals and reported in such a careful, objective manner. The studies revealed that many kinds of sexual activities previously assumed to be quite rare and "immoral" were in fact engaged in by relatively large segments of the general population of the United States. The Kinsey reports also had the eventual effect of opening up the way to the present-day broad research on many aspects of human sexuality.

KISSING. The act of touching, pressing, or joining lips as an expression of greeting, affection, love, good fellowship, reverence, and so forth, or of touching with one's lips and/or mouth any other part of another's body or any object. Kisses can range from most unEROTIC, quick peck of a grandchild on a grandparent's cheek, through the formal and old-fashioned kiss that a gentleman might bestow on a lady's hand on a social occasion, to a highly erotic, lengthy, and intimate contact of lips, mouth, and tongue with any part of another's body. The amount of kissing, and its significance, sexual and otherwise, differ greatly from social class to social class, culture to culture, generation to generation. *See also* FRENCH KISS; ORAL-GENITAL SEX.

L

LABIA. A Latin term referring to the lips of the female GENITALS. The *labia majora* are the hairy outer, larger lips; the *labia minora* are the smaller, inner pair. All these are parts of the VULVA.

LABOR. In childbirth, the contractions of the muscles of the UTERUS that first dilate the CERVIX and then, with the help of the ABDOMINAL muscles, push the baby through the cervix and on down the BIRTH CANAL into the world. The average length of labor, counting from the first contractions is, for a first-time mother, between fifteen and twenty hours, and for mothers who have previously borne a child, around seven hours. The labor of childbirth is divided into three stages: Stage 1: from the beginning of regular contractions until the cervix is completely dilated; Stage 2: from the end of Stage 1 until the baby is born; Stage 3: the period during which the uterus continues to contract in order to expel the PLACENTA and other tissues. The discomfort or pain of labor is caused almost entirely by the very hard work done by the uterine muscles rather than by friction or stretching. The pain is felt less if the mother is relaxed and feels in control of the situation, and if she understands the process of childbirth and what to expect.

LAPAROSCOPY. A method of seeing inside a woman's ABDOMEN with a miniature telescope provided with a light (called a *laparoscope*). It is used for diagnostic purposes and also for doing a TUBAL LIGATION. The laparoscope is inserted into the woman's abdomen by means of a small incision, usually in her NAVEL so that the scar wil not show. Sometimes the incision is made for the same purposes through the upper end of the VAGINA.

LATENCY PERIOD. The period between the end of active expression of INFANTILE SEXUALITY and the beginning of PUBERTY, roughly between around age four and the early teens when, according to FREUD's now-discarded theory, a person's sexuality and sexual feelings and interests become "latent," that is dormant or tranquil. For years, people have believed that the sexual interests of children in kindergarten and elementary school largely disappeared. The facts are that children during this period, although they usually no longer so obviously engage in the actively SENSUAL body enjoyment of infancy, and have not yet reached the time when the physical and psychological changes of puberty and ADOLESCENCE occur, are still very much interested in sexual questions, do engage in SEX PLAY, and in general are continuing their psychosexual development. They have, however, learned that the grown-up world does not approve of children's sexuality, and so they hide it. There is general agreement among psychological researchers and theorists today that the latency period described by Freud simply does not exist.

LESBIAN. A female HOMOSEXUAL. The name comes from that of the Greek island of Lesbos where, in ancient times, many of the inhabitants were women who enjoyed a homosexual way of life together, among them Sappho, the Greek poet (ca. 620–ca. 565 B.C.).

LIBIDO. Sex drive. A psychoanalytic term referring mainly to the instincts that urge the individual to seek to be satisfied by sexual pleasure. The term was invented by Sigmund FREUD and derives from the Latin word for "desire, lust, willfulness."

LESION. A hurt or injury, especially a sore or wound, in some part of the body.

LICE. *See* CRAB LICE.

LOVE. An emotion far too complicated and varied to be defined or explained in an entry of a short encyclopedia. Love is not simply sex, nor is sex simply love. However, the two are often—but certainly not always—closely related. It may be enlightening to note the forms of love that were distinguished by the ancient Greeks: *eros:* sexual love, including the urge toward good human relationships; *philia:* brotherly love, the love between friends; and *agape* (ah-GAH-pay): universal, selfless love.

LOVER. One who loves in an EROTIC way. Used especially to refer to a person who sexually loves another person to whom he or she is not married. However, married couples certainly can be lovers too. The term is used to describe HOMOSEXUAL as well as HETEROSEXUAL relationships.

LUBRICANTS. Substances that cause slipperiness and reduce friction. For pleasant, satisfying SEXUAL INTERCOURSE, lubrication of the entrance and walls of the VAGINA is important. If a man inserts his PENIS into a woman's vagina before she is sexually aroused, the intercourse, especially at the start, may be uncomfortable for the woman and difficult for both partners. If time is taken so that the woman becomes sexually aroused through FOREPLAY, the vaginal walls will have "sweated" mucus, the vagina will have become moist and slippery and the LABIA and area around the CLITORIS also will have been lubricated. Many sexual partners will be helped by applying a lubricant or CONTRACEPTIVE cream before they start intercourse. Saliva is also useful. Petroleum jelly (like Vaseline) works as a lubricant, but should not be used with a CONDOM or DIAPHRAGM since it causes deterioration of the rubber.

LYMPH NODE. One of the masses of tissue that are a part of the system of flow of lymph (a colorless fluid) through vessels of the human body, helping to prevent and fight infection.

LYMPHOGRANULOMA VENEREUM (LGV). A SEXUALLY TRANSMITTED DISEASE. *Cause:* the CHLAMYDIA bacterial organism. *Symptoms:* infection of the LYMPH NODES resulting in a small lesion on the GENITALS or PERINEUM that is usually painless and generally disappears quickly. However, other symptoms are sometimes chills, fever, abdominal pain, backache, and loss of appetite. *Time from contact to first symptoms:* from a day or two to a week or more. *Method of diagnosis:* a special test called LGV-CF. The earlier the diagnosis, the quicker the cure.

M

MAIDENHEAD. An old-fashioned term for the HYMEN.

MAKING OUT. A term used today—especially by young, unmarried people—to refer to physical sexual contact beyond hand-holding and light KISSING. May include anything from NECKING to PETTING, may also refer to actual SEXUAL INTERCOURSE. Making out can be unwise and irresponsible when it leads to the risk of unwanted PREGNANCY.

MALE CHAUVINISM. A state of mind in some men that involves an unreasoning belief in the superiority of males over females and of the rights of males over those of females. A term of disapproval used against such men is "male chauvinist pig." Some males who have been brought up or choose to treat women with a special sort of politeness and respect and who believe that "the weaker sex" enjoys such chivalrous treatment are chagrined to have such a label applied to them, especially since even "liberated" women often enjoy being treated chivalrously, provided their basic needs and desires as equal human beings are respected. *See also* DOUBLE STANDARD.

MARRIAGE. A legal and often religious contract entered into by a man and a woman to live together as husband and wife. It is a complicated and persistent social institution and—despite reports to the contrary—still very popular.

MARRIAGE COUNSELING. *See* COUNSELING. (It is important to distinguish between marriage counseling, which should involve the entire range of the relationship of husband and wife, and SEX THERAPY, in which the emphasis is specifically on sexual DYSFUNCTIONS and satisfactions.)

MASOCHISM. A form of VARIANT SEXUAL BEHAVIOR in which a person receives primary sexual satisfaction from having pain inflicted on him or her. The word derives from the name of Leopold Ivan Sacher-Masoch (1836–95), an Austrian novelist who described it. Masochism is not illegal in any state. *See also* SADISM.

MASTURBATION. Stimulation or SELF-PLEASURING of one's own SEX ORGANS, usually to experience ORGASM. Stimulation of each other's sex organs (mutual masturbation) usually forms a part of SEX PLAY.

MENARCHE. *See* MENSTRUATION.

MENOPAUSE. The period, usually between ages forty-five and fifty-five, when a woman ceases to MENSTRUATE. Although she can no longer become PREGNANT after menopause, it does not mean the end of, or even reduction in, her SEXUAL DESIRE and enjoyment of sexual activity, but often quite the opposite. *See also* CHANGE OF LIFE; CLIMACTERIC.

MENSTRUAL CYCLE. The more-or-less regular female FERTILITY cycle. It begins with Day 1 of one MENSTRUAL PERIOD, is followed in about two weeks by OVULATION, and continues for another two weeks until Day 1 of the following menstrual period. On the average, women's menstrual cycles last about 28 to 30 days but can vary from 21 to 35 or 40 days, or even longer.

MENSTRUAL FLOW. *See* MENSTRUATION.

MENSTRUAL PAD. A disposable pad or napkin used to absorb the MENSTRUAL FLOW. It is made of cellulose or other absorbent material in a gauze covering and can be held in place along the opening of the VAGINA by an elastic panty, belt, or adhesive backing that clings to the panty. *See also* TAMPON.

MENSTRUAL PERIOD. *See* MENSTRUATION.

MENSTRUATION. The monthly discharge of the UTERINE lining (the ENDOMETRIUM), the flow being composed of minute blood vessels and tissue that have been built up during the preceding two weeks (approximately) in anticipation of a possible PREGNANCY. Menstruation takes place if no FERTILIZED EGG has been IMPLANTED in the endometrium, that is, if there is no pregnancy. The *menstrual period* lasts from three to six days, during which a woman may say she is "having her period." If a woman's period does not occur within two weeks of the time she usually expects it, she should see a doctor to determine the cause. It may mean that she is pregnant, although there can be other reasons. The first menstruation is usually called *menarche.* It is considered the beginning of a girl's ADOLESCENCE and is a sign that she can become pregnant. (Some sexually active girls become pregnant even before menarche; some do not ovulate until a year or so after menarche.)

MIDWIFE. A person, not a physician, who is trained to assist women in child-birth. These days, midwives are usually nurses (male as well as female) who have received special training and who work under the general supervision of a doctor. In former times, or in less-developed societies, midwives might simply be women who gathered experience and expertise in helping in childbirth. The practice of midwives is called midwifery.

MISCARRIAGE. A spontaneous ABORTION, when the EMBRYO or FETUS is expelled. Between 10 and 15 percent of PREGNANCIES end in spontaneous abortion, most before the end of the third month of pregnancy. Frequently, a miscarried fetus is found to have been defective in some way. Most women who have had miscarriages will usually have an undiminished chance of carrying their next pregnancy to full term. Sometimes women cannot recognize that they have aborted and think they have merely had an especially heavy menstruation.

MISTRESS. An old-fashioned term for a woman who provides sexual and other companionship to a man—not her husband—over an extended period of time in return for his providing continuing financial support, usually including a place to live. The relationships between men and their mistresses can range from those based mainly on the exchange of sex for money and support, to those that involve a deep and long-standing exchange of affection, understanding, and even commitment.

MOLESTER. *See* CHILD MOLESTER.

MONILIAL VAGINITIS. *See* YEAST INFECTIONS.

"MORNING-AFTER" PILL. A pill containing a heavy dose of a synthetic ESTRO-GEN, which can usually prevent PREGNANCY if taken within seventy-two hours after SEXUAL INTERCOURSE, preferably within twenty-four hours. In many women it has the side effects of nausea and vomiting.

MORNING SICKNESS. A feeling of nausea and aversion to food or even the odors of food that many women experience during the first six to eight weeks of PREGNANCY. It is felt most commonly upon awakening but may occur at other times of the day. Sometimes vomiting is involved, and if this is severe and frequent, prompt treatment is necessary.

MUCUS. A slippery, rather thick substance that lines body cavities that open to the surface and other interior parts of the body. Despite its association with runny noses when a person has a cold, mucus is an essential body fluid and helps facilitate various kinds of sexual activity. It is produced by *mucous membranes.*

MULTIPLE BIRTHS. The most common multiple births are twins, two babies CONCEIVED, GESTATED, and born at the same time. *Fraternal twins* are the products of two EGGS FERTILIZED by two SPERM, and so are no more alike than any other brother or sister would be, except they are of the same age. Fraternal twins may not resemble each other at all, may be of the same sex or different sexes, and always develop in separate PLACENTAS and AMNIOTIC SACS. *Identical twins* are the products of a single egg which, after being fertilized, has split into two cell masses, each of which develops separately. These twins are therefore always of the same sex, being the results of fertilization of one egg by one sperm, and they usually are so alike in appearance that often they are hard to tell apart. They also share a single placenta and sac. Other multiple births—triplets, quadruplets, and quintuplets—are quite rare, and the babies may be identical, fraternal, or any combination of both.

N

NATURAL CHILDBIRTH. A term coined by the British physician Grantly Dick-Read in the early 1930s. Dr. Dick-Read developed a method of preparing women for childbirth based on his observation that the pain of giving birth is related to the fears the mother feels and the tension arising from them. The natural childbirth method educates and trains expectant mothers to break the cycle of fear, tension, and pain—all this without the use of painkillers—by teaching her to understand the process of childbirth and to work along with it by relaxation methods so that they may actually enjoy the experience. The method is well described in Dr. Dick-Read's book *Childbirth Without Fear* (1942).

NATURAL FAMILY PLANNING (NFP). A system of FAMILY PLANNING based on sexual ABSTINENCE during the portion of a woman's MENSTRUAL CYCLE when she is presumed to be FERTILE. It involves teaching a woman to use various physical signs, such as body temperature and consistency of CERVICAL MUCUS, to indicate when she is about to OVULATE, so that she can avoid SEXUAL INTERCOURSE during the calculated fertile days. Terms such as the RHYTHM METHOD and the CALENDAR METHOD are no longer appropriate as synonyms for NFP, since natural family planning techniques have become much more sophisticated and effective than these. Because it is complicated, requires a special NFP training course, and must be very carefully used, natural family planning is not usually nearly so effective as some medical CONTRACEPTIVE methods.

NAVEL. The roundish depression on the ABDOMEN where the UMBILICAL CORD entered the body of the FETUS until it was cut off just after birth. The navel is also called the *umbilicus* and, less formally, the *belly button.*

NECKING. The lighter forms of PETTING and MAKING OUT, involving such activities as arms around neck and waist, sitting close, and simple KISSING.

NIPPLE. The tip of the BREAST. After a woman gives birth, the milk ducts carry the milk manufactured by the breast to the nipple for the baby to suck. For many women the nipples are also important as EROGENOUS ZONES and they become ERECT during sexual arousal. (Men's nipples may also become erect during sexual arousal, and some men experience sexual pleasure when their nipples are stimulated.)

NOCTURNAL EMISSION. The involuntary EJACULATION of SEMEN during sleep, often called a *wet dream.* In many boys, it signifies that PUBERTY has arrived, although more often a boy's first ejaculation of semen occurs during MASTURBATION.

NONGONOCOCCAL URETHRITIS (or *nonspecific urethritis*). Also called *NGU* or *NSU.* Painful inflammation of the URETHRA. *Cause:* until recently, doctors were not sure exactly what caused it, which is why it was called *nonspecific.* Now it is known to be caused by the CHLAMYDIA microorganism. It can often appear without sexual contact, so it is not only a SEXUALLY TRANSMITTED DISEASE; but it can also follow sexual activity, perhaps from mechanical irritation. *Symptoms:* in women, there may be no symptoms or there may be a slight burning or bleeding on urination; in men, most often a discharge from the PENIS and slight burning on urination; the symptoms are usually milder than those of GONORRHEA. *Time from contact to first symptoms:* overnight (in the case of mechanical irritation) to three weeks. *Method of diagnosis:* smear and CULTURE to make sure the condition is not gonorrhea. *Complications:* discomfort but not danger; the disease has a high frequency of recurrence, even without SEXUAL INTERCOURSE.

NONMARITAL SEX. SEXUAL INTERCOURSE unrelated to MARRIAGE. *See* EXTRAMARITAL SEX.

NORMAL. A term often too loosely used, even in science. Dictionaries define it as "corresponding to the median or average of a large group in types, appearance, achievement, function, development, etc." It should be made clear that the term used in this way by scientists is simply a statistical description and does not imply that "normal" is the same as "good" or "desirable." *See also* ABNORMAL.

NUDITY. Without clothing or covering; naked; bare. The feelings, traditions, and TABOOS relating to nudity vary greatly from culture to culture, group to group, generation to generation, family to family, and individual to individual—and also from time to time. Our feeling is that nudity should not be forced on anyone who feels uncomfortable with it or whose sense of modesty it offends. However, within families in which it does not go contrary to the in-family customs and beliefs, it can provide an easy, comfortable means of education in what the human body looks like and how it acts. As children reach PUBERTY, they often develop a strong desire for privacy and don't want to be seen nude or to see members of their families nude. This desire should be respected.

NURSING. *See* BREASTFEEDING.

O

OB/GYN. Short for a physician who is an OBSTETRICIAN and a GYNECOLOGIST, or for the field of medicine that combines these two specialties.

OBSCENITY. Material, language, or behavior which is socially or legally defined as *obscene,* that is, indecent, disgusting, repulsive, lewd, causing (or intending to cause) sexual excitement or lust in a manner or place that is objectionable. What one person finds obscene, of course, another may find unobjectionable and pleasure-giving, and it is unlikely that there will ever be general agreement on just what is and is not obscene. There are those, for example, who find the tasteless depiction of violence on TV and in literature more obscene than tasteless explicit sexual materials. The word "obscenity" probably derives from the two Latin words *ob* (toward) and *caenum* (filth). *See also* PORNOGRAPHY.

OBSTETRICIAN. A physician who specializes in *obstetrics,* the care of women during PREGNANCY, childbirth, and immediately after childbirth. *See also* GYNECOLOGIST.

ONANISM. An old-fashioned term for MASTURBATION. The word comes from the name of Onan, an Old Testament biblical figure who "spilled his seed on the ground" rather than IMPREGNATE his dead brother's widow (as Jewish law then required) so that the brother's name might be carried on. The sin consisted in not honoring the brother by impregnating his wife.

ORAL CONTRACEPTIVE. A BIRTH CONTROL method taken by mouth—"the PILL."

ORAL-GENITAL SEX. Sexual activity involving contact between the mouth and the GENITALS. Attitudes toward oral-genital sex range from the many HETEROSEXUAL or HOMOSEXUAL couples who practice it as a major source of sexual pleasure, to those who consider it "unnatural" or repulsive. In some states it is illegal. *See* CUNNILINGUS; FELLATIO; SODOMY.

ORGASM. The peak or CLIMAX of excitement during sexual activity. Although, in males, EJACULATION and orgasm usually occur simultaneously, some male adults and boys who have just reached PUBERTY, may experience orgasm without ejaculation. The idea, originated by FREUD, that females have two types of orgasm, clitoral and vaginal, has been shown by scientific research to be false. The complex group of physical responses that constitute orgasm in the human female is the same whether produced by stimulation of the CLITORIS, the VAGINA, the BREASTS, the ears, or other EROGENOUS ZONES, or by FANTASIES. Similarly, orgasms have been shown to be the same in HOMOSEXUALS and HETEROSEXUALS.

ORGY. Wild, passionate, abandoned revelry and pursuit of pleasure, usually sexual pleasure, by a number of people together.

OVARY. One of the pair of female SEX GLANDS in which OVA are matured and from which usually one ripe ovum is ovulated once a month. The ovaries also produce the sex HORMONES (ESTROGEN and PROGESTERONE) important in the development of sexual maturity in women, for regulation of the MENSTRUAL CYCLE, and for achievement and maintainance of PREGNANCY.

OVULATION. The release, about once a month, of an OVUM from an OVARY. After ovulation, the ovum is carried into the FALLOPIAN TUBE, in which it may or may not be FERTILIZED by a SPERM.

OVUM (plural, ova).The egg—the female reproductive cell. A newborn female baby contains in her two OVARIES about 400,000 immature ova, some 400 to 500 of which will mature and be OVULATED during her reproductive lifetime, beginning with menarche and ending with MENOPAUSE. *See also* MENSTRUATION.

P

PAD. *See* MENSTRUAL PAD.

PANDERER. A person who supplies customers for PROSTITUTES or prostitutes for customers. *See also* PIMP.

PAP TEST. Also called *Pap smear test.* Taking a sample of mucus from the opening of the CERVIX by means of a cotton swab or wooden applicator and smearing the fluid on a glass slide, where it may be examined under a microscope for evidence of disease, most often for cancer cells. Women should have a Pap test at least once a year as a part of their physical checkup. It is named after its inventor, George Papanicolaou, a Greek-born American GYNECOLOGIST.

PEDERASTY. A term meaning "love of boys" or, often, ANAL INTERCOURSE between a man and a boy. A pederast is one whose sexual satisfaction comes from sexual activity with boys. The word comes from the Greek *pais-* (boy) and *erastes* (lover). PEDOPHILIA has a different meaning.

PEDOPHILIA. A form of VARIANT SEXUAL BEHAVIOR in which an adult desires or engages in sexual activity with a minor of either sex. The word derives from the Greek words *paedo-* (child) and *-philos* (loving).

PEEPING TOM. A person who obtains sexual gratification by watching the NUDITY (as when undressing for bed) or the sexual activities of others who do not realize they are being watched. Of course, many people are turned on by seeing pictures of such activities, but only when they go to some length to obtain such pleasure by secretly observing live people can they be called Peeping Toms. Peeping Toms are harmless, though they may be a nuisance. The name comes from the name of Tom the Tailor, who peeped out from behind the shutters when the nude Lady Godiva rode down the street of Coventry, as told in *Godiva, a Tale of Coventry,* a poem by Alfred Tennyson. *See also* VOYEURISM.

PELVIC INFLAMMATORY DISEASE (PID). A SEXUALLY TRANSMITTED DISEASE of women, usually a complication resulting from untreated GONORRHEA, CHLAMYDIA, and other infections of the GENITAL area. Over a million cases a year are reported. *Causes:* other untreated STDs. *Symptoms:* pain in the lower abdomen, tenderness, fever. However, the great majority of cases are symptomless, and damage is done before the disease is recognized. *Method of diagnosis:* observing the symptoms. In complicated cases LAPAROSCOPY is used. *Time from contact to first symptoms (if any):* two or three weeks; but "contact" is really the wrong word because PID derives from other diseases. *Complications:* ECTOPIC PREGNANCY, STERILITY.

PELVIS. In the human body, the basin-shaped circle of bones at the bottom part of the trunk. It supports the spinal column and rests on the leg bones. At its center front is the *pubis,* from which come the words *pubic* and *puberty.* The area enclosed by the pelvis is called the *pelvic area* and in both sexes contains the urinary BLADDER, and in the female the organs of reproduction.

PENICILLIN. A powerful antibiotic (germ-killing drug) widely used in treating sexually transmitted and many other diseases. It was discovered almost by accident in 1928 by Alexander Fleming, a British bacteriologist.

PENILE. Having to do with the PENIS, as, for example, in the phrase "penile-vaginal penetration," meaning the entrance of a penis into a VAGINA.

PENILE PROSTHESIS. When a man, because of aging or other reasons, is unable to have an ERECTION and thus to enjoy SEXUAL INTERCOURSE, he may choose to have a doctor insert a prosthesis in his PENIS. One type of penile prosthesis consists of fixed rods inserted in the penis, which makes it permanently rigid enough to enter a VAGINA. A more complex type consists of tubes connected to a reservoir of fluid implanted in the ABDOMEN. By means of a small pump placed in the SCROTUM the man can manually causes his penis to become erect and then, when he wishes, to return to a flaccid state. Insertion of a prosthesis requires rather complicated, expensive surgery. A penile prosthesis provides a man with renewed possibilities for the pleasure of ejaculation and his sexual partner with the pleasure of intercourse.

PENIS. The principal male SEX ORGAN. See the drawing on page 36. *See also* ERECTION; PHALLUS.

PENIS CAPTIVUS. A PENIS "captured" or "trapped" in a VAGINA. There are many wild tales about this, but the fact is that it never occurs in human beings. However, it does commonly happen among dogs.

PERINEUM. The area between the legs that extends from the VAGINA to the ANUS in a female, and from the SCROTUM to the anus in a male.

PERIOD. A word often used to refer to MENSTRUATION, as in "having her period" or "her period did not come."

PERVERSION. A term loosely applied to sexual behavior that the user of the term does not approve of. A person engaging in a "perversion" is called a *pervert,* but a more scientific (and less judgmental) term for sexual behavior that is different from the usual is SEXUAL VARIANCE. *See also* ABNORMAL.

PETTING. Sexual activity that includes caressing the most sensitive parts of the body, such as the BREASTS or GENITALS, and deep KISSING; the kind of lovemaking that tends to make a couple ready for SEXUAL INTERCOURSE. *See also* FOREPLAY; MAKING OUT.

PHALLUS. PENIS, usually in ERECTION. The word *phallic* is the adjective meaning "pertaining to a penis." The phallus has been the subject or theme of much art and of some religious ceremonies. The word derives from the Greek *phallos* (penis).

PHEROMONES. Substances that have an odor and are secreted by the bodies of many species of animals and insects, the smell of which produces or affects sexual behavior in other members of the species. They are especially important in the sexual stimulation of one animal or insect by another of the opposite sex. Anyone who has observed dogs, cats, or farm animals has seen the strong effects of pheromones (*see* HEAT). The sense of smell has a strong effect on human sexual behavior—pleasant odors and perfumes turn many people on; foul odors turn most people off.

PHIMOSIS. A condition in which the FORESKIN is so tight that it cannot be pulled back over the head of the PENIS. The condition can be corrected by stretching or by CIRCUMCISION.

PILL, THE. A type of BIRTH CONTROL medication taken by mouth and containing synthetic HORMONES that prevent a woman from OVULATING. The pill is available only by doctor's prescription, and the directions for its use must be followed exactly. In general, a woman takes a pill a day for three weeks and then stops for a week. Taking one or a few pills is useless, and if a woman forgets her pill for a day or two, she may become PREGNANT unless she uses another means of birth control or abstains from SEXUAL INTERCOURSE during that MENSTRUAL CYCLE. Especially during the first few months of using the pill, a woman should consult with her doctor about any side effects she may experience. Correctly used, the pill is a highly effective means of CONTRACEPTION.

PIMP. A "business manager" of one or more PROSTITUTES who usually collects all or most of their proceeds but pays their expenses. *See also* PANDERER.

PIMPLES. *See* ACNE.

PITUITARY GLAND. The master GLAND or "time clock" that largely governs the functioning of the other glands of internal secretion, including the SEX GLANDS. The pituitary thus determines the timing and sequence of body growth and changes occuring during PUBERTY and ADOLESCENCE; it controls FERTILITY, PREGNANCY, lactation, and other body processes. It is located at the base of the brain.

PLACENTA. The thick disk-shaped collection of blood vessels and tissues growing on the inner wall of the UTERUS, through which oxygen, nourishment, and waste products (but not the blood itself) are exchanged between the mother and the baby developing within her. The placenta is connected to the baby by the UMBILICAL CORD, which contains blood vessels leading from the baby to the placenta and others leading from it back to the baby. The exchanged materials pass through the placental blood vessels and filter through their thin walls. Very soon after the baby is born, the placenta and the sac that surrounded the baby—called the AFTERBIRTH—are expelled from the uterus during the third stage of LABOR. This afterbirth is then discarded.

PLANNED PARENTHOOD. An organization in the United States, whose full name today is Planned Parenthood Federation of America. It has affiliates in most cities of the U.S.A. Throughout the world, national independent family planning organizations, both private and governmental, form the International Planned Parenthood Federation. All these groups are concerned with the two problems of unwanted pregnancies and overpopulation, both in families and in countries. They provide CONTRACEPTIVE advice and materials; COUNSELING about ABORTION and, in many cases, abortion services; and information concerning population questions. Although in the United States, young people who use Planned Parenthood services are strongly encouraged to discuss their problems, feelings, and plans with their parents, the family-planning organizations do not require this, and information obtained and given, and services provided, are kept confidential. Basically, the organization urges couples to space the births of their children and to have only the number of children that they want and can care for. Many Planned Parenthood centers also provide INFERTILITY services to couples who want children but have been unable to CONCEIVE them. Planned Parenthood is supported by private donations and foundation and government grants. People who want to be in touch with a Planned Parenthood center can usually find an address and telephone number in their telephone directory.

PLATONIC LOVE. An intimate companionship (or sometimes MARRIAGE) between any two people—man and woman, woman and woman, man and man—based on common ideas, ideals, and needs, but without any physical sexual element; a spiritual relationship. If one says about two people, "Their relationship is platonic," one means that sexual interest and activity are not a part of it. The phrase comes from the name of Plato, a Greek philosopher (427–347 B.C.), who idealized this kind of relationship.

PLEASURING. Activities other than SEXUAL INTERCOURSE that give EROTIC pleasure. Although pleasuring is usually an important preliminary to sexual intercourse (see FOREPLAY), it can also be very often just for physical pleasure, comfort, and intimacy that are ends in themselves rather than being specifically intended to lead to intercourse. SELF-PLEASURING is also known as MASTURBATION.

POLYANDRY. An established MARRIAGE between one woman and two or more men. The word derives from the Greek term *poly-* (many) and *andros* (male). *See also* POLYGAMY; POLYGYNY.

POLYGAMY. Having several SPOUSES—usually referring to wives, although in some cultures it might mean two or more husbands for one wife. From the Greek *poly-* (many) and *gamia* (marrying). *See also* POLYANDRY; POLYGYNY.

POLYGYNY. An established MARRIAGE between a man and two or more women. From the Greek term *poly-* (many) and *gynē* (woman). *See also* POLYANDRY; POLYGAMY.

PORNOGRAPHY. For this word there are almost as many definitions as there are people, and attempts at definitive interpretations even by the United States Supreme Court have not ended the confusion. A useful definition might be: the presentation or production of visual and audiovisual materials specifically intended to be sexually arousing (in art, literature, motion pictures, music, etc.), and sold commercially for this exact purpose. The various laws and regulations in the states relating to pornography are not helpful. One person's "pornography" may be another's great art or literature, or vice versa. The word derives from the Greek words *porne͞* (PROSTITUTE) and *graphein* (to write). Because "I can't define it but I know it when I see it" appears to be a prevailing criterion, a preferable and more scientific term (because it is descriptive rather than judgmental) is "explicit sexual material." *See also* EROTIC.

POSTPARTUM DEPRESSION. The feelings of fatigue, sadness, and being generally let down, rejected, or neglected that occur in many women during the postpartum period, that is, the few days or weeks just after childbirth. Well over half of all women experience such feelings during the first few weeks after DELIVERY. Other terms for the phenomenon are *postpartum blues* or *baby blues*. Fortunately the condition almost always soon passes. If it does not, or if the feelings are severe, the mother should seek COUNSELING. Certainly she will be helped by extra love, help, and attention from her husband and perhaps her own mother, mother-in-law, or other relatives and close friends.

POTENCY. In the field of sexuality, a term that refers to the ability of a male to achieve and maintain an ERECTION and to EJACULATE—that is, to perform SEXUAL INTERCOURSE. Its opposite is IMPOTENCE. (The adjective is *potent.*)

PREGNANCY. The time during which an EMBRYO or FETUS is developing in the UTERUS. It ends in childbirth, MISCARRIAGE, or ABORTION. The usual, "full-term," pregnancy lasts for a period of approximately 266 days, during which the woman is termed *pregnant.* Many women have been pregnant several times in their lives without ever having been aware of it, for research has shown that a FERTILIZED OVUM has perhaps a 30 percent chance of not even IMPLANTING, or else of implanting imperfectly or of being imperfect itself. In these cases the body usually rids itself of the pregnancy very early, appearing as a usual or perhaps only slightly delayed MENSTRUAL PERIOD. *See also* GESTATION.

PREMARITAL COUNSELING. Talking with a trained professional about a forthcoming MARRIAGE. Such COUNSELING can be very useful to a couple, in helping the partners to get to know each other better and more openly, to communicate with each other, and to be sure that they are ready and well prepared for marriage and are entering it with realistic expectations.

PREMARITAL SEX. Strictly speaking, the term means SEXUAL INTERCOURSE between two people who intend to be married, but today it is loosely used to refer to sexual intercourse between two unmarried people who may have no intention of marrying. It should be distinguished from EXTRAMARITAL SEX, in which at least one of the partners is married to someone other than the partner. *See also* ADULTERY.

PREMATURE BIRTH. The birth of a baby weighing less than five and a half pounds. The smaller the baby, the lower its chances of survival as a normal person, but modern medical science is steadily increasing the chances. A premature baby is usually cared for at first in an INCUBATOR. *See also* VIABILITY.

PREMATURE EJACULATION. A sexual DYSFUNCTION in which a man consistently EJACULATES before or immediately after his PENIS enters his partner's VAGINA and thus before she has had a chance to be sufficiently aroused to achieve ORGASM. With proper SEX THERAPY, almost all men so afflicted can learn to prevent it. *See also* SQUEEZE TECHNIQUE; STOP-START METHOD.

PROGESTERONE. The female "PREGNANCY" HORMONE produced by the corpus luteum, yellow cells in the ovary. Its two primary functions are to govern the preparation of the UTERUS to receive the FERTILIZED OVUM, and to maintain the pregnancy so that it will go to term successfully. It also helps prepare the BREASTS to produce milk.

PROMISCUITY. The activity of engaging in SEXUAL INTERCOURSE with a number of different partners on a more-or-less casual basis. As with the term PORNOGRAPHY, however, different people attach different meanings and value judgments to the word. To some, having had sexual intercourse with two people implies promiscuity. Dr. Alfred KINSEY's favorite definition of a promiscuous person was "someone who has had sexual intercourse with one more person than the one applying the term."

PROSTATE GLAND. The chestnut-shaped GLAND that surrounds the male URETHRA just below the BLADDER and that produces certain HORMONES and helps to manufacture SEMEN. The muscles of and around the gland are the principal ones that force the semen through the urethra and out of the erect PENIS during EJACULATION. Cancer of the prostate is the most common form of cancer in men and often requires the removal of all or part of the gland. Also, with age, the prostate may simply enlarge and tend to block the passage of urine. This condition also requires surgery. A "prostate operation" may but usually does not mean the end of a man's capacity to perform sexually and to enjoy sex. It may, however, result in "reverse ejaculation," whereby the semen is forced up into the bladder instead of down through the urethra. This is nothing to worry about, and the pleasurable sensations of orgasm do not change. Reverse ejaculatin does mean, however, that the man can no longer IMPREGNATE a woman.

PROSTITUTE. A person, male or female, who exchanges sexual services for money.

PUBERTY. The period during which a boy or girl enters adolescence. More specifically, the beginning of puberty is marked by the first EJACULATION of SEMEN for the boy, and the first MENSTRUATION for the girl. Children arrive at puberty according to a definite but highly individualized schedule of physical events that it is helpful for them to understand in advance. The fact that a boy or girl has reached puberty does not mean that he or she is an adult or ready for the responsibilities of parenthood, but only that the boy is now capable of IMPREGNATING a girl and the girl of becoming PREGNANT, or conceiving.

PUBIC HAIR. The hair, at first downy but then darker, curlier, and coarser, that appears just above the PENIS in a boy and above and on the upper part of the VULVA in a girl. The arrival of pubic hair is a signal of the onset of PUBERTY.

R

RAPE. Forcible SEXUAL INTERCOURSE with a person against that person's will. *See also* STATUTORY RAPE.

RECTUM. The lower end of the large intestine. Its opening is called the ANUS. See the drawings on pages 34 and 41.

REFRACTORY PERIOD. A period shortly after ORGASM in most men and some women in which further sexual response is not possible.

REPRODUCTIVE SYSTEM. The male and female organs directly involved in reproduction. This system is not the same as the SEXUAL RESPONSE SYSTEM, although closely related to it. For example, the CLITORIS is an important part of the female sexual response system but has no function in the reproductive system. (See the diagrams of the two systems on pages 34 and 39.

RHYTHM METHOD. A method of BIRTH CONTROL which relies on the fact that there is a rhythm or regularity in a woman's MENSTRUAL CYCLE and that by careful recording of the events of her cycle she may be able to predict when she will OVULATE and then abstain from SEXUAL INTERCOURSE around that time. The term is not much used today, since more sophisticated methods of FERTILITY AWARENESS have been developed by specialists in NATURAL FAMILY PLANNING. *See also* CALENDAR METHOD.

RIGHT TO LIFE. A term used to cover the ideas and organizations supporting the concept that the FERTILIZED OVUM from the moment of fertilization is a person and has an absolute right to be born. Regardless of the circumstances into which a baby may be born, right-to-life people oppose ABORTION and state that the EMBRYO and, later, the FETUS, are human life, developing babies, harmless and sacred, with as much right to live as any human being, and that we have no more right to destroy life for what would appear to some to be social convenience than to destroy any person for such reasons. Many right-to-life organizations counsel couples on NATURAL FAMILY PLANNING methods and oppose artificial and chemical methods of CONTRACEPTION.

RUBBER. An informal word for CONDOM.

S

SADISM. A form of VARIANT SEXUAL BEHAVIOR in which a person receives sexual pleasure through inflicting pain upon another person. A person who practices sadism is called a *sadist*. The word comes from the name of the French Marquis de Sade (1740–1814), whose novels described such sexual activity. Sadism is illegal in most states. *See also* MASOCHISM.

SAFE PERIOD. The time during a woman's MENSTRUAL CYCLE during which it might be "safe" to have SEXUAL INTERCOURSE, that is, the days when she is least likely to become PREGNANT. Without expert instruction, it is difficult for women to identify this safe period.

SAFE SEX (or *safer sex*). Ways to have sex without the danger of contracting a SEXUALLY TRANSMITTED DISEASE, especially AIDS. The preferable term, we think, is *safer sex,* since no behavior involving SEXUAL INTERCOURSE, either through the VAGINA or the ANUS, or ORAL-GENITAL SEX, is absolutely safe, unless engaged in by two people known by testing to be STD-free and who have sex only with each other. Use of CONDOMS does reduce the risk of transmitting disease, and their use is an example of safer sex but not completely safe sex.

SAFETY (or *safe*). An informal word for CONDOM.

SALINE ABORTION. The method of induced ABORTION that involves injecting a solution of salt into the amniotic fluid surrounding the FETUS. The salt solution kills the fetus and causes LABOR contractions, during which it is expelled as in childbirth. The method is used after the first three months of PREGNANCY and may lead to some complications. *See also* ABORTION; CURETTAGE.

SANGER, MARGARET (1883–1966). One of the early American leaders in the BIRTH CONTROL movement and founder of the American Birth Control League that later became the Planned Parenthood Federation of America. She believed that the poor especially needed to control the sizes of their families, so that they could have happier, healthier lives and better sexual relationships between the parents. She worked not only in the United States but also in India.

SANITARY NAPKIN. *See* MENSTRUAL PAD.

SCROTUM. In males, the pouch of loose, wrinkled skin suspended below the base of the PENIS. This sac contains the two TESTICLES, the two EPIDIDYMIDES, and the beginning of the two VASA DEFERENTIA. See the drawing on page 34.

SECONDARY SEX CHARACTERISTICS. The physical sex characteristics (other than the main reproductive organs) that develop during PUBERTY, such as PUBIC HAIR, underarm and facial hair, BREASTS, deepening of the voice (especially in the male), and changing body shape.

SEDUCTION. The act of persuading or inducing a person into sexual activity without the use of force. Seduction can be harmful when a person is lured into sex against his or her better judgment and contrary to his or her welfare.

SELF-PLEASURING. MASTURBATION, or the caressing of one's own body for physical pleasure and ORGASM.

SEMEN. The mixture of SPERM (manufactured by the TESTICLES and stored in the VAS DEFERENS) and SEMINAL FLUID (secreted mainly by the PROSTATE GLAND), which is EJACULATED from the PENIS during ORGASM. The function of the seminal fluid is to keep the sperm in lively and healthy condition and transport them safely into the VAGINA. The word *semen* comes from the Latin word for seed, but neither semen nor the sperm are true seeds in the agricultural sense.

SEMINAL FLUID. A fluid that is secreted mainly by the PROSTATE GLAND during EJACULATION and that mixes with SPERM to form SEMEN.

SEMINAL VESICLES. Two small pouches at the back of the PROSTATE GLAND, behind the BLADDER, each attached to a VAS DEFERENS. At the time of EJACULATION, these vesicles discharge a special fluid that constitutes a part of SEMEN and enlivens the SPERM. See the drawing on page 34.

SENSUAL. Interested in and seeking bodily pleasure, but especially sexual pleasure; or, interested in arousing such interest and seeking it in others. *See also* LIBIDO; SEXUAL DESIRE.

SENSUOUS. Enjoying all bodily sensations that involve the five senses.

SEX. A word with a number of meanings, some of which are: GENDER, that is, male or female; SEXUAL INTERCOURSE, as in "having sex"; the GENITALS of a man or a woman; and the sexual attraction felt by one person for another. *See also* SEXUALITY.

SEX-CHANGE OPERATION. A surgical operation performed on a male or female diagnosed as TRANSSEXUAL, that physically changes him or her as nearly as possible into a member of the other sex. The surgery supplies a structural PENIS to a female or a VAGINA to a male and removes the unwanted sex GLANDS (TESTICLES or OVARIES). For the rest of the person's life, he or she must receive maintenance dosages of the HORMONES of the sex into which the transformation has been made. Such surgery is performed only on people who have for years been convinced that they were members of the other sex imprisoned, as it were, in a body that was for them of the wrong sex.

SEX DRIVE. *See* LIBIDO; SEXUAL DESIRE.

SEX GLANDS. Also called *gonads*. OVARIES in the female, TESTICLES in the male.

SEX HORMONES. Chemicals secreted by the SEX GLANDS directly into the bloodstream which affect the characteristics and behavior of males and females. ANDROGEN is the principal male sex hormone and ESTROGEN the principal female sex hormone.

SEXISM. Discrimination against a person because of his or her GENDER. Usually sexism arises from a prejudice against women or a belief, often even by women themselves, that only certain kinds of jobs, activities, behavior, household duties, and recreation are suitable for women, who are, according to the sexist (a person who practices sexism), "the weaker sex." However, sexism is damaging to both men and women insofar as it forces people of either sex into roles and behavior that are not comfortable for them but that they perform because they feel society expects it of them. On the other hand, many people of both sexes feel comfortable and fulfilled in their sex-prescribed roles and do not perceive themselves as damaged by sexism. *See also* FEMINISM; MALE CHAUVINISM; SEX ROLE; SEXUAL STEREOTYPES.

SEX ORGANS. The external and internal organs that distinguish males and females from each other.

SEX PLAY. A term with several quite different meanings, among which are: the activities that precede SEXUAL INTERCOURSE (also called FOREPLAY); the more or less sexually arousing activities involved in NECKING and PETTING, whether or not they are intended to lead to intercourse; the lighthearted, somewhat sexual fooling around that two people may engage in, in a recreational sense; the sexual playing of children as they "rehearse" and learn the roles and activities through which they will later express their sexuality as adults; the activities involved in "playing with oneself," or MASTURBATION.

SEX ROLE. The group of behaviors and activities that people assume to be appropriate to their GENDER, whether male or female. *See also* SEXISM; SEXUAL STEREOTYPES.

SEX THERAPY. Psychological, physical, and perhaps medical treatment with the aim of enabling a person to overcome a sexual DYSFUNCTION. (*See* COUNSELING for the distinction between therapy and counseling.) Sex therapy must almost always be carried out with the two people involved.

SEXUAL DESIRE. A strong feeling of wanting and needing sexual activity and/or ORGASM. Also called *sex drive.* Its opposite is lack of desire, a complaint of many men and women today. Especially in recent years, usually with bad effects, our society has promoted the idea that a person must be sexually very active in order to have a good sex life. It can be a problem if one member of a couple believes this and the other does not, or if one member of a couple feels much less desire for sexual activity than the other member. COUNSELING and SEX THERAPY can in some cases help couples deal with such problems. They can also help couples realize that there are many other rewarding experiences in life and that the desire for sexual activity and the capacity to "perform" sexually may be accepted at a lower level, or even as unnecessary. Many couples consider themselves very happily married even though they do not experience a strong sexual desire or engage in frequent sexual activity, or even any at all. *See also* LIBIDO.

SEXUAL IDENTITY. The conviction a person has of being a male or a female. *See* GENDER IDENTITY.

SEXUAL INTERCOURSE. Principally, the sexual union of male and female in which the PENIS enters the VAGINA. Usually, but not invariably, the male EJACU- LATES and often the female has an ORGASM. On occasion, the partners reach their CLIMAXES simultaneously. There are many varieties of and positions for sexual intercourse, according to the preferences of the partners. Other terms for sexual intercourse are *coitus* and *sexual relations. See also* ANAL INTER- COURSE; HYMEN; STAGES OF SEXUAL RESPONSE.

SEXUALITY. The quality or condition of being a sexual person and of expressing one's sexual nature in a variety of ways; the part of our lives that has to do with our being male or female.

SEXUALIZATION. The process—especially during infancy, childhood, and adolescence, but also during any other period of life—through which we develop our SEXUALITY, or sexual natures. The three primary elements of this process are the development of our GENDER IDENTITY, of concepts of our appropriate GENDER ROLE, and of the capacity for sexual pleasure and response.

SEXUALLY TRANSMITTED DISEASES. Many people still call the STDs *venereal disease* (or VD). The term comes from the name of Venus, the goddess of love in ancient Rome. In the main text, we describe the scope, suffering, and expense caused by STDs (pages 185–93). In this encyclopedia, we give the following essential facts about each disease: its scope, its causes, its symptoms, the time from contact to first symptoms, the method of diagnosis, and the complications. We do not describe the treatment because that should be prescribed by a doctor or an STD (VD) clinic. In alphabetical order, the diseases we explain are: AIDS, chancroid, chlamydia, crab lice, gonorrhea, herpes progenitalis, lympho-granuloma venereum (LGV), nongonococcal (or nonspecific) urethritis, pelvic inflammatory disease (PID), syphilis, trichomoniasis, urethritis, venereal warts, yeast infections.

SEXUAL ORIENTATION. The state of being sexually attracted to and interested in members of the other sex (HETEROSEXUAL), of the same sex (HOMOSEXUAL), or of either sex (BISEXUAL). The orientation is usually quite firmly established during the first few years of life in ways we do not yet understand, and it is not likely to change.

SEXUAL RELATIONS. *See* SEXUAL INTERCOURSE.

SEXUAL RESPONSE CYCLE. *See* STAGES OF SEXUAL RESONSE.

SEXUAL RESPONSE SYSTEM. The parts of the human body involved in the ex-pression and enjoyment of SEXUALITY and EROTIC feelings. Functioning from before birth, the sexual response system should be distinguished from the RE-PRODUCTIVE SYSTEM, to which it is closely related but not identical and which does not begin functioning until PUBERTY. (See the drawings on pages 34, 36, 39 and 41.) *See also* STAGES OF SEXUAL RESPONSE.

SEXUAL STEREOTYPES. Simple, often traditional, ideas of what it is to be a human male or female: males are strong, brave, unemotional, reasoning, etc.; females are weak, in need of protection, emotional, illogical, etc. Without doubt, there are some important inherited and many cultural differences be-tween males and females in all societies, and these should be studied and understood, but they are not simple, and there is a much broader range of differences and potential differences between boys and girls and men and women, as well as more similarities, than used to be commonly thought. *See also* FEMINISM; SEXISM; SEX ROLES.

SEXUAL VARIANCE. *See* VARIANT SEXUAL BEHAVIOR.

SISSY. A young boy who acts in an effeminate manner and seems not to be interested in the rough and noisy behavior that "all-American boys" are sup-posed to display. The opposite of sissy (for girls) is TOMBOY, although the word *sissy* has such overtones of fright and timidity that it is much more of a put-down than *tomboy*. There is no reliable evidence to indicate that effeminate-acting boys are likely to be HOMOSEXUAL, despite a widespread belief and fear to the contrary. A word somewhat similar in meaning to sissy is *wimp*.

SIXTY-NINE. A slang term describing the positions taken by two people simultaneously engaging in ORAL-GENITAL SEX with each other, which positions somewhat resemble the number 69.

SMEGMA. The cheeselike, unpleasant-smelling substance that accumulates under the FORESKIN of an unCIRCUMCISED PENIS or under the hood of a CLITORIS that has not been regularly cleansed. Children should be taught early to pull back the foreskin or the hood and with their fingers wash the area gently but thoroughly with soap and water. This will remove smegma quite easily.

SODOMY. This word has been used biblically and legally to label as "unnatural," repulsive, or wrong various forms of sexual activity that the person doing the labeling doesn't approve of. In the United States, there are three types of sexual behavior legally defined as sodomy: sex with an animal (bestiality), ANAL INTERCOURSE, and FELLATIO. HOMOSEXUALS are more likely than other people to be prosecuted under sodomy laws, although such prosecution is becoming less and less common when the activity is engaged in by mutually consenting adults. The name comes from that of Sodom, an ancient city which, according to the biblical book Genesis, was destroyed by God along with the city of Gomorrah because of the wickednesses of the inhabitants of the two cities.

SPERM. The male reproductive cell, manufactured by the TESTICLES and EJACULATED in the SEMEN. Its function is to FERTILIZE the female OVUM, and initiate PREGNANCY. The plural is either sperm or sperms; the scientific term is *spermatozoon* (singular), *spermatozoa* (plural).

SPERMATOGENESIS. The process by which TESTICLES generate or form SPERM.

SPERM BANK. A place for storing SPERM that have been flash-frozen in a glycerine solution for later use for ARTIFICIAL INSEMINATION. Sperm are also being stored in sperm banks as FERTILITY insurance by men who have VASECTOMIES but who may change their minds about desiring a child in the future. Donor sperm are also stored for insemination of women who wish to have children but whose husbands are unable to produce enough sperm to make them PREGNANT. Sperm stored for as long as five years provide a 50 percent chance of pregnancy, although the longer the sperm are stored, the smaller the chance of their being effective.

SPERM COUNT. The number of sperm contained in an EJACULATION of SEMEN is about 200 to 400 million in the teaspoonful or so of semen usually ejaculated. A man's sperm count is determined when he and his partner have been unable to CONCEIVE children, and is one of the number of tests done to discover why a couple is INFERTILE. *See also* INFERTILITY.

SPERMICIDE. Any substance that, when injected or placed into the VAGINA before SEXUAL INTERCOURSE, will serve to destroy the SPERM EJACULATED in intercourse. Spermicidal creams, foams, jellies, and suppositories are commonly used as CONTRACEPTIVES. They can be purchased at drugstores without a doctor's prescription, are easy to use, and are very effective if the male also uses a CONDOM or the female a DIAPHRAGM. Used alone they are fairly effective.

SPONTANEOUS ABORTION. *See* ABORTION.

SPOUSE. A married partner—husband or wife. The word derives from the Latin *sponsus* (pledged).

SQUEEZE TECHNIQUE. A method used for curing PREMATURE EJACULATION. It involves training exercise and practice in which the man's sex partner first stimulates ERECTION, then squeezes the head of his PENIS quite hard with her thumb and two fingers when he signals that he has arrived at the point just before EJACULATION is inevitable. The technique is highly effective when used as treatment, but it is complicated and subtle to learn, and couples probably should not try it without the guidance of an accredited SEX THERAPIST.

STAGES OF SEXUAL RESPONSE. The patterns of sexual response observed and recorded by sex researchers Masters and Johnson. In brief, the stages of the *sexual response cycle* are: (1) excitement, during which sexual feeling and great interest are aroused; the man has an ERECTION, the woman's VAGINA becomes LUBRICATED and aroused, and various other complex but definite body changes occur; (2) plateau, during which the man's erection increases in size, the woman's body maintains and increases the physical changes observed in the excitement stage, and both men and women maintain a high degree of sexual feeling; (3) ORGASM, the period of CLIMAX, including EJACULATION in a man, lasting only a few seconds, and the not necessarily simultaneous period in a woman, when she has one, or perhaps two or several, orgasms; (4) resolution, the period of declining sexual excitement, when the man quite quickly loses his erection and returns to a calm and relaxed state, and the woman, perhaps much more slowly than the man and possibly after having been reexcited one or more times, finally relaxes and feels satisfied. After the resolution stage, men and some women go through a REFRACTORY PERIOD, during which for variable periods of time both are incapable of further stimulation. There is no such period in some women, who may be capable of almost immediate reexcitement.

STATUTORY RAPE. Any act of SEXUAL INTERCOURSE with a female under the "age of consent," regardless of whether the intercourse is voluntary or involuntary on her part. The age varies from state to state, the most common being from sixteen to eighteen, but in some states as low as ten and as high as twenty-one. *See also* RAPE.

STD. The initials for the term SEXUALLY TRANSMITTED DISEASE.

STERILITY. Being unable to IMPREGNATE (on the part of a man) or to become PREGNANT (on the part of a woman)—that is, the inability to CONCEIVE. The state of INFERTILITY is due in about 50 percent of cases to a difficulty in the woman's reproductive apparatus, in about 30 percent to a problem with the man's FERTILITY, and in 10 to 15 percent is due to both partners.

STERILIZATION. Any procedure or event that renders an individual incapable of producing offspring. The most common procedures are VASECTOMY for men and the TUBAL LIGATION for women. The two most common sterilizing diseases among women are CHLAMYDIA and GONORRHEA, which may infect and then permanently block the FALLOPIAN TUBES with scar tissue.

STILLBIRTH. The birth of a dead child. A stillbirth differs from a MISCARRIAGE in that in a stillbirth the dead FETUS is beyond the sixth month of PREGNANCY and fully recognizable as a dead baby, whereas most miscarriages occur much earlier in pregnancy. The causes of many stillbirths are not known.

STOP-START TECHNIQUE. A term for one of two successful methods to cure PREMATURE EJACULATION. As the man feels himself approaching the moment of inevitable ejaculation, he must stop all stimulation, whether by himself or his partner. Once the moment has passed, he can begin again. As taught in SEX THERAPY, with practice he can learn to gain good control of the timing of his EJACULATION. The advantage of this over the other method is that it can be learned and practiced by the man alone during MASTURBATION. *See* SQUEEZE TECHNIQUE.

STRAIGHT. An informal term meaning HETEROSEXUAL in orientation, as distinguished from GAY, HOMOSEXUAL, or LESBIAN.

SUCTION METHOD OF ABORTION. *See* VACUUM ASPIRATION.

SURROGATE. In general, a person appointed to act for another person. In the field of SEX THERAPY, to be a sex surrogate means to serve professionally as a partner in the sex therapy desired; it is looked upon by some as being a new profession. A sex therapist trains and supervises the surrogate's work with the patient, who is usually a male with no partner to work with him in therapy to overcome a sexual difficulty, such as PREMATURE EJACULATION. The therapist refers the surrogate to the patient, who pays her fee. It is a business relationship, not a personal or social one. In many cases the use of surrogates in this manner has been very successful. However, this is obviously a controversial subject on which many people, including sex therapists, have mixed or strongly negative feelings. Because of this, most sex therapists do not at present routinely use surrogates.

SURROGATE MOTHERHOOD. When a couple is unable to have a baby because the mother is infertile, the fertile father donates sperm for the artificial insemination of a woman who volunteers, usually for a fee, to conceive and bear the child. The practice has brought about serious legal and moral questions. *See also* INFERTILITY.

SYMPTO-THERMIC METHOD. A method of BIRTH CONTROL in which a woman learns to recognize the symptoms of OVULATION and also to predict it by keeping a record of her temperature. *See also* NATURAL FAMILY PLANNING.

SYPHILIS. Also called *syph, pox, lues, bad blood.* One of the SEXUALLY TRANS-MITTED DISEASES. *Cause:* spirochete bacterium called *Treponema pallidum* (meaning pale, twisted thread, shaped like a corkscrew). *Symptoms:* symptoms come in three stages. In Stage 1 there are chancres (pronounced SHAN-kers), usually one or sometimes more painless, round, hard ulcers or "sores," which disappear after three to six weeks. They appear usually on the GENITALS but occasionally on the mouth or BREASTS; in some cases they cause swelling of the LYMPH NODES in the GROIN. The chancres are very infectious. Stage 2 comes usually a month to six months after the first stage has disappeared, but may overlap it; it commonly lasts for from six weeks to six months. The most common symptoms are like those of flu—fatigue, aching joints and muscles, fever. Other Stage 2 symptoms are: (a) a rash of brownish-red, flat pimples, which are painless and appear most often on the palms of the hands or the soles of the feet (this rash is infectious if it touches a cut or scrape or mucous membrane of another person); (b) swollen lymph nodes; and (c) hair falling out in patches. The "Latent Period," after the Stage 2 symptoms are gone and before Stage 3 has set in, is when the disease enters a "quiet" stage; the patient is infected but not infectious, and the spirochetes are traveling throughout the body, entering and beginning to damage various organs. This period may last from one to twenty years. At Stage 3, the disease is called *late syphilis* or *tertiary syphilis,* when the effects of the damage being done by the spirochetes become evident and when the organs of the body reveal that they have become seriously damaged. Here the symptoms vary according to the organs affected (heart, brain, etc.). *Time from contact to Stage 1 symptoms:* ten to ninety days; average three weeks. *Method of diagnosis:* blood test; smear from chancre; examination. *Complications:* if syphilis is treated and cured during Stage 1 or 2, there are no complications. If it is allowed to enter the Latent Period and then Stage 3, the complications are very serious; brain damage (sometimes resulting in insanity), heart and blood-vessel disease, kidney disease, and possible death from any of these. Infants infected during PREGNANCY suffer various kinds of serious damage and disfigurement and may be born dead. For this reason, the law requires that couples have a blood test for syphilis before marriage, and pregnant women must be tested as soon as they become pregnant, so that if the test is positive, treatment during the pregnancy can result in a nonsyphilitic baby. In 1988, about 15 of every 100,000 Americans had syphilis, and recently the rate of new infections has risen about 30 percent.

T

TABOO (or *tabu*). Something forbidden by social custom or religious belief. INCEST is a taboo in almost every society and social class. PREMARITAL or NONMARITAL SEX, male effeminancy, or female mannishness might be taboo among certain groups and entirely acceptable among others. A number of slang words that refer to sex are at present taboo on radio and television, though used far more liberally in literature, magazines, and the press.

TAMPON. The small roll of absorbent material that is inserted into the VAGINA to absorb the menstrual flow. Tampons come in different sizes and absorbencies. *See also* HYMEN; MENSTRUAL PAD; MENSTRUATION.

TESTICLES (or *testes*). The singular is *testicle* or *testis.* These are the two male SEX GLANDS. Carried in the SCROTUM suspended between the legs, the testicles are oval-shaped and each about 1½ inches long in a grown man. These glands manufacture SPERM, the male reproductive cells. In most men, one testis hangs lower than the other. See the drawing on page 34. *See also* EPIDIDYMIS; SCROTUM; UNDESCENDED TESTICLES.

TESTOSTERONE. The primary male sex HORMONE (or ANDROGEN) manufactured by the TESTICLES. Not only is it the inducer and maintainer of the male SECONDARY SEX CHARACTERISTICS, but it is also responsible for the SEXUAL DESIRE (LIBIDO) in males—and in females too, for in the female the adrenal GLANDS always manufacture a certain amount of testosterone.

TEST-TUBE BABIES. Babies who start their lives in a test tube. If a woman's FALLOPIAN TUBES are blocked and she wishes to have a child, it is now possible to take a mature OVUM from her OVARY and place it in a test tube with SPERM from her husband. When the ovum is thus FERTILIZED, it can be placed in the woman's UTERUS, where it may become IMPLANTED and grow normally. The procedure is complicated.

TOMBOY. A young girl with boyish ways. Probably most tomboys are girls who find the limits of behavior that society has set for girls too restricting of their freedom and who simply revolt against these limits and behave the way they want to rather than "the way nice little girls should." The opposite of *tomboy* is SISSY, but this word expresses a more critical attitude about boys than *tomboy* does about girls.

TOXIC SHOCK SYNDROME (TSS). A rare disease contracted by women who use TAMPONS. Among the symptoms are high fever, diarrhea, vomiting, rash, and, in severe cases, shock. The fatality rate is about 5 percent. TSS can be avoided by never using the same tampon all day and all night, or by using a menstrual pad at night and tampons during the day.

TRANSSEXUAL. A person who feels that he or she is a member of the other sex, imprisoned in the body he or she was born in. Many such persons earnestly seek to have their bodily sex changed by surgery and HORMONES. *See also* SEX-CHANGE OPERATION.

TRANSVESTITE. A person, almost always a male, who has a strong desire or compulsion to dress in the clothing of the other sex—that is, to engage in *cross-dressing.* Often a male transvestite depends upon cross-dressing to be able to perform sexually and to achieve sexual satisfaction. The root of the word is the Latin *vest* (garment), which combines with the prefix *trans-* (across).

TRICHOMONIASIS. Often called *trick.* An infection of the VAGINA. *Cause:* A special parasite, *trichomonas vaginalis,* which can be transmitted sexually or by infected washcloths and towels that are moist. *Symptoms:* Many infected women have no symptoms. If a woman does have symptoms, they are a greenish-yellow discharge, itching, and a musty odor. The discharge causes irritation and redness of the VULVA. It may also contain spottings of blood. The GROIN may swell, and sometimes there's a feeling of need to urinate frequently. *Time from contact to first symptoms:* one to four weeks. *Method of diagnosis:* observation of small red dots ("strawberry marks") on the vaginal wall and cervix; microscopic examination of vaginal discharge. *Complications:* infection of the URETHRA and/or BLADDER; increased risk of cancer of the CERVIX.

TRIMESTER. In PREGNANCY, one of the three approximately three-month time divisions. The first trimester includes approximately the first twelve weeks after

CONCEPTION; the second, the second twelve; and the third trimester the final weeks, at the end of which the child is born.

TRIPLETS. *See* MULTIPLE BIRTHS.

TUBAL LIGATION. The method of female STERILIZATION in which a surgeon ties and cuts a woman's FALLOPIAN TUBES so that OVA cannot pass down the tubes or SPERM pass up. A more modern and frequent procedure involves electrically cauterizing (searing closed with heat) rather than tying the tubes. The word comes from the Latin *ligare* (to tie). *See also* LAPAROSCOPY.

TUBAL PREGNANCY. *See* ECTOPIC PREGNANCY.

TUBES. *See* FALLOPIAN TUBE.

TWINS. *See* MULTIPLE BIRTHS.

U

ULTRASOUND. A procedure in which sound waves and a computer are used to enable clinicians to "see" the FETUS in the UTERUS in order to determine the fetal position, growth, and even GENDER. Ultrasound is used in conjunction with AMNIOCENTESIS to make sure that the needle does not touch the fetus.

UMBILICAL CORD. A ropelike cord, filled with blood vessels, that runs from the baby's ABDOMEN to connect the developing baby to the PLACENTA. By means of the umbilical cord the baby is supplied with nourishment and oxygen from the mother; also, the baby's circulatory system passes waste materials into the mother's circulatory system. The baby and mother have separate blood systems and do not exchange blood. What happens is that in the placenta, where a multitude of tiny, thin-walled blood vessels lie next to each other, nutriments and oxygen from the mother and waste materials from the baby can filter through. The NAVEL marks the spot where a person's umbilical cord was attached.

UNDESCENDED TESTICLES. TESTICLES that have failed to descend into the SCROTUM as they should before birth. Normally, in the early weeks of a PREGNANCY, the SEX GLANDS of both male and female are located high up in the ABDOMINAL cavity of the EMBRYO (and then FETUS). By about the tenth week of the pregnancy, the sex glands shift down to the upper edge of what will be the PELVIS. In a female, the OVARIES remain at about that level, but in a male, starting about the third month, the testicles begin to descend toward the scrotum, a process usually completed by the fourth or fifth month of the pregnancy. However, one baby boy out of fifty is born with one or both testicles undescended. In most such boys the descent subsequently takes place before puberty. If it does not, HORMONAL and perhaps surgical treatment are necessary. If the testicles remain within the abdomen, not only will the temperature be too high to permit the making of sperm, but there is also a possibility of cancer development in the GLAND.

UNISEX. The state of affairs in which it is difficult to distinguish by clothing or hair length to which GENDER a person belongs. Some people, especially older ones, are worried that unisex dressing and hair may be the result of, or result in, confusion of GENDER IDENTITY or GENDER ROLE. However, the young apparently have no difficulty making the distinction, and unisex (or ANDROGYNOUS) clothing and hairdos are, on occasion and among some groups, quite fashionable.

UNNATURAL. A term not used by scientists. When applied to sexual behavior by lawyers, legislators, reporters, or the public, the term usually refers to sex-related activities the user of the term does not approve of (or does not understand). *See also* SODOMY.

URETHRA. The tube through which urine is discharged from the BLADDER. In the female the urethra is very short, and urine exits from an opening (the urethral orifice) located between the CLITORIS and the VAGINA. In the male, the urethra extends from the BLADDER to the tip of the PENIS. SEMEN is EJACULATED through the male's urethra, but never at the same time as urine. See the drawings on pages 34 and 41.

URETHRITIS. Inflammation of the URETHRA by several types of infection that cause painful urination, occurring more often in men than in women. *See* CHLAMYDIA; NONGONOCOCCAL URETHRITIS.

URINARY TRACT. In both male and female this consists of the kidneys, ureters (tubes between kidneys and BLADDER), bladder, and URETHRA.

UROLOGIST. A physician who specializes in the treatment of diseases and problems of the URINARY TRACTS of males and females, and of the GENITAL tracts of males. Some but not all urologists are trained as sexologists.

UTERINE. Of or relating to the UTERUS.

UTERUS. Also called *womb.* The organ located in the PELVIS of the female between the OVARIES, in which the FERTILIZED OVUM is IMPLANTED and GESTATES until ready to be born, and from which, if there is no fertilized ovum, the MENSTRUAL FLOW is discarded. The uterus is shaped rather like an upside-down pear and is about 3 inches long in a mature female who has not had children. It is tremendously stretchable, so that it can contain a fully developed FETUS, and it is made up of very powerful muscles, which push the baby out through the BIRTH CANAL when the time comes. *See also* ENDOMETRIUM.

V

VACUUM ASPIRATION (or *vacuum curettage*). Today this is the most common and safest method of performing ABORTIONS, but it is possible only during the first TRIMESTER of PREGNANCY. A small plastic tube is inserted through the cervical canal (*see* CERVIX) into the UTERUS and attached to an aspirator—a suction machine. Through holes in the tube, the EMBRYO and other products of CONCEPTION are vacuumed out of the uterus. The procedure is simple, relatively painless and brief, and it can be done on an outpatient basis.

VAGINA. The soft, non-muscular, usually collapsed tube, about 3 or 4 inches in length, that provides a passageway between the CERVIX and the outside of a woman's body. It is the passageway, or BIRTH CANAL, through which babies pass to be born and through which the MENSTRUAL FLOW passes. The vagina is also the passageway into which the PENIS is inserted during SEXUAL INTERCOURSE and into which SEMINAL FLUID is EJACULATED. See the drawing on page 39.

VAGINAL INFECTIONS (VAGINITIS). *See* TRICHOMONIASIS; YEAST INFECTIONS.

VAGINISMUS. A condition in which the muscles surrounding the VAGINA go into such powerful, uncontrollable contraction that it is difficult or impossible for the PENIS to enter during SEXUAL INTERCOURSE. *See also* DYSPAREUNIA.

VARIANT SEXUAL BEHAVIOR (or *sexual variance*). The preferred term for sexual behavior that is not engaged in by most people. The term *variant* is simply descriptive, whereas terms like "perverted," "unnatural," or "abnormal" are judgmental.

VAS DEFERENS (plural, vasa deferentia). The two ducts that convey SPERM from the TESTICLES and store them. Each vas is about 18 inches long, but convoluted. See the drawing on page 34.

VASECTOMY. A relatively simple surgical procedure for STERILIZING a male by tying, cutting, and removing a portion of each of the two VASA DEFERENTIA and cauterizing the cut ends, thus preventing passage of SPERM into the SEMEN. Vasectomy is a method of CONTRACEPTION, in most cases irreversible.

VD. *See* SEXUALLY TRANSMITTED DISEASES.

VENEREAL DISEASE. *See* SEXUALLY TRANSMITTED DISEASES.

VENEREAL WARTS. Can be a SEXUALLY TRANSMITTED DISEASE. *Cause:* a virus. *Symptoms:* small warts in the GENITAL area, pinkish-red and soft, or yellowish-gray and hard, that itch and become irritated. *Time from contact to first symptoms:* up to two months. *Method of diagnosis:* examination. *Complications:* can spread enough to block opening of VAGINA; highly contagious.

VIABILITY. The state of being viable, that is, capable of living and developing normally, as a newborn infant. By the sixth or seventh months of PREGNANCY, a FETUS has matured enough so that it would have some slight chance to live in the event of PREMATURE BIRTH. Some people believe that an ABORTION is morally defensible only as long as a fetus is non-viable, but not afterward. This seems a questionable basis for argument, since medical science has steadily reduced the age of viability as techniques for caring for premature babies have improved, and a baby born full-term, that is, after nine months of GESTATION, is still very far from being able to live independently, needing for a number of years the help of a complex support system called a mother, or a mother substitute.

VIBRATOR. An electric mechanism that vibrates, or causes the hand that holds it to vibrate. When such vibrations are applied to the area in and around the CLITORIS or, with a PENIS-shaped soft rubber vibrator, to the clitoral area and outer end of the VAGINA, they cause many of the women who use them (or whose sexual partners cooperate in using them) to experience an intense ORGASM or series of orgasms. Vibrators have been notable in helping women experience orgasm for the first time in their lives, even as late as at forty years of age. A vibrator also helps a woman analyze what it is that causes her to reach orgasm, so that she can then communicate this information to her sexual partner. In this way it can serve as a bridge to orgasm in SEXUAL INTERCOURSE.

VIRGIN. A term used for a person, female or male, who has not had SEXUAL INTERCOURSE. In some societies—for example, Islamic ones—virginity in a female is essential if she is to find a good husband. In our society, there are many young people, both females and males, and more of their parents, who consider premarital CHASTITY important. The word *virginity* is used to describe the state of being a virgin. *See also* DOUBLE STANDARD; HYMEN.

VOICE CHANGE. *See* CHANGE OF VOICE.

VOYEURISM. A form of VARIANT SEXUAL BEHAVIOR in which a person, almost always a male, derives sexual pleasure from observing, usually from a hiding place, the sexual activities of others or even their simple undressing. *See also* PEEPING TOM.

VULVA. The external female SEX ORGANS, including the LABIA, the CLITORIS, and the opening of the VAGINA.

W

WARTS. *See* VENEREAL WARTS.

WET DREAM. *See* NOCTURNAL EMISSION.

WHORE. An old-fashioned word for PROSTITUTE. A whorehouse is a house of prostitution, or BROTHEL.

WITHDRAWAL. A method of CONTRACEPTION in which the man withdraws his PENIS from the woman's VAGINA just before EJACULATION. Also known as *coitus interruptus.* Withdrawal is not an effective method of contraception, because a man's penis often releases SEMEN containing SPERM even before ejaculation and because many men find it difficult to withdraw at the height of sexual excitement. However, it is better than using no method at all.

WOMB. *See* UTERUS.

WOMEN'S LIBERATION. *See* FEMINISM.

Y

YEAST INFECTIONS. A set of vaginal infections, some of which are called *monilial vaginitis, candida, fungus, vaginal thrush. Cause:* a yeast-like fungus, normally present in the mouth, intestines, and VAGINA of a healthy woman. An infection is more likely to happen when a woman is pregnant or diabetic, has gone through MENOPAUSE, or is taking antibiotics, cortisone, or birth control pills. Obviously, therefore, yeast infections are often not considered a SEXU-ALLY TRANSMITTED DISEASE, but they do affect a woman's sex life and can be spread by sexual intercourse. *Symptoms:* white, cheesy, smelly discharge from the vagina; inflammation inside vagina; swollen LABIA. *Time from contact to first symptoms:* there is no "first contact" but rather a change in bodily conditions, as described above. *Method of diagnosis:* observation of the cheesy patches on the vaginal walls or in the mouth; microscopic examination of the vaginal discharge. *Complications:* difficult to get rid of; can cause mouth or throat infections in newborn infants.

Z

ZOOPHILIA. A form of VARIANT SEXUAL BEHAVIOR, quite rare in our society, involving sexual contact with animals.

ZYGOTE. Scientific term for the single cell that results from union of SPERM and OVUM at the instant of FERTILIZATION. The zygote immediately begins to grow by cell division as it proceeds down the FALLOPIAN TUBE toward the UTERUS.

Family Reading About Sexuality

It is helpful to read widely about human sexuality, and readers' needs and interests differ. Many of the books listed below are in the SIECUS 1987 *Human Sexuality: a Bibliography for Everyone,* which, however, we have considerably shortened. We are deeply grateful to SIECUS for this excellent publication. Also, we have added a few books known to us as especially useful.

The brief descriptions of books are our own, although we have not hesitated to use SIECUS's words when, as often is the case, they seem particularly apt.

Young Children

Better Safe Than Sorry Book: A Family Guide for Sexual Assault Prevention, by Sol and Judith Gordon. Ed-U Press, P.O. Box 583, Fayetteville, NY 13066, 1984.
Tells which parts of the body should and should not be touched by various people. Tells children what to do when confronted by an abuser and how to seek help. Includes a parents' guide.

Did the Sun Shine Before You Were Born?, by Sol and Judith Gordon. Ed-U Press, P.O. Box 583, Fayetteville, NY 13066, revised 1982.
A book for parents to read with their children, ages 3–7. Answers the question "Where do babies come from?" clearly, and deals with how different kinds of families live and grow.

Growing Up—Feeling Good: A Child's Introduction to Sexuality, by Stephanie Waxman. Panjandrum Books, 11321 Iowa Ave., Suite 1, Los Angeles, CA 90025, 1979.
An excellent introduction to many concepts about sexuality, presented with simplicity and dignity.

How Babies Are Made, by Andrew C. Andry and Steven Schepp. Little, Brown and Company, 34 Beacon St., Boston, MA 02108, 1984.

The story of reproduction in plants, animals, and humans, with a brief, large-print text and color photographs of paper sculptures. Accurate and simple enough to be understood by the youngest group. An excellent book, since there are no "embarrassing" photographs, to be read aloud to kindergarten classes.

Making Babies: An Open Family Book for Parents and Children Together, by Sara Bonnett Stein. Walker Publishing Company, Inc., 720 Fifth Ave., New York, NY 10019, 1984.

Excellent color photos of pregnancy and the time just after childbirth. Includes the famous Lennart Nilsson pictures of the fetus in the amniotic sac. Two texts on each page; one very simple to be read to the child, one more detailed for answering questions children may have. Contains photos of nude small children.

Preteens

Love and Sex and Growing Up, by Eric W. Johnson. Bantam Books (Skylark Edition), 666 Fifth Ave., New York, NY 10103, 1989.

Provides all the facts in simple, direct language that readers as early as grade 3 can understand. Aimed mainly at grades 4 through 7. Based on Surgeon General Koop's dictum that "information is the best protection." The main text is well, but not provocatively, illustrated and is followed by a complete word list that often gives more detailed information. Contains a multiple-choice test on the facts. Useful as a school text or in the family.

No More Secrets for Me, by Oralee Wachter. Little, Brown and Company, 34 Beacon St., Boston, MA 02108, 1984.

Four vivid, realistic stories depict children in sexually abusive situations and who deal with their problems by talking to adults who respect their rights, and by then taking action to protect themselves.

People, Love, Sex, and Families: Answers to Questions That Preteens Ask, by Eric W. Johnson. Walker Publishing Company, Inc., 720 Fifth Ave., New York, NY 10019, 1985.

Concise answers to questions asked anonymously by over a thousand 4th, 5th, and 6th graders. Some of the questions are surprisingly specific and advanced; all are dealt with honestly. Addressed to the kids themselves, but good for sharing with parents. Covers more than just sex.

Early Teens

Am I Normal? An Illustrated Guide to Your Changing Body and *Dear Diary: An Illustrated Guide to Your Changing Body,* both by Jeanne Betancourt. Avon Books, 105 Madison Ave., New York, NY 10016, both 1983.

Based on award-winning films of the same titles. The first depicts Jimmy's successful efforts to learn the truth about boys' sexual development. The second describes two weeks in the life of Jamie, during which she comes to understand the normalcy of her own body and its internal time clock.

Boys and Sex and *Girls and Sex,* both by Wardell B. Pomeroy. Delacorte Press, 1 Dag Hammarskjold Plaza, New York, NY 10017, both 1986.

Classic sexual guides for young teenage boys and girls.

Facts About Sex for Today's Youth, by Sol Gordon. Ed-U Press, P.O. Box 583, Fayetteville, NY 13066, 1985.

A short, direct approach in explaining anatomy, reproduction, love, and sex problems. Includes slang terms when giving definitions, and a section answering the ten questions most frequently asked by young teenagers.

Love and Sex and Growing Up. See Preteens list.

Love and Sex in Plain Language, by Eric W. Johnson. Harper & Row, Publishers, 10 E. 53rd St., New York, NY 10022, fourth edition, 1985. (Bantam paperback, updated fourth edition, published by Bantam Books, 666 Fifth Ave., New York, NY 10103, 1988.)

Provides basic information on sexuality for about grades 6 to 10, ages 12 to 16. Written to be acceptable in both family and school settings. Based on stated, generally acceptable values. Contains multiple-choice test on facts.

The Teenage Body Book, by Kathy McKoy and Charles Wibbelsman, and *The Teenage Body Book Guide to Sexuality,* by Kathy McKoy. Simon and Schuster, 1230 Avenue of the Americas, New York, NY 10020, both 1984.

Resources for early and middle teens that cover both factual and emotional aspects of puberty and adolsecent sexuality.

Late Teens

Changing Bodies, Changing Lives: A Book for Teens on Sex and Relationships, by Ruth Bell and others. Random House, 201 E. 50th St., New York, NY 10022, 1987.

An excellent book for teens that deals forthrightly with their concerns about sex and relationships. Sprinkled with quotes from adolescents.

Learning About Sex: The Contemporary Guide for Young Adults. Barron's Educational Series, P.O. Box 8040, 250 Wireless Blvd., Hauppauge, NY 11788, 1986.

Without neglecting basic factual information, focuses on attitudes and the process of sexual decision-making.

A Way of Love, A Way of Life: A Young Person's Introduction to What it Means to Be Gay, by Frances Hanckel and John Cunningham. William Morrow, 105 Madison Ave., New York, NY 10016, 1979.

A unique, sensitive book, written by people who are coming to terms with homosexuality, for others who want to understand it.

A Young Man's Guide to Sex, by Jay Gale. Holt, Rinehart & Winston, 383 Madison Ave., New York, NY 10017, 1984.

Source book for late teen and young adult males who want to understand the pleasures and problems of their sexuality.

Adults

Coming Out to Parents: A Two-Way Survival Guide for Lesbians and Gay Men and Their Parents, by Mary V. Borhek. Pilgrim Press, 132 W. 31st St., New York, NY 10001, 1983.
Sound, sympathetic, and helpful advice from a parent who has herself been through the experience of her child's "coming out." Includes a section on religious issues.

Contraceptive Technology, 1988–1989, by Robert A. Hatcher, M.D., and others. Irvington Publishers, 740 Broadway, New York, NY 10003, 14th revised edition, 1988.
A comprehensive, detailed book written primarily for professionals, but invaluable for anyone who wants to know the latest medical facts, statistics, and medical advice.

How to Make Love to the Same Person for the Rest of Your Life (and Still Love It), by Dagmar O'Connor. Doubleday, 666 Fifth Ave., New York, NY 10103, 1985.
Offers many practical suggestions for avoiding sexual boredom and exploring a variety of sexual options, such as sensate focus exercises. Stresses the idea of responsibility for one's own sexual pleasure.

Incurably Romantic, by Bernard F. Stehle. Temple University Press, Broad and Oxford Sts., University Services Bldg., Room 305, Philadelphia, PA 19122, 1985.
A beautiful book of photographs about love relationships where one or both members of the couple is severely disabled. Includes text of their tape-recorded statements.

Love and Sex After 60, by Robert N. Butler, M.D., and Myrna I. Lewis, A.C.S.W. Harper & Row, Publishers, 10 E. 53rd St., New York, NY 10022, revised edition, 1988.
Explores the social, medical, and psychological problems relating to the sex lives of men and women over sixty. They discuss the effects of illness, medications, drugs, and alcohol as well as the importance of loving relationships on sex and intimacy in later life.

Love, Sex, and Aging, by Edward M. Brecher and the editors of Consumer Reports Books. ABC-Clio, 2040 Alameda Padre Sierra, P.O. Box 4397, Santa Barbara, CA 93140, 1986.
The findings of a 1978–79 Consumers Union study of love and sex. Over 4,000 respondents aged 50–93. Includes both statistics and direct quotations.

Masters and Johnson on Sex and Human Loving, by William H. Masters, Virgina E. Johnson, and Robert C. Kolodny. Little, Brown and Company, 34 Beacon St., Boston, MA 02108, 1986.
Revised edition of college text titled *Human Sexuality.* Provides information on all aspects of human sexuality.

Midlife Love Life, by Robert N. Butler, M.D., and Myrna I. Lewis, A.C.S.W. Harper & Row, Publishers, 10 E. 53rd St., New York, NY 10022, 1986.
Deals with the psychology of aging and sexuality as well as with the medical

aspects, such as new diagnostic and surgical procedures relevant to this age group.

New Conceptions: A Consumer's Guide to the Newest in Fertility Treatments, by Lori B. Andrews. Ballantine, 201 E. 50th St., New York, NY 10022, 1985.
Explains the causes of infertility, the practical and psychological aspects of fertility tests, the technical and personal sides of genetic screening and counseling, and the emotional effects of infertility, as well as the remedies available.

The New Our Bodies, Ourselves: A Book by and for Women, by Boston Women's Health Book Collective. Simon & Schuster, 1230 Avenue of the Americas, New York, NY 10020, 1985.
Covers sexuality, contraception, relationships, health care, sexual physiology, and reproduction.

Now That You Know: What Every Parent Should Know About Homosexuality, by Betty Fairchild and Nancy Hayward. Harcourt Brace Jovanovich, 1250 Sixth Ave., San Diego, CA 92101, 1981.
Informative, sensitively written guide for parents of gay children.

Older and Wiser: Wit, Wisdom, and Spirited Advice from the Older Generation, by Eric W. Johnson. Walker Publishing Company, Inc., 720 Fifth Ave., New York, NY 10019, 1986.
Treats elders generally, with many wise and humorous quotations. Three especially useful chapters: "What Does 'Old' Mean?"; "About Our Health"; and "About Our Sexuality."

Parents Talk Love: The Catholic Family Handbook on Sexuality, by Susan K. Sullivan and Matthew A. Kawiak. Paulist Press, 997 MacArthur Blvd., Mahwah, NJ 07430, 1984.
For Catholic parents in their homes, or for use in discussion groups in parish settings. Nine chapters, each concluding with a list of questions for discussion.

Raising A Child Conservatively in a Sexually Permissive World, by Sol and Judith Gordon. Simon & Schuster, 1230 Avenue of the Americas, New York, NY 10020, 1986.
Chapters on coming to terms with your own sexuality, becoming an "askable" parent, self-esteem, the role of schools, and the questions most frequently asked by parents and children, with suggested responses.

Reaching Your Teenager, by Elizabeth C. Winship ("Ask Beth"). Houghton Mifflin, 1 Beacon St., Boston, MA 02108, 1983.
Discusses the concerns parents have about their teenagers' emotional and social development, including puberty, premature sexual experiences, working out rules and guidelines, choice of friends, discipline, and self-esteem. Lively and practical.

Recovery: How to Survive Sexual Assault, for Women, Men, Teenagers, Their Friends and Families, by Helen Benedict. Doubleday, 666 Fifth Ave., New York, NY 10103, 1985.
Information about the mythology surrounding sexual assault, along with discussions of both short- and long-term traumatic effects, reporting assaults, medical care, finding and giving support, and self-defense.

Sexual Interactions, by Albert R. and Elizabeth Rice Allgeier. D. C. Heath
   Company, 125 Spring St., Lexington, MA 02173, second edition, 1988.
   An excellent, comprehensive textbook for college and sexology students.
   Explains the most modern developments but also gives well-selected histo-
   rical background. Well-written, with touches of humor (even Rothco *Punch*
   cartoons); sprinkled with interesting case studies and revealing quotations
   for discussion. The best general text we know of for sex ed teachers, for
   learning and for reference.

The Silent Children: A Parent's Guide to the Prevention of Child Sexual Abuse,
   by Linda Tschirhart Sanford, McGraw-Hill, 1221 Avenue of the Americas,
   New York, NY 10020, 1982.
   Advice to parents to help their children feel good about themselves, to
   know how much others have a right to ask of them physically and emotionally, to trust their instincts, and to act in their own best interests.

*Talking with Your Child About Sex: Questions and Answers for Children from
   Birth to Puberty,* by Mary S. Calderone and James W. Ramey. Ballantine,
   201 E. 50th St., New York, NY 10022, 1984.
   Divided into six sections, from birth through age 12, each beginning with
   an introduction describing that stage of development and then presenting
   a series of questions that children (or their parents) at that stage might ask,
   each followed by suggested answers. Practical; gives many specific facts.

General Index

Page numbers in *italics* refer to illustrations.

Selfish use of sex, 155–57
Self-knowledge, 211–12
Self-pleasuring, 14, 253
  See also Masturbation
Semen, 37, 253, 254
  for artificial insemination, 219
  ejaculation of, 34, 53, 228
    first occurrence, 251
  manufacture of, 251
  mistaken beliefs, 158
  nocturnal emission, 244
  sperm count, 257
  after vasectomy, 88
Seminal fluid, 253, 254
Seminal vesicles, *34*, 36, 254
Senses of newborns, 66
Sensuality, 254
Sensuousness, 254
Separation, in marriage, 115–17
  single-parent families, 126
Sex:
  development of interest, 23–25
  and love, 240
  and marriage, 119–20
  problems of, 154–84
  and romance, 118
  uses of word, 1–2, 254
Sex-change operations, 182, 254
Sex counselors, 27
Sex drive. *See* Sexual desire
Sex education, 11
  for adolescents, 140
  for disabled people, 146–48
  in early childhood, 104–5
  families and, 3–4
  language, 141–43
  parents and, 24–25, 134–36
  programs, 194–210
Sex glands, 254
  prenatal function, 102–3
  testicles, 260
Sex hormones, 254
  therapy, 235–36
Sexism, 254
Sex organs, 254
  female, 13
    external, 265
  incomplete, 235
  prenatal development, 57, 59, 103
  See also Genitals
Sex play, 255
  by children, 23–24, 138–40
Sex roles, 255
  nongenital, 20–21
  See also Roles, gender-related
Sex therapy, 28–29, 241, 255
  for premature ejaculation, 258, 259
  surrogates, 259
Sexual, use of word, 2

Sexual activity:
  in adolescence, 140
  decisions, 100–101
  in old age, 152
  of parents, 129
  studies, 157
Sexual Behavior in the Human Female,
  Kinsey, 238
Sexual Behavior in the Human Male,
  Kinsey, 238
Sexual desire, 229, 255
  androgen and, 218
  and breast size, 220
  and castration, 221
  lack of, 29
  and menopause, 222, 241
  stimulation of, 219
  testosterone and, 261
Sexual development, prenatal, 4–6
Sexual deviancy, 226
  See also Variant sexual behavior
Sexual dysfunction, 227
  impotence, 237
  premature ejaculation, 251
  vaginismus, 264
Sexual identity, 255
Sexual intercourse, 53–54, 225, 255
  AIDS transmission, 190
  extramarital, 217, 229
  first occasion, 236
  foreplay, 231
  fornication, 231
  and heart disease, 234
  lubrication, 240
  painful, 227
  pleasure from, 14
  during pregnancy, 54–55
  premarital, 250
  problems of, 28
  promiscuous, 251
  rape, 252
  refractory period, 252
  and reproduction, 31
  safety of, 253
  statutory rape, 258
  voluntary abstinence, 221
Sexuality, 1, 102, 255
  development of, 3–4
    early, 15–27
    family and, 122–43
  infantile, 237
  and loneliness, 145
  in old age, 152
  uses of word, 2
  variations, 105–6
Sexualization, 255–56
  of children, 103–6
  process of, 2–11
  in single-parent families, 126–27

Symptoms:
of AIDS, 190, 217
of sexually transmitted diseases, 188
See also name of disease
Sympto-thermic method, natural family
planning, 87, 259
Syphilis, 186, 188, 259–60

Taboo, 260
Talk about sex, 160
Tampons, 43–46, *45*, 260
and hymen opening, 42
toxic shock syndrome, 261
Tasks of adolescence, 131
Teachers, sex education, 204–5
Techniques, sexual, learning of, 27–28
Teenagers:
pregnant, 76, 155, 213
reading lists for, 268–69
See also Adolescence; Puberty
Temperature, basal body, and ovulation,
219–20
Tennyson, Alfred, 123
Godiva, a Tale of Coventry, 246
Tertiary syphilis, 260
Testicles, *34,* 35–36, 228, 233, 253, 254,
260
prenatal development, 4, 5, 59
undescended, 262
Testosterone, 228, 235, 261
prenatal production, 5, 103
Tests for pregnancy, 54
Test-tube babies, 261
Therapeutic abortion, 216
Therapy, for sexual dysfunctions, 28–29,
255
Third trimester, fetal growth, 59
Thyroid gland, 228
Time required for intimacy, 30
Tobacco:
and contraceptive pill, 83
during pregnancy, 55–56
Toilet training, 17
Tomboys, 256, 261
Toxic shock syndrome (TSS), 43, 261
Traditional family patterns, 124–25
Training of sex education teachers, 205
Transmission of STDs, 186–87
AIDS, 190, 217, 218
gonorrhea, 233
Transsexualism, 181–82, 254, 261
Transvestism, 180, 261
Treatment of STDs, 187–88, 256
Trichomoniasis, 185, 261
Trick. *See* Trichomoniasis
Trimesters of pregnancy, 56–59, 261–62
Triplets, 69, 243
Trust, in intimacy, 30
TSS (toxic shock syndrome), 43, 261

Tubal ligation, 88, 236, 239, 258, 262
effectiveness of, 91
Tubal pregnancy, 227
Twins, 69, *70,* 243
studies of, 74

Ultrasound, 262
Umbilical cord, 56, *58,* 243, 248, 262
in childbirth, 63
first trimester, 57
second trimester, 59
Uncircumcised penis, *35,* 233, 257
Undescended testicles, 262
Unisex, 20–21, 263
United States:
AIDS victims, 217
family arrangements, 122–24
individual rights, 149
prostitution in, 171
United States Supreme Court:
abortion decision, 97–98
pornography decisions, 167
Unmarried people, 148–49
mothers, 93–94, 213, 236
teenage, 76
Unnatural behavior, 263
Unwanted pregnancy, 213
Ureters, *34,* 220
Urethra, 32–34, *34, 41,* 220, 263
inflammation of, 244
Urethritis, 263
Urinary tract, *34,* 263
Urination, 32–34, 220
and ejaculation, 34
frequent, in pregnancy, 54
after intercourse, 89
Urology, 5, 263
Uterus, 13, *39,* 40–41, 263
in childbirth, 62
and movement of sperm, 53
progesterone, 251
surgical removal, 236

Vacuum aspiration abortion, 95, 263–64
Vagina, 13, *39,* 41–42, *41,* 43, 220, 264
chlamydia symptoms, 223
in intercourse, 53
lubrication, 240
artificial lubricants, 115
trichomoniasis infection, 261
yeast infections, 265–66
Vaginal thrush, 265
Vaginismus, 28, 264
Values:
in sex education, 197–200
and sexual decisions, 212–14
taught by parents, 125
Variant sexual behavior, 105–6, 215, 264
bisexuality, 112–13

About the Authors

MARY S. CALDERONE, M.D., M.P.H., was one of the founders of SIECUS (Sex Information and Education Council of the U.S.) in 1964 and served as its first Executive Director and President. She has also been Medical Director of Planned Parenthood Federation of America and has received honorary degrees from a dozen universities. Dr. Calderone is the author of several books and many articles on sexuality, including *Talking with Your Child About Sex* (with James W. Ramey). She is the mother of three daughters and has three grandchildren and three great-grandchildren. She lives in Princeton, New Jersey.

ERIC W. JOHNSON, a graduate of Harvard College and the Harvard Graduate School of Education, has taught English, history, and sex education for more than thirty years. He has also worked for the American Friends Service Committee in Portugal, Morocco, Algeria, Egypt, India, France, Haiti, the U.S.S.R., Poland, and Sweden in the fields of relief and rehabilitation, international relations, and education. He is the author of over forty books, including *Love and Sex in Plain Language; Love and Sex and Growing Up; Sex: Telling It Straight;* and *People, Love, Sex, and Families.* He lives with his wife in Philadelphia and has three children and three grandchildren.